Praise for *Tied Up in Knotts*

"I love thi~~s~~ book!"

"Don Knotts knew how to be funny w~~ith~~ chest and look weaker. He could preten~~d~~ ~~an~~~~gry and~~ become laughable. Whatever he did, you reverse and read the opposite. He was truly a comic genius!"

—Ed Asner

"Personal, revealing, compelling—Karen Knotts's book about her iconic father is an irresistible page turner. It's a delightful documentary in written form about the legendary actor Don Knotts, descriptively told through the lens of his daughter, who gives us a unique look into the man so many of us grew up with. Rich with Hollywood history, too, Karen shares her dad with us . . . and we're left feeling gratefully entertained for her generosity."

—Craig Shoemaker

"Don Knotts's daughter Karen has captured the essence of her dad as only a daughter can. One of the great comedians of our time. How lucky I was to cross paths with this kind and genuine man."

—Beau Bridges

"Since my father Tim Conway stole all his comedy from Don Knotts, it just seems honorable to continue the tradition and steal *Tied Up in Knotts* from the local bookstore."

—Tim Conway Jr.

"Don and I had fun together in a long-running show, *Search for Tomorrow*. It was a wonderful time."

—Lee Grant

"Don Knotts has made such lasting impact—*who didn't grow up watching him?*—that it's easy to forget there was a person behind all those iconic characters. Karen Knotts's memoir reveals the struggle before the success and the hard work behind the brilliance, a family-inside look at a brilliant actor and a complex man."

—Dana Gould

"Don Knotts was a unique and brilliant comedic actor. I knew him,
and he was a wonderful person as well. The 'nervous guy' on the
Steve Allen Show was one of my favorites. . . . In this book,
his daughter Karen beautifully captures his life and career."

—David Steinberg

"Karen Knotts's memoir reveals the untold sides of Don
and explores his creativity. I loved knowing him in Yarmy's Army."

—Peter Marshall

"Karen takes you back to the heartland of America from which Don and
his values and insecurities sprang. It is a wonderful portrait of a simpler
yet fraught time in our country's history, and how a man with brilliance,
talent, and drive made it into Hollywood history. I feel so lucky to have
known the gentle, humble Don, and the wild and crazy Mr. Furley,
during the many years of *Three's Company*."

—Nancy Morgan Ritter

"The cardinal rule for an actor to be a comedic hit on a sitcom
or the movies is 'Show me a man in trouble and I'll show you a funny man.'
Don Knotts personified that man in trouble with his brilliant acting skills
whenever the light hit him, and he made it look
effortless. I loved this book, and the millions he made laugh
week in and week out will love it also."

—Tom Dreesen

"Karen Knotts has a strong love for her legendary comedian dad.
She's also very honest about the challenges of being the daughter
of a beloved famous person. Her writing is witty—I laughed
out loud in places. I really enjoyed the book!"

—Rocky LaPorte

Tied Up in Knotts

My Dad and Me

KAREN KNOTTS

CHICAGO
REVIEW
PRESS

This book is dedicated to all the "Nip It in the Budders"
who come together to laugh and prove what Dad loved to say:
"A good joke or a funny story can get you through
just about anything."

CONTENTS

Foreword by Betty Lynn   vii

Preface   ix

Introduction xiv

1 Down by the River 1

2 *Stars and Gripes* 32

3 College Man Plays the Fool 42

4 On Live TV, It Pays to Be Nervous 50

5 The Legend of Mayberry: A Town Is Born 69

6 I Was Only Funnin' 85

7 The Mountain Folk 94

8 The Women 104

9 Dad and Andy 116

10 A Fish, a Ghost, an Astronaut, and a Mule 121

11 Beverly Hills Hideaway 149

12 It's All in the Family 172

13 Mr. Furley Lands, and Mayberry Returns 205

14 Barney Takes to the Stage 224

Epilogue   253

Acknowledgments   255

FOREWORD

---

by Betty Lynn

"Thelma Lou" on *The Andy Griffith Show*

I REMEMBER WHEN KAREN was a girl how surprised she was the first time she came to the *The Andy Griffith Show*. She said, "The sets all look like toys!" And I said, "You're right, nothing looks real."

She had a real good time whenever she and her brother, Tommy, came to visit. They were darling—both of them were so cute. They took after their father, because Don was so darling.

People all say he must've been a riot. Everybody thinks he was like Barney Fife, but he was nothing like Barney! I'd say he was quiet, sweet as he could be. He smiled. His mind was fast; he was thinking of different things he could do. And he loved to write poetry.

We loved *The Andy Griffith Show*, all of us who were on it. We were so privileged to be on that show. When they put a call in for

Thelma Lou, I couldn't wait to go to set, because I loved doing it so much. And everybody on it was wonderful, as actors. They were all great to work with. And that doesn't happen every day of the week in show business today. I did a lot of movies and things, but the thing that I'm proudest of, really, is being on *The Andy Griffith Show*. I loved it so much.

And Don was so proud of Karen—you could just see by the way he looked at her. When Don left this world, Karen decided to pay tribute to him with her funny, touching show *Tied Up in Knotts*. The first time she did it at Mayberry Days, she asked me to introduce her, and I said I would be honored. She was so nervous. I said, "Oh, honey, they'll love you just like I do. And I know you're a very good actress, so don't worry about it." And she knocked them dead. I know that's a strange expression, but she did.

And I'm so proud to be the first one to tell you about her wonderful book!

Betty Lynn and Karen Knotts at Mayberry Days, about 2014.

PREFACE

I N MARCH 2019, just before the COVID-19 pandemic paralyzed life as we know it, I was preparing to perform my show *Tied Up in Knotts* at the Whitefire Theatre in Sherman Oaks, as part of its Solofest. The main subject of the show, like this book, is Dad's career and the relationship between him and me.

One of the other solo performers told me she had met Dad, and I interviewed her. Lisa Sosenko: "Fifteen years ago my husband, Gary, called me from LAX Airport. He said, 'Guess who is in the Continental Club, and who is flying on the plane back to Cleveland?' I said, 'Who?' He said, 'Don Knotts.' Gary said, 'No one knew who he was; he looked sad.' I got to the Cleveland airport, and then we found him! He was waiting for a ride. That ride was Tim Conway, who was visiting his family in Chagrin Falls."

Her story is important to me because it expresses the shock and sadness we often feel when we discover that a famous person from our childhood has become virtually unknown to the younger generation.

Over the years, many people have told me I should write this book. I would explain that I had no time—I wanted to pursue my acting career, yada, yada, yada. That was true, but also Dad was a very private person, and I was concerned I'd be trespassing on forbidden territory.

When Dad passed on February 21, 2006, I became haunted by the opportunity I was missing. Just as the iconic film *Back to the Future* expresses, many people desire to walk in a parent's shoes for a day. Writing this book didn't allow me to travel through time, but it enabled me to see his life through others' eyes. And I realized I was in a unique position. As the daughter of a famous person, I could locate and talk to strangers who had known him.

In addition to preserving Dad's legacy, my interest in writing the book was to understand him, to explore his many facets, and to share his remarkable journey with you, dear reader. So I took the plunge.

When I started, Dad had been gone more than ten years, as were most of his closest friends. Fortunately, I had started collecting interviews years before I made the decision to write a book, just in case.

I started by interviewing members of my immediate family: my mother, Kay, and my brother, Tom. It may seem strange for me to interview members of my own family, but I was amazed how much I learned by doing so. I didn't know some of the things Dad and Tom had done together, and it informed me about their relationship. Tom and I began to have conversations about things we'd never discussed, including Dad's fame and our own experience with it. I included my mother's story too. So many of Dad's fans have expressed interest in her. It turns out that Mother had kept a journal of several events in our family's life, as well as her own, and she gave me access. Thanks, Mom!

I soon realized I needed more information on Dad's childhood. I flew to his hometown of Morgantown, West Virginia. I announced on radio that anyone who had reliable information about my father was invited to meet me for wine and cheese at the Hill & Hollow restaurant. A nice crowd gathered and shared their memories—or, more accurately, their parents' or relatives' memories.

I wanted to know more about his high school days, so I inquired and was advised to go to Gene's Beer Garden on Wilson Avenue. I wandered into the bar, ordered a beer, and started talking about my project. A man said, "Don Knotts! My mother-in-law dated him in high school!" I later interviewed the woman, Doris Harner, and she gave me insight into Dad's life prior to his entrance into World War II. Later, when I returned to Los Angeles, I interviewed Dad's friend actor Al Checco, who had entertained with Dad in the army show *Stars and Gripes*.

But my greatest *Back to the Future* moment came when I visited Dad's alma mater, Morgantown High School. Dad had often talked about the school as the turning point in his young life. That's when he really began to channel his charismatic personality and brilliant comedic talent. I was excited when I walked through the door of the school I'd heard so much about. I talked with a former MHS student, Lorenzo Turner, who told me, "When I was fifteen I got my summer job at MHS. It was to clean the desks, get rid of gum, and so on. We were in the old auditorium, and carved into the proscenium arch with a knife was DON KNOTTS."

I interviewed a gym coach and learned how Dad had used his ventriloquism to flirtatiously engage with other students. And while in Morgantown, I also reconnected with the children of Jarvey Eldred, Dad's best friend in high school. I hadn't seen Judy, Karen, Jenny, or Jarvey Jr. since we were kids, when our fathers introduced us.

I continued my search for people and eventually met a woman in her nineties, Fern Hall Giessman, who had been Dad's close child-hood friend! She told me how she and Dad, as children, had coped with the difficulties of the Great Depression.

After I had exhausted all the connections I could think of, I realized that a great many of *my* friends had met Dad. When I interviewed them, I was surprised by the interactions they'd had with him. My school friend Gina reminded me that her mother had interviewed Dad for a class she was taking at UCLA, and she shared the recording with me.

At the Mayberry Days festival in Mount Airy, North Carolina, I work with *The Andy Griffith Show* "tribute artists," and I interviewed a few about their conversations with Dad. I'm grateful for the fans who continue to participate in Mayberry Days festivals over the years. Speakers have included actors and people like Bruce Bilson, *The Andy Griffith Show*'s first assistant director. Bruce coordinated a visit to the former Desilu Studios (today, Red Studios) with *The Andy Griffith Show* Rerun Watchers Club and me. He showed us how the studio had been arranged when the show was filmed there.

Before I started to write, I made a list of topics I wanted to cover. Of course, there's enormous interest in Barney Fife, and I would explore the visits Tom and I made to the set of *The Andy Griffith Show* when we were kids. The memories are still vivid and a unique part of our childhood. In addition to the *Griffith Show* days, I would talk about his work on *Three's Company*, as well as his live TV days in New York during the 1950s and his ill-fated variety show in the 1970s. I would also cover his amazing film work and career in legitimate theater.

Another area of interest, I discovered in my early interviews, was the ladies' man side of Dad. I decided to ask his leading ladies to comment on it.

As his daughter, I made it my main goal in writing this book to discover for myself, and reveal to readers, who was the "real" Don Knotts. I think of him like the man behind the curtain in *The Wizard of Oz*. He had a laser beam of concentration that dazzled audiences into believing, one hundred percent, the character he was playing. In addition, he had human qualities we don't normally associate with big stars: he was considerate and kind, generous to those he cared about. And his painful childhood informed his art; he understood what people needed to make them feel good and delivered, even when it didn't benefit him personally.

He kept the friendships from his hometown close, and he kept our extended family together. It makes me sad when I hear news that a celebrity has died and left relatives fighting over the will. In our family, ex-wives and ex-girlfriends were never excommunicated. He created a spirit of inclusiveness that has enabled Tom and me to stay close to both our stepmothers, Loralee and Francey. I interviewed other family members, including dad's first cousin Ray Lewis Knotts, cousin Sandy Knotts, and cousin Bill Knotts. I also interviewed my mother's brother, author Robert Metz.

In order to pay proper tribute to Dad, I felt the need to mention comedy legend Stan Laurel, who originally inspired him to act and go into show business. Dad had the opportunity to speak with Stan two weeks before he passed. Stan told him, "Nobody will remember those little pictures of ours [Laurel and Hardy]."

Dad's greatest legacy, hands down, is Barney Fife. But I want to make sure his other work won't be forgotten, including those "little pictures" he made, which include *The Incredible Mr. Limpet*, the all-time classic *The Ghost and Mr. Chicken*, and the *Apple Dumpling Gang* movies with Tim Conway.

The first celebrity I interviewed was Gary Busey; the interview took place in the back of a limousine. His wife, and my standup comedy pal Steffanie Busey, was driving. It never occurred to me to ask if their chauffeur had the night off or if she was in training to be a chauffeur herself. I was excited and turned my recorder on, because I didn't want to miss a thing! Here's what I recorded:

Gary Busey: "Don was the Nervous Guy! I thought it was real! I said, 'I have never seen anybody stand up in front of an audience and show how nervous he is naturally.' I bought it, I bought it! Next day, I tune in, gotta find the Nervous Guy! Talk show—Andy Griffith was talking about Mayberry! Fulcrum of the teeter totter is Don, one bullet right there. Andy, his stoic expression dealing with Don, he wouldn't drop character! Everyone would guffaw at the end. It was like a prairie fire with a big wind—it's blowing down, forget the water!"

INTRODUCTION

W HEN I THINK OF DAD, the image that most often comes to mind is of
him sitting in his favorite armchair, fingers tapping, eyes wandering the room, saying nothing. I would lean forward and study
his face intently. It was as if the shape of his mouth, deep creases in
his cheeks, and the blueness of his eyes were a treasure map to the
secrets of his mind.

My father was, and shall remain, the greatest enigma of my life.
He was known for playing characters that were simple, yet he was
incredibly complex. People were often surprised when they'd meet
him, whether they were awestruck fans or other celebrities. When
introduced, they half expected an overexcitable man to jump out of
his chair and do something wildly unpredictable, like his most famous
character, Barney Fife. Instead, they saw a shy and quiet man who
looked at them with direct, intelligent eyes. And yet, it's probably
the greatest testament to his immeasurable talent that people think
of Barney not as a character but as a living, breathing person. The
genius of his craft was inspired by a fascination with the people he
watched and studied. In coffee shops, at airports, and on film sets,

his mind was absorbing the human spirit. I think his young widow, Francey Yarborough, expressed it perfectly when she said, "He was moved by peoples' poignancy and pain, and he turned it into something endearing and hilarious."

The first time Dad took me to Morgantown, West Virginia, where he grew up, I was nine and he was a celebrity. We arrived at the Hotel Morgan, which had been there since he was a boy. We went to the front desk, and I rang the bell until, finally, a lanky young man appeared. He drew his words out slowly, and there was a gap in the center of his teeth. I didn't know what to make of it. When our family traveled, we'd stay at a fancy hotel like the Beverly Wilshire or the Chateau Marmont; I didn't know there was any other kind.

The hardworking life in Morgantown had left an indelible impression on Dad. This town, as well as Andy Griffith's hometown, Mount Airy, North Carolina, would form the basis of the mythical place called Mayberry, which vibrates with life like so many towns across America. There's something about a hometown that irresistibly pulls at the heartstrings. Many people who find fame and fortune in the city return to live in their hometowns. And they share what they've learned in the wider world to help their towns grow stronger.

The lure of the hometown is a sense of belonging; it's having the lowdown on local gossip or understanding its offbeat humor. City dwellers can relate to this feeling if they identify with a neighborhood. As I've travelled across the country with my one-woman show honoring Dad, I have explored many small towns and marveled at their individuality and how much they have to offer. Far from becoming a thing of the past, these towns are stronger and more vibrant than ever.

Just as in Mayberry, residents of Morgantown and other towns in the American South possess a talent for storytelling, colorful colloquialism, and humor as part of their identity. According to Morgantown resident Chris MacFarlane, there's a lot more: "In Morgantown there was a belief in God that was deeply rooted. People took care of each other. It was just a simple way of life. All people had value. I remember my father telling me the story of how he got sick, he had polio. He ended up living with two ladies in Morgantown who took care of him. They forced him in their way to read, read everything. There was something about us in *The Andy Griffith Show*; our roots, and who we are as people. When I was young, I'd watch the show with the feeling of 'this is home.'"

Today, Morgantown is a midsized city, and West Virginia University is internationally known. The gentle country folk have drifted away. But their memory lives on in the prayers of the departed, in the echoes of the holler, and on black-and-white TV, still being watched by millions.

After *Griffith* and for the rest of his life, Dad would run into clones of Barney Fife. When he arrived somewhere, there might be a squad car parked nearby. A guy with a knowing grin would appear and say, "Bob from the office looks just like Barney Fife." He'd step aside, and presto, another "Barney Fife" would appear! Barneys were everywhere, and still are.

Dad's characters, as well as his life, are legendary. Morgantown paid tribute to Dad with a boulevard named after him and a statue in his likeness. The statue beautifully captures his essence: he's sitting on a bench, deep in thought. Yet some have asked, "Why isn't the statue of Barney Fife?"

My answer is that a statue honors the creator. Dad was a modest man of infinite talent, an artist whose work celebrates the meaning and joy of living a simple life.

1

DOWN BY THE RIVER

O N ANY GIVEN school night, one might have found me up late talking to Dad in his bedroom. His feet would be pointed in the air, his head down by the floor. His right leg had a blood clot—phlebitis—and the doctor had ordered him to spend time on a slant board. I'd sit beside him and look into the eyes of my "patient." At twelve, I was his amateur therapist. At that time, he was preparing to make his second feature film, *The Reluctant Astronaut,* the second of five he would star in for Universal Pictures. Our conversations, often repeated, went something like this:

Don: "If this picture doesn't work out it's off to the poor house."

Me: "Dad, we have enough money."

Don: "You're young, you think money is always going to come. I've got a lot of pressure on me to keep making more."

Me: "But you will, because people love you."

Don: "It's not that simple. When people have money on you, it's not about love anymore."

Me: "'When people have money on you'—you make yourself sound like a racehorse!"

Don: "I've got to make the audience keep coming to see me."

Me: "Why won't they? I think the script is very funny."

Don: "You do?"

Me: "At least, it made me laugh."

Don: "If it doesn't work . . ."

Me: "What's the worst that could happen?"

Don: "I'll go back to square one."

Me: "No, you won't, because they loved *The Ghost and Mr. Chicken*, and they still love Barney."

Don: "When you're famous and you fall, everyone knows."

Me: "You failed before. Remember the first time you went to New York?"

Don: "Sure."

Me: "You couldn't get an acting job that time, so you had to go back to Morgantown and ended up—"

Don: "Plucking chickens at Raese's Grocery store. I had to face my brothers. They knew I wasn't going to make it."

Me: "You didn't that time, but later you did."

Don: "My poor mother had to use her wits every week to pay our rent on time. I wanted to save her from that worry."

I could see his thoughts defeating him in an endless loop of negative thinking. I looked for any glitch that might break the spiral. Memories of the past don't go away because you're famous.

———————————

Ever since the time his mother, Elsie Knotts, conjured up enough coins to treat her youngest son to his first Laurel and Hardy picture at the Warner Theatre, Jessie Donald Knotts knew he wanted to act. Elsie loved the pictures and was well-read on movie stars. Movie theaters offered live entertainment before the feature in those days. When they went to the Metropolitan Theatre on Saturdays, Donald would get up and sing during open mic time. He would do anything to get on stage. All he could think about was *How can I get into show business?*

Dad's family couldn't be *any* farther from the golden lights of Hollywood. Morgantown was in rural West Virginia, surrounded by farms and the rugged mountains of Appalachia. Most people got where they needed to go on foot.

But one thing Morgantown did have was variety. In the late 1800s, rich coal deposits were discovered that led to a boom in gas and oil until around 1920. Buildings in the Queen Anne and Neoclassical Revival styles gave elegance to downtown High Street, due to the talents of architect Elmer Jacobs, who had settled in Morgantown in 1893. There was the Cosmopolitan Hot Dog stand, Bailey's Hardware, and a shoe shop run by a jovial Italian, Nicolas DiPetta, who could repair just about anything. The five-and-ten-cent stores—McCrory's, Murphy's, and Woolworth's—had soda bars or a lunch counter. The town's main economy was coal mining and farming. Most remarkable was West Virginia University, boasting some four thousand students. The Knotts family lived just seven blocks from the university's open-air stadium. It hosted sports and occasional events; even former President Harry Truman once appeared there.

Morgantown had miners and truckers and farmers and shopkeepers and glass workers. Hand-blown glass factories had caught on at the turn of century and attracted skilled craftsmen from all over Europe. But now, the times they lived in were not just bad, they were terrible. Starting in 1929, West Virginia began to suffer dramatically—it was one of the states hit hardest by the Great Depression, and unemployment in some counties was as high as 80 percent. But most people did get by. They gossiped and teased, helped out, and "made do." They had the Good Lord and a funny bone all their own. Jesse Donald Knotts absorbed these people into his soul. (A boy who was to have a huge influence on his life, Andrew Samuel Griffith, was growing up in a similar rural Southern town, Mount Airy, North Carolina.)

When we were growing up, Dad told my brother, Tom, and me some great stories about his own brothers, none of whom went by their given names. There's a cultural mystique about Southerners and their nicknames. Dad's brother William Earl was called Shadow, because he was "so skinny he didn't have one." That makes sense. But how does Jesse get shortened to Don? How did Ralph become Sid? Why did we kids refer to Bill as Uncle Pete? It's a secret of the South that's found only in the sauce.

When I decided to write this book, I met Dad's first cousin Ray Lewis Knotts for the first time and asked him how Dad's family ended up so poor. I was surprised to learn that Dad's father, Jesse, had originally come from money.

Cousin Ray: "Our dads were brothers. Don and I were first cousins. He was my older brother's same age, so he knew your dad much better than I did. He used to go see his act when he was in college. Yeah, he used to perform in taverns and so forth with his dummy. That was in the 1940s."

Me: "How did Dad's father come to own his farm?"

Ray: "The original Knotts farm, owned by Don's and my grandfather, was one of the largest in the Whiteley Township. It was near what they call Claughton Chapel—that was the name of the area—near Mount Morris, Pennsylvania. When Grandfather died and they settled the estate, each of the twelve children, including Don's dad, Jesse, got a pretty good sum of money. Two of the aunts bought farms, and Jessie bought a farm. I think the other brothers were farmers, and the oldest one bought land that had a coal mine. They were very successful."

Jesse and his wife, my grandmother Elsie, were successful farmers. They raised three boys, until one day, Jesse collapsed from a mental illness in the fields and could no longer work.

According to Dad, "When my dad fell ill, one of his brothers stepped in and bought part of our farm, paying Mom a trifle. He later resold it to DuPont before World War II. *He* got rich. Mom tried to farm the rest of the land, but even that was too much for her. Finally, money ran out and she lost the property. She was stone broke." The Great Depression sealed their fate.

Ray: "Then came the crash in '29. . . . My dad lost a lot of his money, and the banks closed. People lost their properties and land—everything. There was no subsidy. There was no unemployment, nothing. There was nothing! And it was just a very, very tough time, I'll tell ya. So people just kind of made out on their own. They had their gardens and had their food and things like that, you know."

When Elsie sold the farm, the family moved into a house at 82 Jefferson Street in Westover, a suburb of Morgantown. Dad was born there on July 21, 1924. According to Morgantown native Melody Siracusa, "The maintenance man who took care of that house told me once that he found Don's signature on the wall of one of the rooms while doing work there." When they outgrew it, Elsie found a large house with lots of rooms in Morgantown, close to the university. She figured she could take in students as boarders.

This house was built in the 1890s and had very odd construction. It had different levels, and there was only one bathroom. The kitchen and living room were on one level, and the rooms they let to boarders were on another.

Elsie was thirty-nine years old when she got pregnant with Donald. When Elsie asked her youngest boy, Earl, "Would you rather I have a baby boy or a baby girl?" he answered, "Well Mama, if it wouldn't push you out'a shape too much, I'd like a pony!" Dad was an unexpected arrival, and Elsie was thrilled, even though she had another mouth to feed.

Don: "Mom and Dad slept in the living room, and I slept on a daybed in the kitchen. Sid and Shadow shared a bedroom with our [long-term] boarder, Tom Helfrik, who was a WPA foreman. The reason for all this doubling up was to leave the remaining four rooms free for rental." Sid and Shadow were in their teens and only able to

Dad as baby, before the family went bust, 1924.

get temporary work here and there. Shadow was a naturally gifted comedian who had such terrible asthma, he had to sleep sitting up. Brother Bill had a steady job but had his own family to support. As a child, Dad even tried to help out with his newspaper route. Rose Anne Childs: "My Mom used to tell me that Don was her paper boy when they lived on Sixth Street."

Nicolette DiPetta Cognetti: "My father had a small shoe repair shop in Sunnyside where Don and many other paper boys would come to pick up their newspapers for delivery. He'd invite the boys into his shop to get warm on cold winter days."

I tried to picture Dad as a boy on his daybed in the kitchen. The nights were long, he was hungry, and what little coal they had would burn out before daylight. The hardest part of the night was anxiety and fear. His father would come in, stare at him with a haunting look, then disappear. To steady his nerves, he gave each of his freezing toes a voice, a personality, and he'd have a conversation with his feet. I came across a man named Chuck Flumm, whose dad had played with my dad when they were kids. Don was five years old when Chuck's grandfather, "Papaw," was taking care of Chuck's dad, Wayne; Wayne's friend Vern; Don; and the rest of the kids.

Chuck: "Papaw had a dairy farm. He invited all the neighbor kids to a birthday party. When Papaw took Don home, his dad and mother were having a spat." Papaw had noticed Jesse looking at Don in a strange way. In fact, everyone seemed on edge around Jesse. "Papaw said, 'If it'd be all right, we'll take Don to our house, and he can spend the night there.' Elsie said that would be fine. Don spent the night, and they had a good time. From then on, if he was ready and wanted to, Don would ride to school in the milk truck with Daddy and his five brothers and sisters."

From what Chuck's grandfather said, Jesse was kind of mean to Dad; he may have been drinking. Papaw would check up on him when he was on his milk delivery route, and if there was trouble, he'd take him home.

The kids got along great milking cows. Chuck: "They'd squirt each other in the face with the milk. Daddy had a favorite cow, and Don had a favorite cow, Daisy. Don said the milk tasted sweeter from his cow. He would milk her and carry the milk home for his family." Papaw would let the boys drive his dairy truck short distances. There were big hills on the road coming from the barn. Chuck: "Don was driving and he was trying to dodge that mud hole. Daddy and Vernon were outside the truck shouting, 'Turn to the left!'—'No, to the right!'—'That's too far!' The truck was wobbling and about to flip over. Don was scared to death; his eyes were bulging! The boys tried to grab the back bumper of the truck but they couldn't hold it. It flipped over with Don in the truck! He pulled himself up and fell down again! His arms and legs were flying every which way. All the milk bottles flipped over and milk was pouring out of the truck." Papaw, who was watching, sat down, slapped his knee and had himself a belly laugh! Then he got up and turned the truck back over.

When the boys got to be eight or nine, he taught them how to shoot the old .22 rifle. It had a real sight and everything. It was the uncle's gun, but Papaw would take them out and let them practice with it. They were told, "You don't kill nothing you don't eat."

Don delighted in his brother Shadow's humor, which I imagine was like the verbal wit of Groucho Marx combined with expressions of Red Skelton. Don would follow him around the house, egging him on. When Shadow would leave to look for work, the house swallowed Don in gloom, so he'd go outside. One morning he decided to practice some baseball moves. He had no equipment, so he pantomimed striking out batters, fighting with referees, and catching the ball in triumph. Suddenly he heard laughter—neighbor kids were pointing at him and cheering. He had been their entertainment! It made him feel so good, he thought he might try it again.

Baseball continued to be part of Don's life. Delores Eddy Moore: "I first met Don Knotts when we were students at Seneca Grade School in 1934. I was in the third grade and he was in the sixth grade. I remember the entire school playing baseball in the schoolyard. I recall him as being a nice fellow" (*Dominion Post* [Morgantown, WV], March 19, 2006).

The Knotts boys cracked a lot of jokes about going "over the hill to the poor house." Sid would say, "It's bad enough to go to the poor house without climbing a hill to get there." However, it was a very real fear. Poor houses and poor farms started in England in the seventeenth century when poverty was institutionalized. They didn't begin to disappear in America until after social security became a federal program in 1935. They were built out of public view because of the stigma.

Despite poverty, everyone listened to radio. There were shows with great stars like W. C. Fields, Jack Benny, Fred Allen, Kate Smith, and Milton Berle, who was sixteen and already a showbiz veteran. Since there was no picture, listeners had to use their imaginations. The Knotts family listened to shows on their five-foot-tall radio and repeated their favorite lines at dinner. Dad's favorites were Jack Benny and Edgar Bergen, a ventriloquist, and his dummy, Charlie McCarthy.

I was able to connect with a woman who played with Dad as a child, Fern Hall Giessman. I asked her what it was like for them as kids growing up during the Great Depression. Fern: "Oh, listen, I prefer to forget it because people were knocking at doors and begging for sandwiches. Don didn't want to beg, and neither did I. But I can remember three doors away from my house, this woman would invite six kids in and give them each half a sandwich. I'd get my cousin and Don. We'd sit there and be very quiet because we didn't want anybody to know we were being fed. Oh, heck. Oh, those days!" They walked to Seneca Elementary School together, and right across the street was Phillips Grocery, a converted garage. Fern: "If somebody would come in and say, 'Could you spare a glass of milk?' They would not only give them a glass of milk they'd give them a pint of milk and say, 'Now, take this home to your family.'"

The nights Don spent on the dairy farm gave a respite from that misery. Chuck: "Grandma made clothes and quilted socks for the cold winter nights. One day she couldn't find her quilting. She looked up and saw Don and the boys wearing the socks on their hands." They were using them for puppets! They put on a show with Dad as writer, director, and head puppeteer. Papaw invited the neighbors—his sisters, brothers, aunts, and cousins. Seated comfortably in the barn, they watched the puppet show in the treehouse.

Dad was very thin and had a slight curvature of the spine, so he didn't stand completely straight. People would look at him and say, "You're gonna get sick if you don't eat," often knowing full well there was little to eat. He began to believe their theories and it eventually led to full-scale hypochondria.

As Papaw had recognized, Dad's home life was like a ship tossing in a storm. Even as he got older, Dad slept in the kitchen, and Sid would come home drunk in the middle of the night as if he weren't even there, singing off key, and fry up some eggs. When Dad protested, Sid smacked him with the spatula.

The Knotts brothers couldn't find much work, so in those desperate times they had to be creative. Once, Dad was listening outside their bedroom door, as he often did, and heard their plans. It was Shadow, Sid (who was tipsy), and big brother Bill, who was wearing a suit for his job as a store manager. Sid opened a suitcase. Sid: "This is just the beginning! Folks'll soon be coming to the Knotts boys for all their smokes." He lit one, but Bill waved the smoke away: "Put that out—Ma's gonna smell it." Sid: "No she ain't. I got it covered." He put the cigarette on top of his head and covered it with his hat. Shadow and Bill counted: "Five, four, three, two . . ." Sid yelped, "Yeow!" He pushed his hat off. Shadow deftly caught the cigarette as it fell, stuck the unlit end in his own ear, and amazingly exhaled smoke from his mouth while doing an Irish jig. They heard a high-pitched giggle and turned to see their little brother in convulsions, which spurred Shadow to make his dance even sillier. Sid pushed the suitcase under the bed and growled, "Have you been here the whole time?" Dad felt his intensity and scrambled away to find his mother, who always managed to cheer him. In these tough times she had to be wise. But the specs perched on her nose couldn't hide her twinkling eyes.

Soon after Sid, Shadow, and Bill acquired their secret "business acquaintance," young Cousin Ray's kin had a surprise visit. Ray: "Sid would come over to our house a lot on Sundays when he needed a drink; you couldn't get any booze in West Virginia, so he'd come over to Pennsylvania. One Sunday morning Sid and Shadow drove up to our house with two guys in the car. They'd just came from Chicago and said they hadn't had breakfast yet. That was in the bad old days when Al Capone was there. They had their holsters under their coats

Clockwise from upper left:
Dad's father, William Jesse
Knotts; his mother, Elsie Knotts;
the Knotts boardinghouse at
2147 University Avenue in
Morgantown; brothers Sid and
Bill with Dad; and brother
Shadow Knotts.

like the old-time movies. My dad said, 'OK, you guys put your guns up on the mantle and Elle will feed ya.' It was somethin' to see, I tell ya. My mother fed them, and they got back in the car and left. We always had a lot of fun with Sid. He was kind of a character, ya know."

One night, Dad woke to the sound of an argument in the hall. Sid was singing drunkenly. Elsie hissed, "Don't you dare go in there with that gun, the boy's sleeping!"

Sid: "The boy? You mean the *baby*?" He laughed and sang louder.

Elsie: "Shhh! Quiet down. Who do you think you are, Roy Rogers?"

Sid: "Hell, no, I'm Rudy Valee."

Elsie: "Quit cussing! And I told you not to bring that gun in the house. As drunk as you are, you're gonna shoot yourself in the foot!"

Sid: "Ain't happened yet, Ma, it ain't happened yet." There was a series of loud *thumps*. Sid: "Ow! Cut it out! Alright, I'm going!" Dad heard footsteps going downstairs and the front door slam shut. Elsie literally swept him out of the house. Sid went on a bender and didn't come home for a week.

As a welcome distraction from the chaos, Dad had an active life in the neighborhood. Fern: "Don lived on University Avenue and I lived on Grant Avenue. There was just an alley between the two backyards. We were the same age—he was like a brother to me, and I was his sister, because he didn't have a sister. There was a Mickey Mouse Club at the Metropolitan Theatre. Nobody had money to go anywhere, so we just got together for free." A couple of dance teachers had started the club for children, which offered them a chance to perform onstage. Fern had been given a special pair of tap shoes. Fern: "Don would come over and sit on my garage steps and watch me dance, then he'd practice his routines on me. My older cousin was an artist who also made puppets and he gave one to Don." As she described it, the puppet had a straw hat and a corncob pipe attached to its mouth. Fern: "He'd come out with the puppet in a bag and say, 'I want to talk to somebody that no one has ever seen,' and he'd take the puppet out of the bag." He would do a little routine:

Don: "I'm so mad I could spit money. Ptui! There's a dollar!"

Puppet: "Ptui! There's your change!"

Fern: "Then he'd ask, 'Is this OK? Can I go on with this?' I'd say, 'You certainly can.' I would be excited or unexcited, and he built his routines like that. He loved Edgar Bergen and he tried to do the same routines. But my cousin said, 'Nope, you've got to do it another way. This character has to be somebody else; you can't copy.' I was trying to develop a dance, and Don was trying to develop a routine with the dummy."

Over the years, Dad loved many dummies, and he left many. You can imagine if they could *really* talk, what stories they might tell! When he started to outgrow his current puppet, he noticed a sign in Harner's Grocery advertising a small Charlie McCarthy dummy with lips that moved! He started saving up. That afternoon, Elsie put some coins in his hand and said, "Go on over to Galusha's and get half pound of ground beef. We've got six for dinner." Don told her about the dummy. "How much do you need?" she asked. He gave her a pathetic look: "Ten cents?" Elsie sighed. "All right." She took a dime from his hand and put it in a piggy bank. "Make that a *quarter* pound of ground beef."

Don ran over to Galusha's Grocery, which was right next door— he was excitable and ran everywhere. The store was owned by two brothers, Harold and Sleepy. They also owned the house the Knotts family occupied. Don said, "Mom needs a quarter pound of ground beef."

Sleepy: "You hear that, Harold? The Knotts are entertaining."

Harold smirked, "Is the mayor invited?"

Don puffed out his chest. "We got plans. My brothers and I are starting a business. It's gonna be *big*!"

Harold: "Yeah? What kind of business?"

Don: "A cigarette factory!"

Sleepy: "Aw, now you're just blowin' smoke." Their loud cackles followed him home.

West Virginia University's Mountaineers had an exceptionally fine football coach from 1931 to 1933 in Earle "Greasy" Neale. The team lost quite a few games, but Greasy would later be inducted into the Pro Football Hall of Fame as coach of the Philadelphia Eagles in 1969. When a reporter asked how he got his nickname, Greasy said, "There was a boy I grew up with in Parkersburg, West Virginia, who was kind of a Huckleberry Finn. One day I called him 'Dirty Face' or 'Dirty Neck' or some such thing, and he got even by calling me 'Greasy' because I had worked as a grease boy in a rolling mill. The other kids picked it up and it stayed with me for life."

The usually cynical Shadow found a hero in Greasy. They were both tall, thin, looked somewhat alike, and had catchy nicknames. The Knotts boys couldn't afford tickets, but they never missed a game. Don would get there early and hang out in the tunnels with his buddies. When the stadium was just about filled, they'd come out of cover and find a seat. Shadow might have a date or act as a goofy shill for Sid selling hot cigarettes.

John Pyles, a younger friend of Dad's from Morgantown, remembered: "There was a guy they used to call 'Chop 'Em Down.' He was a country guy who came in from River Road. Everyone could hear him yelling in the stands, 'Wash them out! Wring them out! Hang them out on the line! We can beat Pitt any old time!'" Rumor also had it that he would look for things like an orange or a hat and juggle them. If he saw a guy with a pretty girl next to him, he'd jump on the guy's lap and try to kiss her. If the fellow was a good sport, the crowd would egg him on. He'd take a drink and gargle to the tune of the Mountaineer fight song. This bit was a hit and always got applause.

After the game, the brothers would find each other and walk home together. They'd reenact the game for Elsie, vying for her laughter with their impressions. They did a mock debate like two sports announcers. Sid claimed the team lost because "they tried too hard." Shadow answered as Greasy: "Fellas, think *small*. It's hard by the yard but it's a cinch by the inch!" Don imitated the referee and got laughs from everyone! Their father did not join the fun; Jesse would hover in the background, or he'd suddenly lurch forward and frighten them.

––––––––––––

Sometimes Jesse's paranoia would come out in force. Once, when Don was out playing with a friend, his father came and ordered him home, forcing him to walk at knifepoint. He also attacked Elsie on occasion. Ray: "In those days, no one spoke of the mental illness that Don's dad had; you didn't talk about it. All I knew was that Don's daddy had a breakdown, which was probably due to the bad times."

Bill remembered his father before the illness had devoured his soul. He'd been an elder of the church, a big, strong man who did well with his farm, raising tomatoes, potatoes, and corn that were trucked to nearby grocery stores. He took pride in his family. One day Jesse was led home from the fields, unable to see. He lay in bed, blind, for two weeks. He got his sight back and never lost it again, but he remained distant and disturbed.

It was common in those days for a mentally ill person to be taken care of at home. Public opinion didn't start to change until the writings of Dorothea Dix, who died in 1887, began to penetrate in the 1930s: "Leaving an insane person in a household is very disturbing, and especially difficult for the children present." It was also believed that mental illness was hereditary.

Jesse was committed to Weston State Hospital for the mentally insane sometime between 1936 and 1938. Ray's wife, Molly: "I remember seeing that place as a child. It was a huge building with lots of land and probably eight- or ten-foot iron fence all the way around. Once you got in, you just didn't return. Back then, mental illness was thought of as, you could never be cured."

Bill once visited his father at Weston. He followed the directions he'd been given at the desk, passing rooms filled with patients. From within were sounds of moaning, shouting, and nonsensical talking. He turned the corner to a hallway that was deathly quiet. An unpleasant odor assaulted his nose. He located the room number and went in, looking among beds of patients passed out or staring off into space. Then he saw him: Jesse had been confined to his bed and had little room for movement. His frame was gaunt, and his eyes, like a vulture's, stared into a void. Bill knelt beside him but could only manage, "Pop." Jesse raised his head stiffly and growled, "Son, get me out of this hell hole!" Bill fought back tears and thought, *He doesn't deserve this.* For lack of an alternative, Jesse was reinstated to his perilous perch in the living room.

———

Boarders at the Knotts home could be anyone from students to transients. Some of them skipped out on the rent. Others took an interest in Elsie or her youngest son. A magician, Master Curtiss, taught Don tricks with tarot cards. The special deck, he explained, had been a gift to him from a Mesopotamian princess. Master Curtiss: "Young Donald, when you work in circuses and carnivals, you learn a whole new vocabulary, kind of a pig Latin we speak to one another when we don't want 'marks' or non-carnies to understand. And you learn how to be a pitchman. I'll show you." In a deep, mysterious voice, he recited; "Step right up, folks. The show is about to begin! Inside this tent is the one and only Gozi, the Wild Boy from Borneo. Come and watch as Gozi tears and eats the flesh of live, poisonous snakes, a wild boy who is immune to his vicious, slithering, reptile playmates."

Donald came downstairs as if in a trance. Elsie asked, "Did he give you the rent?" He absently shook his head. Elsie: "Oh, that man!" She marched upstairs with Donald hiding behind her skirt. She called his name, but got no answer, so she flung the door open. The carny's window was open; he had fled. Elsie was fit to be tied until she saw Donald excitedly holding some colorful cards. The magician had trimmed them to fit his small hands. Donald presented the deck to his mother, commanding, "Pick a card, any card!"

Dad's friend Robert A. Moore remembered, "One fall while at Morgantown Junior High, Don and I went to the Westover Fireman's Carnival, we had very little money. Don spent his and mine trying to win a dummy at the spinning wheel concession run by Ralph Spittler, a Westover fireman. After several times trying, we were most likely out of money, Ralph gave him the dummy. As I recall, he named it Oscar" (*Dominion Post* [Morgantown, WV], March 19, 2006).

———————

Cousin Ray: "It was a tough time for Aunt Elsie to raise boys. You had to take your hat off to her. She was always a happy person; she had this giggly laugh." But her laughter wasn't heard the day they came for her piano. She did not play, but she admired its sturdy black frame in the foyer, proclaiming, "We're middle class!" Now, the illusion was gone.

Shadow was hilarious at dinner that night. When everyone noticed an extra portion of meat on the platter, he "machine gun" spat on it, then politely asked, "Seconds anyone?" He did a Chaplinesque

impression of the ice man who would deliver an ice cake, supported
on his shoulder by a leather pad to keep his shirt dry. He pantomimed
dropping the ice into a drip pan, splashing the water everywhere,
before slipping and falling into the tub. The performance inspired
Sid to jump in with wisecracks. Using his ventriloquist's talents,
Don threw his voice into his mother's apple pie: "Great show!" Elsie
laughed so hard, tears streamed down her cheeks. She was the audience her sons strived to please, and there was a competition to see
who could make her laugh hardest.

Don: "If you'd have asked me when I was twelve years old who
would be the famous comedian in the Knotts family, I'd have answered,
'Shadow.' Mom thought I was talented, but not that funny. She thought
Shadow was the funniest man alive. I was so much younger—I was
just the baby. Shadow was always thinking of something funny to
do." Don had a natural gift for comedy, but he hadn't learned how
to harness it yet.

Elsie was sick for a while, and Bill chipped in so they could hire a
helper. Marie Halle Warren: "My father, Ernest Snyder, was a trucker
hauling timber. . . . Don's mother was not well and needed someone
to give her a hand with housework. I was doing this at a very early
age to earn some of my keep. My father was struggling, I was the
oldest of my family of eight brothers and two sisters. So my father let
me stay with Don and his family. I was 13 years of age. They lived in
what I called the oil fields. Every Saturday, Don and I went to 'Texas
Lunch' in the city for one of those very special hot dogs. The first
sermon I ever heard was in a Pentecostal church and was preached by
Don's other uncle, and what a preacher he was. I accepted my Jesus
that very day" (*Dominion Post* [Morgantown, WV], March 19, 2006).

Dad described the frustration he had with his "preacher uncle,"
Lawrence: "Time stood still on those rare occasions when Uncle Lawrence came to dinner. I would cringe when Mom asked him to say
grace. Every time he started, he'd end up speaking in tongues. Maybe

thirty minutes later Uncle Lawrence finally said 'Amen' in *our* tongue. By then dinner would be as cold as John Brown's body."

Uncle Frank, on the other hand, was considered a playboy who had given up the old-time religion for Old Crow whiskey. Uncle Lawrence wrote him off: "One sip and you slip!" They were both barbers and rarely on speaking terms, though their shops were four doors apart. Lawrence would give Donald a free haircut after he finished with his paying customers. The wait could be hours, but Lawrence was witty, too! He had a rhyme: "Snip a little, quip a little, snip a little, quip a little, and zowie! A crew cut in jig time." A few customers would get up and dance that jig! They'd probably had a couple of nips with their snips.

———————

Elsie was raised a born-again Christian, and she was deeply religious. She disagreed with the church's prohibition on dancing, movies, and card playing, but she did feel that sex outside of marriage was a major sin. Dad told a story about the irreverence Shadow felt for some of her more respectable friends. Don: "Mom was enjoying an afternoon of bridge with some of the uptown church ladies. Shadow sauntered by the card table while a lady shuffled; he casually mentioned he was going to the john. He went upstairs and opened the door to the bathroom. The ladies could hear the door swing open—*thunk!*—as it hit the doorstop. Then came the sound of water dribbling into the john. Mom and her friends tried to concentrate on the game but activity stopped, as the trickle went on and on and on. I was upstairs and heard the stream of water. I sneaked to the door of the bathroom. There was Shadow, chuckling quietly as he poured water from a large bucket into the bowl, ever so slowly. Mom barely managed to hide her mirth from her friends."

Once, Shadow took him along when he was running an errand for Elsie. They passed through the campus by Woodburn Hall, and there was a man on a scaffold washing the face of the tower's clock. Shadow yelled, "Hey buddy, you wouldn't happen to have the time, would you?" The man didn't hear people laughing below. He took out a pocket watch and yelled, "*It's three thirtyyyyy.*" Shadow yelled back, "*Thank youuuu!*"

Dad came home by himself, and they didn't see Shadow for a while. He had to serve a ten-day stint in the town jail for being drunk and disorderly. Don: "Shadow and Sid were periodically in trouble. When they drank a lot, they did fight a lot, and that frightened me a whole lot."

———————

Dad liked to roam the neighborhood with his pals. Elsie trusted him and gave him a wide berth. Don: "I palled with lots of guys in the nine blocks between my place and my friend, Bill Law's. Bill's family was rich and lived in a fancy duplex, but everyone was welcome to use his basketball hoop. When Bill and I were twelve, we'd ride out to his father's farm on the dairy truck, milk cans banging, just to hang out."

At the time, the movie *Dead End* was all the rage. Dad and Bill felt inspired by the young, tough characters, known as the Dead End Kids. They made a secret plan to head for the river, which was strictly forbidden. After a four-mile trek, they found themselves in Osage, by the mines. They climbed a low bridge over the river. The Monongahela shimmered invitingly in the breeze, but Bill had a funny feeling. "It's later than I thought. We better get out'a here. Come on." Suddenly the wind swelled up, pushing them to the edge—and over. They landed with a heavy splash. Dad started flailing his arms, and Bill yelled, "Don't do that!" Dad croaked: "I can't breathe!" His arms and neck were covered in weeds. Bill made his way over and pulled them off. Shivering and exhausted, they made it out. The sun was going down as they hightailed it for home. Donald tiptoed to his front door. It opened on its own. There stood Elsie with her broom.

"I smelled you from a block away. You went down to the river!"

"I'm sorry, Ma," he said, breaking into sobs. "It was awful terrible!" The broom fell to the floor as she swept him in her arms. In the morning, he faced a lecture from brother Bill.

Good, kind, loving Elsie. God and family were everything to her. Don was the baby she nurtured. Bill was her reliable son and a born salesman. Sid and Shadow were her "lost boys." The two had been through so much in their young lives. When their proud Papa collapsed, they left school to help out. Now they were unskilled misfits with only their wits to guide them. They tried to find escape with booze and town girls, who they slipped out the back before Elsie's broom could find them. They wanted to be good, to please her. They loved to watch her humming on the porch, gently sweeping leaves away. They would join her, singing, "We are climbing, Jacob's ladder, soldiers, of the Lord"—moments of joy in a chaotic world.

Dad finally had enough money to buy the dummy he had seen in Harner's Grocery Store, and he headed out in the pouring rain. When he got back, he stood in the door with his umbrella, proudly showing off the dummy. Shadow came running over, but ignoring the dummy he grabbed the umbrella and sat with it on his knee. Shadow: "Who was that lady I saw you with last night?" Umbrella: "A walking cane from uptown." Dad threw in, "That umbrella's quite a fella." Making Shadow laugh was the best!

Dad was asked to perform at a neighborhood gathering with his dummy, and his show was a hit. He made over $1—that was a fortune! He began performing his ventriloquism at banquets and civic events all over Morgantown. But by this time, his department store dummy had developed a case of terminal dry rot. A university professor in the neighborhood, sort of a jack-of-all-trades, fashioned a very professional-looking dummy for him, and Dad was thrilled. He was practicing constantly. One time he threw his voice into a glass of whiskey Shadow was drinking and gave him quite a start. He was in junior high and starting to find his legs as a comedian. According to Clarence Hess, assistant principal, "He was a comical nut. He could act crazy when he wanted to. I remember he would go up to the water fountain and pretend to drink, but there wouldn't be any water coming out. He liked to be laughed at" (*Dominion Post* [Morgantown, WV], March 19, 2006).

Jim Sennett's mother, Shirley Hamilton Sennett, and Dad were in the same sixth-grade class together. Jim: "My mom used to say your dad would get all his friends together and play courtroom. He'd play the lead defense lawyer, and the others would be judge and jury. One particular game he cajoled them to play was B Line. He would set the course, and the group had to move in a straight line toward the goal, no matter what the obstacle in front of them."

———————

When Dad was thirteen, the principal came to his class and told him to go home right away, his father was very ill with pneumonia. He went home to a horrifying scene. Don: "My mother was crying, my father was wild-eyed, and Uncle Lawrence was talking in tongues. There was a preacher there from the church. He took me over and stood me close to the bed. Much later, my father rose up and died. It was a highly emotional scene. But after a few weeks, my mother settled down. She seemed relaxed and relieved, actually."

That demon in the closet was gone, and Dad was about to exorcise the other. He had grown a few inches, and the next time Sid started his bullying tactics, Dad rose up and pushed him down the stairs. Sid never bothered him again.

Dad was about to enter a new phase, high school, and he was ready. The first day he walked into Morgantown High School in the more upscale neighborhood of South Park, he was filled with excitement. He soon became a very well-loved student. By his senior year, he was voted the wittiest, the most popular, the best all-around senior boy, and Most Pleasing Personality. He was voted class president three out of four years. Dad said, "I didn't know what to do, so I just made jokes."

Gary Green: "I was the senior class president in 1966 of our class. Sandy Knotts was in my graduating class. I had to give a speech, and I didn't have a clue what they were like. Miss Byrd, our senior class advisor, had a three-by-five file card filled with notes from various people who had given the speech before at spring banquets. I was surprised to come across Don Knotts's file from 1942. His notes were absolutely hysterical. I mean they were just a class above what anybody else had written. It did give me some ideas."

Dad wrote a gossip column for the school newspaper, the *Red and Blue Journal*, called "Dots and Dashes by Knotts." He was active in several clubs, and he continued to round up kids to put on shows. Sean Malone: "Don and my grandfather Tom Jackson and a guy named Jack Feck used to perform the Three Stooges at Morgantown High."

Barbara Palumbo: "Don would walk over to my mom's house in Westover and talk her into doing a show. He'd round up a team of performers, and Mom was proud to be part of it. She played piano and tap danced and he did his ventriloquist act at Morgantown High."

At the same time, Don was hustling ventriloquist gigs. Joe Vincent Kilianski was the esteemed Polish American leader of the Joe Vincent Orchestra, which entertained in the region. According to his son-in-law, John M. Panza, "On several occasions he hired a young and upcoming entertainer to perform during orchestra breaks. Money was hard to come by in the early 1940s, so Mr. Knotts' fee was just a few dollars per session" (*Dominion Post* [Morgantown, WV], March 19, 2006).

According to Ina Dennis Bruceton Mills, "He was scheduled to do a show somewhere in Fairmont with his puppet. At the time, he had no transportation and someone asked my aunt if she could take him. Of course, she did. She thought he was such a nice young man. Her name was Beatrice Scotchel Cundiff, and she had a restaurant, Bea's Restaurant in Westover, for several years" (*Dominion Post* [Morgantown, WV], March 19, 2006). He met her at the corner of High Street and Fife Avenue.

Everybody was jitterbugging. They had lunchtime dances in the school, and the girls would hurry and eat their lunch, hoping a guy would ask them to dance. There were special shows on holidays at the Met; the biggest was on New Year's Eve. Morgantown had a lot of big bands coming through from DC, Pittsburgh, Cleveland, and Baltimore. They were big acts, live productions.

There was a path around the gym where the older kids would go to flirt. According to the gym teacher, Barbara Solly, "From what I understand [from her dad and uncles, the Wotrings], your dad used to stand by Senior Alley, throw his voice, and whistle at the girls. He would do it in a way that didn't look like it was him. So the girls would turn and look at the guy that *wasn't* doing the whistling."

Don: "I met a boy named Jarvey Eldred, and we became inseparable. We hung out together in school, and on weekends we'd double date. Jarvey's mother would let him use their 1929 DeSoto, and we'd go dancing or head to the roller rink. Jarvey was smooth with the ladies."

They did shows together. Jarvey played the musical saw and Don would get a few laughs with his latest dummy, Danny. The boys would harmonize a couple of numbers and do a little soft shoe. Don: "Later on we added a third man to the group. His name was Richie Ferrara, he had a beautiful singing voice, and he played mandolin and banjo." They called themselves the Radio Three.

One of Dad and Jarvey's many high school performances, 1939–41.

Bill Hart: "The Z-1 Moose club probably gave Don his first pay-ing job, certainly one of the first. He was a young, skinny kid in high school and he was throwing his voice. When we hired him for $5 to perform at a Loyal Order of Moose clambake . . . Moose were really going to town. Knotts was hired for part of a floor show and he brought along another young skinny kid named Jarvis Eldred, who played a saw like you never heard one played. The acts were smash hits, and we had to raise the going pay for these budding young stars. He did start here and the Moose got their money's worth" (*Dominion Post* [Morgantown, WV], January 25, 1969).

The high school drama department was active in competitions with other schools. Dorothy Stone White directed Dad and another student, Mary Ellen Duncan, in a competition. Mary's son and daugh-ter, Les Wylie and Jenni Greco, brought me a letter his mother had received. It read, "Miss Duncan is charming and unaffected and your direction of her was a joy to see." It also said, "the same goes for

Mr. Knotts who is one of the few high school actors I have ever seen who could play a sophisticated Coward role convincingly."

In high school, Dad continued his tradition of playing practical jokes. Jane Maddox Bishop: "Your dad grew up with my father, Max Maddox, and his brother Bob. Don and Max had a class together in high school. One time, Don, my father, and another friend went to a store and bought some cheap perfume, then poured it on the seats in a classroom at the high school. My grandfather had a department store on High Street called O.J. Morrison's. Several young men would paint the floor once a year. One time my father and his brother lined up on each side of Don, winked at each other and started painting. As they crossed the floor, they sped up and painted Don into a box as they closed in behind him."

Girls were crazy about Dad and Jarvey, one for his looks and the other for his humor. Of course, they were both great guys and fun to be out with. One girl Dad knew, Doris Coddington Harner, dated him as a friend. Doris: "Don was two years ahead of me. My oldest brother, Delroy, was in his class. His neighbor Bob Spangler, who I was dating, and Jarvis Eldred were two of Don's very best friends. Bob joined the Marines; when he was telling everyone goodbye, he said, 'I'm going to have Don look out for you while I'm gone.' So Don took me to the movies and took me out dancing—he was a wonderful dancer. He was a very friendly person, and everybody loved him. We didn't have a car, and his family didn't either. He would walk from downtown to South Elkins, where I lived. In school we had assemblies every Friday, and Don was in a lot of them." An assembly was where a couple of drama and dance teachers collected anyone who had talent and put on a show for the whole school. He performed with Danny, and he told funny stories and jokes. It was just for the kids.

Mary DeAntonis: "He was so funny in school. When he walked into a classroom, without a word he would make everyone laugh with his eyes and gestures. The kids would laugh, and even the teachers would laugh, and finally get class under control."

Bill Mason: "During his senior year at high school, some students worried that Don spent too much time on his motorcycle, driving out to Cheat Lake" (*Dominion Post* [Morgantown, WV], March 19, 2006). Dad and Jarvey were dared by some fellow classmates to climb the treacherous Coopers Rock, which is perched atop Cheat Mountain and rises up from Cheat Lake. They accepted the challenge. Don: "Jarvey and I imagined ourselves adventurers, so one night, Jarvey told his mom he'd be staying overnight at my house, and I told mine I'd be staying at his." Elsie happened to call Mrs. Eldred that afternoon for her recipe for hummingbird cake, and they realized they had been duped. *What are they up to?* Elsie wondered.

Emma Belle, Elsie's sister, was the person to call for help. It was risky, though—she had always been a wild child. Their grandpappy worried about it so much he had given her a Remington Derringer for protection but regretted that when he noticed Emma's aim wasn't so good. He dared not insult her by taking it back, so he simply disabled the gun by dislocating the barrel's pivoting mechanism. He reasoned, "When she gets mad, she'll scare the pants off any man, anyhow." Emma never found out. She would smooch in the parlor with her favorite beau, the gun in the drawer beside her.

This afternoon, Emma was preparing a basket for the church picnic when she got Elsie's call, and she announced she was on the case! She put on her overalls and her prettiest flowered hat and rode her bicycle into town. Since it was a warm summer's day, it occurred to her they might go fishing. Sure enough, Jarvey's car was parked right in front of Bob Mayola's Sporting Goods. She hid in the brush and watched as the boys came out and drove off. Emma ambled into the store and started to chat with Bob. She smiled and batted her lashes, but her prattle was interrupted when Bob's wife came in. So Emma changed tactics and commenced to gossip. A while later, Elsie's telephone rang and Emma reported that Don and Jarvey were headed to Cheat Lake!

"Oh, Lord," Elsie sighed as she sank into her chair. "Not the river again!"

From the start, it didn't go as planned. Karen Eldred: "They got a rowboat and took it to the bottom of the mountain. There was a boy named Howard Ward Christopher—he was a spoiled kid. He was gonna help them, but he said his nanny or maid would be upset, and he left his friends right there." So they set up camp and started the precarious climb, hugging the mountain face. The higher they went, the scarier it got. Rocks would slip and hit the lake with a barely audible splash. It was terrifying. By the time they finally reached Coopers Rock, they realized they were no adventurers.

———————

Another event occurred that sobered Dad even more. Don: "I was taking tickets at the movie theater where I was an usher and saw my brother Sid walking into the lobby. He said, 'You'd better change your clothes and come home with me. It's Shadow; Shadow's dead.' He had died during the night of an asthma attack. He was just thirty-one. The next night, I was sent into town on an errand. Woodburn Hall is one of the most beautiful buildings on the campus of WVU. I looked up at the tower and was so startled I came to a sudden halt. The light on the old clock was out. I had never seen the light out in that clock."

———————

The Great Depression that had dragged on for a decade finally ended, but it took an attack on American soil to do so. The Japanese bombed Pearl Harbor on December 7, 1941, forcing the United States into World War II. Imagine having lived through the Great Depression, only to end up fighting the most terrible war of the twentieth century! The Greatest Generation is aptly named. Doris Harner: "A lot of the boys volunteered early so they could get into what they wanted. Bob [Spangler] wanted to be in the Marines, and so did Delroy."

At the final senior high school assembly, Dad told the tale of a parson who preached about the evils of alcohol. Don: "If I had all the whiskey in this county, I'd throw it in the river. If I had all the whiskey in this state, I'd throw it in the river. If I had all the whiskey in the country, I'd throw it in the river. Now let us rise and sing, 'Let's All Gather at the River.'" He got a big laugh, and he got it without using his dummy, which was a turning point. He still performed with the dummy, but he now had the confidence to be himself on stage, as well.

When he graduated from Morgantown High School in 1942, his confidence was so high that he felt he was ready to go to New York City and pursue a professional acting career. He vowed to his mother and anyone who would listen that he was going to "bring the Big

Dad's first professional picture, about 1940.

Apple to its knees!" He and his friend Ray Gosovich made their way via farm wagon and Greyhound bus and found lodgings at the YMCA. Dad got a job as an elevator operator at the Cornish Arms Hotel. He saw some shows and got to talk to an idol of his, the dancer Ray Bolger. He went to a couple auditions but landed neither part. He had done everything he could to prepare himself, but casting directors only made fun of his accent.

The pair ran out of money and had to go home in defeat. To make things even more humiliating, the only job he could get was chicken plucker at the grocery store. The whole experience left a deep scar that seemed to confirm his fears that he could never escape. He had given his small cash reserves to folks who said they were in need; they had taken the money and laughed at him. The neighborly thing to do in Morgantown was seen as foolish in the city.

When he looked in the mirror now, he saw a ridiculous hayseed who had dared to dream. Fortunately, Elsie had taken the precaution of enrolling him at WVU "just in case." He started classes, but he didn't perform or socialize. He studied and became like Mr. Peepers, a nebbish schoolteacher character Wally Cox would later play. The only thing he did toward a possible acting career was take a speech class. He knew if he ever did try again, he'd have to get rid of his accent or be labeled a "hillbilly comedian."

As the school year dragged on, a nagging feeling grew that he ought to enlist. Just about everybody he knew had joined, except for a couple of 4-Fs. This included Shadow before he died; he insisted after his exam that the army doctor had written on his application "fit as a fiddle." Dad could be facing the same fate, but, if accepted, the fear of war was crippling. He was never going to be a heroic soldier, so what could his place be in this war? He did enlist, however, so apparently, he really wanted in.

Emma Belle wrote in her journal, "Donald went to the recruiter's office and took Danny with him. He started his ventriloquist routine, and the recruiter was laughing so hard he didn't notice that Danny added a few pounds to Donald's weight." However, he was still one pound underweight, and had to sign a waiver saying he was "skinny, not shaky." (I'm kidding. Who knows what the waiver said? There's always a waiver!) On the army application, Dad listed his profession as ventriloquist because he had been earning money with it since he was thirteen.

Dad enlisted in 1943. Before he left, he went to see his friend Doris Harner: "When he went into the army, he asked me if I would take his fraternity pin. I had already had a boyfriend and wasn't ready for that. I said, 'I will not wear it. Give it to your mother or sister or somebody.' He said, 'Please, just keep it for me.' So I kept it in a box and gave it to him when he got back. I enjoyed going out with him because he was so entertaining; he made everyone laugh. Always had a smile on his face, never said a bad thing about anyone."

He joined the artillery outfit at Fort Bliss, Texas, for basic training. While there, he got a telegram from the War Department telling him to join "Detachment X." Hmmm? It turned out that "X" was a unit of Special Services, an *entertainment* unit. The army was forming a company to entertain the troops with a show called *Stars and Gripes*. He was in show business at last! He later wrote, "To this day, I bless the nameless army officer who, long before the computer era, turned up that ventriloquism entry on my sheet."

2

STARS AND GRIPES

THE PENTAGON KNEW how difficult this war was going to be and wanted to take care of the morale of the soldiers. It formed an entertainment unit called Special Services, which would report straight to the Pentagon, and found a show for this troupe to perform. *Stars and Gripes* was a musical comedy revue by a well-known writer, Harold Rome, which had received good notices. The Pentagon decreed that Special Services would perform the show only when there was a suitable stage. Otherwise, they would perform a variety show with different acts, like *The Ed Sullivan Show*. That meant they would have to use their creativity to put another show together.

The Special Services unit consisted of entertainers who had also been trained to use a gun. They were told, "You're going to be good-will ambassadors and help the soldiers forget the ugliness of combat," but in an informal way. They would treat it like putting on a show for their buddies, the soldiers. Don: "Talented guys from all over the country were sent to Fort Meade, Maryland, to join the show. We were thirty-five in all. We had a top-notch band, two good singers, a magician, a few tap dancers, and a guy who got music out of a tire pump. I'm not sure how he did that."

The unit also had a fine comic actor named Al Checco. Don and Al became very close friends and had a camaraderie with a couple of musicians—a sax player named Dave Rafferty, and the troupe's drummer, Joe Damiani, the only guy smaller than Dad. There were also professional comedians: Donald "Red" Blanchard and Red Ford. A lot of guys were named Red in this era, like Red Skelton and Red Buttons. I guess if you were male and you had red hair, people thought that was your name, somehow! There was also a third professional comedian named Mickey Shaughnessy.

The Special Services unit travelled for forty days in a troop ship called the *Seawitch* and finally arrived at Milne Bay, New Guinea. Don: "When I arrived in port, I have to admit it was lush. At the outset, before I realized it rained all the time, I thought it was the most scenic, beautiful place I had ever gotten a chance to look at."

Bob Metz: "Just like in a movie, friendly natives with fright wig hair rowed out in long canoes to sell coconuts. Everyone, including the Japanese, feared the cannibals. At the time, the nearly impenetrable jungles on the islands were unexplored thirty miles in from the beach. When an airplane crashed, no one dared to look for survivors. Aboriginals hunted within the tall grass marshes. A scouting party once stumbled upon aboriginals worshiping the mysterious metal birds that had fallen into the forest, loaded with usable goodies. Natives created special ceremonies begging the gods for more 'tin birds.'"

There were no orders for the performing troupe at Milne Bay, and the captain wouldn't let them off the ship. Morale sunk to its lowest point as they listened to the never-ending rain. Mickey said, "I'm fed up with the set up." Al: "I'm nervous from the service." Don: "I'm skinny off New Guinea." Suddenly, they were laughing. A tap dancer who rarely spoke, "Silent Ben," tapped out some beats, and they got a rhythm going. They kept at it until they had a musical number.

Mickey and the two Reds contributed material from their own shows. Sometimes they got so creative they didn't stop.

As an army unit, they were kind of sloppy, but they did what they were supposed to do—they rehearsed and put a show together. Since they were a special outfit, they had no standard operating procedure and there was no sergeant in charge, but that was a good thing. They were busy preparing a show; they had no time for sergeants. They were living under difficult conditions: the constant rain and mud, the fear of getting malaria, the terror of a violent attack from the enemy. The Japanese tortured their prisoners and left their bodies for the soldiers to find. Things were tense, and if an argument began to escalate, the four Italian accordionists who had formed a musical act called the New Guinea Quartet would start to play. The music was upbeat, and with their cutting up, nobody could remember what the heck everybody was fighting about.

Al: "After the army, or navy, or whoever had gone through these little towns, we performed in all these places, Milne Bay, Hollandia, Finschhafen; we were all over New Guinea. New Guinea was and still is an unbelievable jungle. It's huge—a continent almost. We went through all of that. They had to take it island by island, section by section, where the Japanese were, and we would advertise our show. We'd get in the truck and our drummer, Joe Damiani, kept his fingers going—he practiced the drums all the time. He would play paradiddle, paradiddle, so we called him "Paradiddle." Soldiers would come with boxes and sit down. If they had any kind of a stage, wherever it was, there might be surrounding companies come, and we'd have a nice, big audience."

Lanny Ross was a popular singer who was an officer in *Stars and Gripes*. He saw their show and told Dad to look him up in New York City after the war. The Red Cross was always there with writing paper, crackers, and cookies. If the lights came up in the tent, members of the unit could read or write a letter. Dave Rafferty's letter home read, "We ended up in hot New Guinea and began rehearsals on April 16, 1944." On April 18 he wrote about starting their show that Wednesday:

"Frequent cold showers and clothes washing made conditions more tolerable." On July 7, it was raining all the time but they had a good show on the stage that was constructed under a tent. On July 8, they rehearsed in the morning and had a good show later for a navy unit. Dave wrote, "Yesterday was another nice day. Played for Negro troops and they just about went wild. They'd stand up and hit one another over the head with their caps convulsing with laughter. It did us good to see someone enjoying themselves so thoroughly. Did some music arranging for the show, it has improved steadily."

The troupe usually had Sunday as its regular day off. Al Checco: "We had a guy who was weird and would complain about not being well and wouldn't appear in the show. He was a very good piano player, but what he really wanted to do was magic. He was amazingly good at throwing knives at trees." By this time the troupe had been assigned an interim sergeant. Al: "One night he got drunk on jungle juice and held a knife at the sergeant's throat because the sergeant wouldn't let him do his magic act. He was arrested and put in the guard house. The psychiatrist who interviewed him let him talk his way out again. Anybody who stepped on his toes, he'd threatened to kill. So we had to be careful with him and try to talk him out of it. We'd tell him a joke, but many's the night we were worried he might do something, so all of us would stay up all night. I heard Don praying to the Lord, 'Please get me out of here.' I saw that on several occasions. He wanted to do things with his life." This was bizarrely similar to the situation with his father; his dad threatened him with a knife and talked his way out of the state hospital. It affected Dad mentally, and he feared he was going insane like his father. Around that time something like a miracle occurred. He ran into Jarvey!

Judy Eldred: "My dad was in the navy. Was your father in the army?"

Me: "Yes, he was."

Judy: "I wish I could remember exactly where they were. But my dad was in his tent or whatever, and all of a sudden somebody comes in and says, 'Hey there!' and it was your dad, and here they were overseas! They talked about that the last time they were together, before my dad passed away. My dad was saying, 'Yeah, I remember when you came in.' There was Don in his army uniform, and here he was in his navy uniform, and they just couldn't believe it, you know."

Me: "I see how that could happen. My Dad traveled by ship most of the time."

One day, Dad was cutting up with some of the guys when he caught Red Ford staring at him, then he came over and said, "You know something? You're a funny little son-of-a-bitch." Red was a seasoned performer at the age of thirty. That was quite a difference in age, but there was nothing regular about a World War II soldier. A recent high school graduate might train alongside a twenty-seven-year-old coal miner, Glen Miller, or Clark Gable. Don: "Red gave me a few jokes to try at the Washington USO. We got huge laughs with it. In fact, we scored so well he wrote me into his act as a second banana. This turned out to be a great break. Rather than use a dummy, I preferred to 'play the dummy' with Red Ford."

Dad on stage (second from right) with *Stars and Gripes*, about 1943.

Dad's ventriloquist act went over well, but not as well as it had at home; this was a very different audience. Besides, he was tired of doing it. What a pain it must've been, lugging the dummy on and off ships. But the main reason he wanted Danny *out* was that his dummy had been getting the laughs. In the routines with Red, he played a deadpan comedian who walked in and interrupted. This "crossover" originated in vaudeville; it was used as a distraction when the show needed to change a set. When Red was sent home due to illness, Mickey Shaughnessy incorporated Dad as a second banana into *his* act.

Following protocol, Dad asked the sergeant for permission to lose the dummy and just do comedy bits. The sergeant, who was gay and a bit of a ham, said, "Mr. Knotts, you are the only ventriloquist we've got out here. And Danny is no ordinary dummy. He's got USA carved on his chest. He's a wooden American!" A few weeks later, the guys were helping each other load luggage for their next port. Al noticed the dummy's case was missing, and he blew the whistle: "Where's Danny?" Everyone scattered to look for him. Don whispered to Al, "I threw him overboard when we were unloading." But in Dad's autobiography, *Barney Fife and Other Characters I Have Known*, Dad wrote that he left Danny on the beach. Was he worried he had committed "dummycide" as Al teased? At any rate, he had no regrets.

The older comics started coming up with more bits for him to do. Al: "We were in the middle of the jungle and the Japanese were bombing every night. We were traveling with carbines, and we had to jump into foxholes. The Japanese would bomb us nightly; there were some that got pretty close. When we were in the foxhole, we knelt with our guns just in case something happened." That old saying that the show must go on was true even in wartime. Al complained to Dad, "Every time the Japanese start bombing around 7:30, I'm right in the middle of my song!" When the air raids started, they would jump off stage, run to a foxhole, wait for the raid to end, and get back up on stage.

Clowning with Al Checco in the South Pacific during World War II,
1943–1945.

Al: "After Don got rid of Danny, he was in all the sketches. Before that, he only had a few crossovers. In one bit, he'd go across the stage carrying a long stick like a fishing rod."

MC: "Oh, Don, where are you going?"

Don: "I'm going *fithing*."

MC: "What do you have in your mouth?"

Don: "*Wormth*."

He stopped the show just with that. Two numbers later, Dad would come back.

MC: "Well, Don, how was the fish today?"

Don: "OK, but I had better luck last night. I had my girlfriend out with me all night long."

MC: "Wonderful! Did you catch anything?"

Don: "I hope not!"

He stopped the show again. For their closing, since they didn't have any women, a lot of them dressed in drag, posing like pinup girls.

MC: "And here she is, Donella Knotts, the prize pinup girl."

Al: "Don enters, who was skinny as a broomstick. The audience just died! It was a great finish. He was the star of the show, and we all loved him like mad." I didn't realize Dad had become the star. He had started as a nineteen-year-old freshman; learned from the experienced comics; traded his dummy for any quip, bit, or walk-on he could get; and ended up in all the sketches! And in the process, was beloved by all. At the end of the shows, the MC would announce, "Don Knotts, hailing from Morgantown, West Virginia," and "Al Checco from Pittsburgh," and the soldiers would cheer. They loved to meet guys who lived anywhere near their hometowns. They'd come over and talk. "Where are you from again?"

Army buddies: Al Checco standing behind Dad (bottom center), Joe Damiani in cap (bottom right), 1943–1945. *Courtesy of Richard Joseph Damiani*

Headline, January 9, 1945: THE US SIXTH ARMY INVADES LINGAYEN GULF ON LUZON IN THE PHILIPPINES. A US fleet of about seventy ships carried 175,000 troops from the Sixth Army to the beaches of Lingayen Gulf, on northwest Luzon, where a major invasion took place. On January 15, a second smaller invasion took place forty-five miles southwest of the capital, Manila. Fighting continued until March 4, 1945, when the city was officially declared liberated.

Al: "We were at one of the islands that had been taken only two or three days before. Either the Red Cross or Special Service showed us around. As we got into where we were going to be billeted, we saw crossbones and skeletons; it looked like a graveyard. Some of the guys collected the bones and put them up in front of their tents. The machine guns were gone, but the bodies were still there. Little Joe Damiani was one of the youngest in the group. This is how psychological it gets. When we were on a tour, we saw this embankment where the Japanese had machine guns. We weren't carrying guns because they said it was pretty clear now. We were on a hill looking down at the water below, maybe two or three feet, and there was a dead Japanese guy's body there. Joe picked up a rock and threw it at the body, which was so unlike him! He was so conscientious about being a drummer. We saw maggots come out. And we said, 'Joe, come on. Don't do that, Joe, he's dead already.' He said, 'He's a Jap, ain't he?' He wasn't that kind of a person at all, but it got to him, the islands and all that."

Bob Metz: "After the invasion of the Philippines, *Stars and Gripes* followed quickly. They did a lot of hospital entertaining for the soldiers who were wounded. Late in the war they saw virtually all of the Philippines. As the war was nearing its end, the surviving prisoners of the infamous Bataan death march were freed. General MacArthur gave direct orders for them to fly to their island outpost and entertain them." Don: "These guys had been in prison for four years, were half starved, and had been tortured by the Japanese. They watched but didn't laugh once. They barely applauded; it was an eerie experience, but we were happy to try to entertain them."

By the end of the war, Dad had been awarded a World War II Victory Medal, an Asiatic-Pacific Campaign Medal, an Honorable Service Lapel Button, and a marksmanship badge. So he did become a soldier hero, after all.

3

COLLEGE MAN PLAYS
THE FOOL

WHEN WORLD WAR II ended, the returning soldiers, including Dad, took advantage of the GI Bill to pay for a college education. In 1946 Dad had just gotten out of the army. His brother Bill was living with his family in Tucson, Arizona. Bill now had a son he had named after Dad, so he was also Don Knotts. Dad decided to take the summer off and go visit Bill and his family.

Dad told nephew Don that he'd met a fellow in the service who was in production and casting with Hal Roach Studios and who had invited him to come see him if he ever got to L.A. He said he was going to L.A. to meet the guy, and his nephew wanted to go. Don: "We pooled our resources and jumped a Greyhound bus. We took the long ride down to Culver City, and I was so excited to meet these people. We got to the studio and there was a long line around it. They were on strike! I never did get to meet the guy." He spent the rest of the summer at Bill's home and in the fall returned to WVU. He also reconnected with Jarvey and Richie Ferrara, and they revitalized their act.

Kay Metz was a high-spirited student at WVU. Her freshman year had been like a girls' school with all the men at war, but she loved the freedom of being on her own. Kay: "The restrictive rules for freshman women at WVU made an easy transition from the sheltered environment of the preacher's home to the semi-grownup world we were entering. Things changed drastically by the second semester. The campus was overwhelmed by returning soldiers. The ratio was five males to every female. These young men were older and much more serious than those previous high school grads before the war. Many were anxious to settle down and get married before starting school. Several female students were happy to oblige. I was not one of them."

That spring all the sororities decided to invite the guys returning from the army to an open house. The invitation said it would be held from 1:00 PM until 5:00 PM. However, at 5:15 two late arrivals came to the door. They were returning former students Don Knotts and Kent Jones. When they walked in, Dad spotted Kay chatting with a couple of guys, and Kent joined in. They were all asking her out; she seemed embarrassed about all the attention. Finally she said, "Well, this lamp hasn't worked for two weeks. Whoever can get it working can take me out for a soda." While Kent and the other two checked the plug and wiring, Dad simply walked over, put the lamp shade on his head and ordered her to turn him on!

Kay dated both Dad and Kent for a while. Dad was going crazy over Kay, who in turn drove Richie crazy talking about how much in love he was with her. One thing Don and Kay had in common was they both came from strong religious backgrounds and had fathers who dominated from the living room. Kay's father was Reverend Carl, a Baptist pastor who would nap on the sofa during the day, forcing everyone to tiptoe around him. He was an excellent speaker, but he had a difficult time connecting with people. He was quick to judge and expressed his views without much sensitivity. On the other hand, he was emotional in matters involving family and would cry easily, sometimes without control. When his wife broke her arm, he became so emotional that he had to call three times before he could get the words out.

Kay and her brothers, Bob and David, were known as preacher's kids. The label fell more heavily on her, being a female. She studied music and played the pipe organ, often for her father's service. Kay: "The organ is an important part of the service. The organist practices with the choir and is responsible to accompany the music the way the director wishes it to be sung and leads the audience in hymns—not too fast, or too slow—and most importantly, keeps the service moving in an orderly fashion to support the minister." One Sunday she gave an organ recital at the church. A teacher added one of her piano students to the program at the last minute. Her father was to announce her selection, a Chopin piece. He pronounced it "chop in." Kay: "Mother's audible gasp and correction were loud enough to hear all the way to the organ loft. The faux pas gave the audience a chuckle."

Dad had grown up around tent revival meetings. He was questioning those beliefs, and he talked to Kay about it. Don: "At tent meetings in the summer, some of the possessed climbed poles wailing and crying. They believed the unanointed were doomed to hellfire. It troubled me, and I asked some Pentecostal believers, 'What about the Jews?' They said, 'They're lost. We have to save the Jews.' And I asked, 'What about the people in other parts of the world who never heard of Christianity? Are they going to hell too?' They'd say, 'Yes, they are.'"

Kay told him her father had warned against that: "We sat in the car and watched those people out there in the tent who were emotionally involved. He wanted to warn us that these things were bad. He said, 'I do not like this. I do not want you to ever be associated with something like this.' He meant associated with those kinds of religions; a lot of people became mentally ill because there was no escape. If you had even a bad thought you were condemned."

Stars and Gripes, the army show he was in, had given Dad a surge of confidence, and he quickly bounced back from his sad freshman year. He later realized that he probably never would've gone into show business if *Stars and Gripes* hadn't helped him recover his nerve after that first bad trip to New York City.

College was beginning to feel like the glory days of high school. But when he entered a talent contest and didn't even place, he was stunned. He was walking out of class with a heavy heart when he heard "Mr. Knotts!" He turned to see his teacher, Armand Singer. Armand: "He was proud of his skit, sure he had won. But he didn't even get second or third. He spent a sleepless night—if he couldn't make it on campus, what chance did he have? I was one of the judges and I was also his Spanish teacher that 1946 spring. I explained privately that it wasn't fair for a budding professional to compete against rank amateurs" (*Dominion Post* [Morgantown, WV], March 19, 2006). Dad told Mr. Singer that he was so glad he had told him; it helped him eventually make the decision to try his luck again in New York.

Dad was heavily pursuing Kay during this time and romanced her at his former haunt, Cheat Lake. He took her out in a canoe, rowing all by himself. They got caught in a rainstorm and were scared, but once again luck was with him and they made it back. They were becoming a very close couple.

Kay: "Don was a charismatic person, and his sense of humor made him popular. He had more loyal friends than anyone I know, and several of them went out of their way to tell me how much they thought of him." Some of them probably did so at his urging—he really wanted to get married.

Dad was in Kay's sophomore acting class. Kay: "He had already starred in several plays at the university plus his semi-professional performances, and the class members were in awe of his ability. I, on the other hand, couldn't do any of the class exercises without getting a case of the giggles. For the final exam, I did a skit about a scatterbrained lady trying to balance her checkbook. At the conclusion, the class burst into applause. Professor Boyd announced to everyone that he had been ready to flunk me, but instead I was to get an A for the semester due to my splendid performance in that skit!"

Kay's college budget was about depleted, so she asked the housemother to give her a paid job as lounge hostess. Part of the job was making sure everyone was checked in after curfew. Kay: "This was challenging because I had to pry my sorority sisters and their sweethearts apart before the last gong of the campus clock. But the hardest part was to first tear myself away from Don, my fiancé. We were all convinced our food was laced with saltpeter to suppress our sexual desires, and it was rumored that Dean Arnold spent her evenings looking for couples making out in the bushes."

In addition to doing college theater, Dad found time to hustle gigs in West Virginia and Pennsylvania. Bill Kurilko: "When I was 17 years old, I was playing the saxophone and singing with an 11-piece orchestra at the New Martinsville Inn in Mount Morris, Pennsylvania. One Saturday night when we were taking an intermission, a skinny young man of about 21 years of age carried a chair and a microphone out to the floor in front of the stage and sat down. He explained to the audience that he was going to pantomime a person sitting in a movie theater and disturbing people around him. He started out by pretending to unwrap a candy bar, holding the bar close to the microphone where it made a loud noise that only cellophane can make. His facial movements were hilarious when he pretended to apologize to those seated by him. He continued these antics while the audience was in stitches. Next, with his nose, he pantomimed smelling a gas someone near him had let loose, sliding farther and farther down on his chair. By this time, the audience was really breaking up! Later at the bar upstairs, he complimented me on my singing" (*Dominion Post* [Morgantown, WV], March 19, 2006).

Dad, Jarvey, and Richie also looked for bookings for the Radio Three, but venues in the area were not only scarce but also scary. Kay: "Because of the laws, you could only drink beer. They had these roadhouses, and people had parties in their homes." On one of these trips to acquire alcohol, they went to Maryland. Kay: "It took a couple of hours driving and they found this guy who had on a white suit and was very furtive when they got the alcohol back in the car. You could get ninety proof alcohol. Believe me, everybody got smashed very quickly. And then the guys would put on a show."

Dad knew he needed an agent to get any real work in Pittsburgh and complained to Richie that he couldn't get anyone to book him. Richie said, "I'll go with you next time." They went to see a lady agent who gave him the usual "your work is not known here" routine. Richie told her he was studying to be a doctor, and she mentioned she had a medical condition. Richie started to rattle off a couple of prescriptions. She was impressed and grateful, so Richie asked if she would take a look at his friend's act, and she did.

I always thought it was serendipitous that Dad got his first big break in showbiz thanks to a case of irritable bowel syndrome! Don: "She started booking me regularly on weekends. After she booked me in one club, a second booked me, then another. Once I got started, they all wanted to use me."

Kay was working too. She got a summer job through WVU working at a Victorian hotel in Beach Haven, New Jersey. The hotel was huge and took up the whole block. Dad decided to drive up with her. He checked out the competition and figured he'd better get a job there too. Kay: "The hotel guests had few options for entertainment on the island, and Don got an idea. He would put on a musical comedy show, writing and directing the production himself. As soon as we got permission to produce it and the word got out, everyone wanted to get in the act. Among staff, we found a couple of dancers, a few singers, and one guest who was a very good banjo player. Before long we were deep in rehearsals." Kay was the accompanist.

Every day after they finished work, they'd go down to the ocean and swim. One day Kay looked up and saw flames coming out of the hotel, so they tore back! All the crew and everybody was there. They joined a line of people holding the hose, which got yanked and they both flew off! So they snuck back to the hotel's dorm. Kay: "I had some pink panties hanging on the upper bunk bed. I threw them over and under there was our drama teacher, Sam Boyd. He was saying, 'Well!'" After the fire, the ballroom became the dining room. They let some people go, but Dad and Kay were kept on because they were preparing for the big show—they'd been rehearsing every night. Finally, it was the night of the performance, and everybody came to the hotel. It was a full house and the show was a smashing success. They got paid for it too!

When Kay went to see her parents, Rev. Carl told her he would be willing to provide financial support if she and Don got married. Kay: "His fatherly concern was based, no doubt, on his fear that those romantic evenings in Beach Haven had proven too great a temptation. I was furious and told him not to say anything to Don because I didn't want any more pressure." She had always dreamt of having a career, but when she talked to her practical father he had told her, "If you're a girl you have two choices. You can become a teacher and be underappreciated and underpaid, or you can become a nurse emptying bedpans and looking at men's private parts."

Kay: "As the semesters progressed, I found the twenty hours of work in the library more challenging than my previous jobs, and I was losing weight and felt tired most of the time. It occurred to me that if I got married, I wouldn't have to work or struggle so hard financially. So I took the most important step of my life and agreed to get married."

Don and Kay married in her junior and his senior years, two days after Christmas 1947, in her father's First Baptist Church. They found an apartment they could just barely afford, 2.5 miles from campus, and walked to school on bitterly cold mornings. Kay: "We took lunch with Don's mother, who fed us wonderful food including homemade pies and cakes. She would not miss her favorite soap opera, broadcast during the noon hours, and Don's comical interjections kept us in stitches. Afterwards, I would take the long walk back to the room and study while Don attended class. Later, there was the reverse walk back to town to join him for dinner at Richardson Restaurant."

Dad after graduating from West Virginia University, 1946.
Courtesy of Sandy Knotts

4

ON LIVE TV, IT PAYS TO BE NERVOUS

———————

W HEN THE SEMESTER ENDED, Dad graduated, and Kay left school in her
junior year. They moved to New York; Dad was champing at the
bit to pursue his career. They found a cute brownstone apartment near
Central Park. Kay met a relative of Dad who, I believe, had conned
Elsie out of the mineral rights to their land, which caused them to
end up in such terrible poverty.

Kay: "We went to this Fourth of July dinner. It was out in the
country in a big, big house that had a wraparound porch. He was an
uncle of Don's. They would spend the winters in Florida—they were
well-off; they could do that. So all the relatives were invited. And I
can remember nobody ever said a word to me. While his mother
and he were struggling and his father was out of it, they would be
invited out there for Sunday dinners. This man was such a . . . I don't
know what! He treated his wife and everybody badly. If there were
some peas left in the dish at dinner, Don would want them, and he
wouldn't let him have them, things like that—mean, nasty things.

And they told a story about the '30s. They went to the movies and on Wednesday night they'd give out a gold watch and maybe some dishes or something to get people to come. So this man won a watch. Well he had a nice watch, and his wife did not have a watch, but he took another watch for himself, not for her. A lot of the wives were unhappy. There was another story about a woman who was so unhappy with her husband she took to her bed for twenty years; she never got up."

Dad insisted Kay go with him to his gigs in New York. Those audiences were different from those of the taverns and roadhouses. Kay: "He performed at a movie house that had a stage show with acts, like singers. Your dad did a monologue, the fast patter one. I don't think the people understood it, they might have been Russian. The baseball one they understood a little bit more. He would always get huge laughs from the college kids. I thought, *My gosh, why aren't they laughing?* I was cringing in my seat, and the man sitting next to me thought I was after him. I had to get out of there!"

They survived mostly on the thirty-three dollars a week she made working for the Celanese Corporation. Don: "There's no turning back. You have to stay with it. When I first started, I knew lots of kids who were totally committed but hadn't worked in years. There's an actors' joke that goes, 'I haven't had a job in five years. I wish I could find a way to get out of this business!'"

Bob Metz: "My father somehow got wind of the fact that Don was hurting financially. He wrote a letter to Kay, saying, 'If he can't support you, come back home.' Don was devastated and angry about that. He was struggling, and that came at the wrong time for him." Kay reminded him of Lanny Ross's invitation to get in touch after the war, and Dad wrote him a letter. Don: "To my huge surprise, I received an immediate reply inviting me to drop by his studio. What a nice guy Lanny was! He introduced me around, telling all his people how talented he thought I was, and he gave me a shot on his radio show.

I did the comedy routine he saw me do in the South West Pacific. My routine was a football sportscaster who bobbled *huddle* among words, as in, 'The players are in a muddle . . . puddle . . . *huddle!*'"

Through Lanny, Dad met comedy writers Bill Dana and Hal March and the director Perry Lafferty. Perry was a director for television shows, including episodes of *Studio One*, *Kay Kyser's Kollege of Musical Knowledge*, *The Hazel Bishop Show*, and several others. Perry told Dad to keep in touch. Dad heard that Perry was going to direct a comedy series with Imogene Coca and Hal March, so he wrote him a postcard that said, "He also serves who stands and waits," and Perry gave him a part.

Comedians who had not yet made it in their careers, like Buddy Hackett, Jerry Stiller, and Howard Storm, hung out at two popular showbiz coffee shops in New York City, Cromwell's and Hanson's. At Hanson's they could buy a cup of coffee for a nickel and make phone calls to their agents. If there was a part they weren't right for, they'd tell the other comics and help each other out. Milton Berle was the big shot of the bunch. In the late 1940s he was starring in the *Texaco Star Theater* on radio. When it was telecast, Berle became the first TV superstar, with the moniker "Mr. Television."

Another of these actors was Frank Behrens, who was primarily a radio actor with a well-known voice. Frank: "We were at Cromwell's reading the trades and checking out the actresses' legs parked under the counter. This skinny guy walks in, and he looks nervous. He says his name is Don Knotts, and he's new in town. I introduce myself and the gang. Buddy says, 'Sit down, Don, take a load off.' And Berle goes, 'He's a toothpick! What's he gonna take off, his head?' Buddy: 'It's not as big as yours! Don, have some coffee.' Berle: 'Don, the coffee beans were roasted in the crankshaft of Buddy's car.' . . . Don picked up the cup, and his hands were shaking. He took a drink and did a perfect spit take! It was hysterical; he'd been putting us on the whole time! Berle: 'That's your little joke? Don't worry! We'll mop it up later.'"

Howard told Don, "There was a comedian named Sonny Sands. He was older than us by about ten years. Somehow the man who owned Hanson's banned him; I don't know what he did. So Sonny stayed away for about two weeks, and then he came back. Hans saw him and said, 'Sorry, Sonny, you can't come in. I want you out!' Sonny said, 'Come on Hans, don't be like that. All my friends are in here.' Hans said, 'I'm the proprietor and I don't want you here. I'll give you two minutes to leave!' Sonny says, 'Are you kidding? Solomon gives me six!'"

Frank: "Don told them he had an act, but he didn't have any wheels. Buddy said, 'Hey, I got a gig tonight in Greenwich, Connecticut. Come with me and meet the club owner.' Don went with Buddy in his Volkswagen. After the show they went to get the car and the two front seats had been stolen—common in those days. Buddy whipped out a gun and said he was gonna track the hoodlums down. Thinking fast, Don shoved a tree branch into Buddy's back and yelled, 'Stick 'em up!' Buddy, startled, raised his arms and fired a shot in the air. The club owner came out, mad as hell! They grabbed a couple boxes from the curb and got in the car. That was all they had to sit on, two Coca Cola boxes. Buddy held on to that steering wheel like mad, and Don was flying around inside the car. They got to New York, but it was a real wild ride."

Don and Jerry Stiller went to audition for a show that all the comedians in New York were trying to get in on. The casting people had seen so many actors, and they were bored. Jerry: "Your dad said, 'We gotta do something different to make them pay attention to us.' I remember the baseball routine he had. You felt you were at a baseball game watching this weird, strange pitcher making so many faces. . . . He's got a baseball cap on, he stands at the 'mound.' He peers down, shakes off a sign from the catcher. He's chewing tobacco, bobbing in his mouth as he tries to block out the sun. At one point he walks off the mound and yells at the umpire. He did everything under the sun to make it real. He was a genius, one in a million!" I guess those pantomime practice games as a kid paid off.

It was a very creative time for Dad. Once he was sitting at a banquet table when the speaker got up to make a speech. The man was so nervous his hand was shaking, and when he took a drink, he spilled water on Dad. It struck him so funny that he had a dream about it. He woke up and wrote it down. He ended up with a polished monologue he called the "Nervous Speaker."

Dad made a point to drop by Lanny's studio now and then. He got to know Peter Dickson, Lanny's writer, who had a long list of radio credits. Peter was putting together a western series about a twelve-year-old boy, Bobby Benson, who owns a ranch called the B-Bar-B. Dickson cast Dad in the role of Windy Wales, an old-timer along the lines of Gabby Hayes. Pete hired him on blind faith, no audition. That first day, Dad found himself at the microphone with a cast of veteran radio actors. He was terribly nervous, knowing the final word had to come from the vice president of the Mutual network, on which the show aired. Don: "I went home fully expecting to get an official phone call, advising me of my release. My body ached so much from worry and tension I thought I was coming down with the flu. These aches and pains were to become very familiar to me in live TV."

Even once you got a part, you had to sweat out the standard thirteen-week cancellation option. Dad made it through those hurdles, and the show, *Bobby Benson and the B-Bar-B Riders*, became a hit. But that didn't mean he escaped getting pranked! The real Gabby Hayes showed up in the studio one day and acted like he was furious with Don for stealing his voice. It scared the pants of him, but it was all in fun—Gabby actually loved what he was doing.

The *Bobby Benson* show went from airing once a week to five times per week. Scale for an actor on a half-hour show was $33, so Dad ended up with a nice income and started to make a name for himself. He was becoming known for his amazing voice, and that

led to a part on television playing a mute! He got the role of Wilbur
Peterson on the soap opera *Search for Tomorrow*. Wilbur was a neurotic man who could only speak in the presence of his sister, played
by Lee Grant. There was no video, tape, or film, so there was no such
thing as a retake. On one episode Les Damon, the actor he was live on
camera with, went blank on his next line. Normally if that happened
the other actor would start vamping until the first actor got back on
track. But Dad was playing a mute! They couldn't do sign language,
so they started doing face language. Their heads were going back and
forth, they looked like a couple of bobbleheads. The stage manager
couldn't believe it when Les finally called, "Line!" After that, Dad gave
the boot to ever playing mute.

———————

Dad's life became frantic. He was still doing *Bobby Benson*, racing
from one show to the other. He was making enough money that he
and Kay were able to buy a house in Dumont, a small commuter town
in New Jersey about forty-five minutes from the George Washington
Bridge. I was born in 1954, and a few years later, my brother Tom
made his entrance. We settled into a comfortable family life.

There were girls in the neighborhood I played with when I was
three and four years old. I contacted them to see how much they
remembered. Diane Cappio: "Your dad used to mow the lawn with
the push mower, that little hand mower in his Bermuda shorts. He
was the first man in the neighborhood to wear shorts."

Mary Dalidunas-Linder: "I remember playing Ginny dolls in your
living room in Dumont and we would have a little break. Your dad
would come in and I'd sit on his lap. And he would say something funny,
and I'd laugh. Always had something funny and a smile on his face."

Diane: "I remember your dad walking down Blanche Court,
and my mom would say, 'Oh, there goes Mr. Knotts. He's probably

catching the bus to go to New York, I would imagine." Mary: "He would get the bus to go into Manhattan at the corner of Pershing and Madison, the 166. You would take it to West New York." Diane: "It's still running, the 166." Still running! I'm glad New York hasn't changed. If it ain't broke, don't fix it.

Dad's career was running on four cylinders, but mother was feeling housebound. They had one car, and she had her hands full with Tommy and me. Kay: "It sometimes felt as if the world was passing me by. My neighbor Rita Mulvaney and I tried to keep each other from going berserk. We prided ourselves that our close friendship allowed us to discuss issues without anger. It was our way of keeping mentally stimulated."

Dad's radio and TV shows were unexpectedly cancelled within a few months of each other! Dad was terrified; he didn't know how he was going to feed a family of four. Beginning in 1950, Jackie Gleason hosted a variety show, *Cavalcade of Stars*, produced by the Dumont Television Network in New York. Comedy writer and producer Leonard Stern was called in to help with the writing of a six-minute weekly sketch, "The Honeymooners." When Jackie Gleason got too heavy, he would check himself into New York's Lennox Hill Hospital to diet. Leonard was sent to the hospital to see Gleason in his suite and told the nurse, "I'm here to see Jackie Gleason. I'm his writer." The nurse said, "Oh, Mr. Gleason wasn't feeling well, so he went home."

Dad idolized Jackie, so he decided to call the show for work. Jackie was known for having tough guys working for him, and he was quickly turned down.

Then Dad remembered how nice Bill Dana was and gave him a call. They met up at Times Square. Bill said, "Don, you look so down. What's the matter?"

"I can't get enough work to feed my family. I'm gonna have to move back to Morgantown," Dad glumly replied. "Maybe I'll get a job at the university drama department."

"Come on, you're crazy. I'm writing *The Steve Allen Show*. You have that monologue, the nervous man speech, I saw you do it—"

"At the rehearsal for Imogene Coca's show."

"That's right," Bill said. "Listen, you're a talented guy. I'll bring you in and introduce you to Steve."

Bill Dana had been very instrumental to the birth of *The Steve Allen Show*. He was a triple threat: comedian, producer, and a great writer. Howard Storm: "Bill once told me he was working in an off-off-off-Broadway play. 'How's the pay?' I asked. He said, 'The pay's good. Actually, they're not paying me at all. But in the second act I get to eat soup.' Bill also told me he was performing for a convention of blind people. He said he knew he was bombing when they started touching their watches."

Bill Dana also discovered a lot of the talent. "I wasn't an official talent scout there, but I was the only bachelor, and I went around and saw people." He brought Dad in, and Steve loved the Nervous Guy. Pat Weaver (Sigourney's dad!), the head of NBC, had been looking for a vehicle for Steve Allen. Finally, Steve Allen's *The Tonight Show* began on September 27, 1954. Don Knotts, Tom Poston, Steve Lawrence, and Eydie Gormé were regulars, along with Bill Dana, who debuted a character who had an accent: "My name, José Jiménez." Jose had many occupations, from baseball player to astronaut. The show was cutting-edge funny.

A talented young fan itching to get into showbiz, watching from Chagrin Falls, Ohio, was inspired by it. That fan was Tim Conway. In a 1991 interview with Raymond Arroyo, Tim said, "I just lived to see that show at night and always admired Don Knotts because he did what I thought. . . . If I was ever going to be in that business, I would want to do that. He had this gentleness and a relationship with an audience."

A year later, there was a reshuffling, and the program went off the air with the intention of returning in a different format. Dad was out of work and again feeling the pressure of supporting our family. One afternoon, he walked into Cromwell's and saw Frank Behrens. Frank looked up startled, "Don, what are you doing here? I thought you'd be at the audition in Greenwich Village." Don: "What audition?" Frank: "Maurice Evans is casting a Broadway show and it's right up your alley. It's about the army and they're looking for southerners!" Even the title struck a chord—*No Time for Sergeants*. It was about a naive farm boy who gets drafted into the army. The lead would be played by a relative newcomer by the name of Andy Griffith. Don: "How late do they go?" Frank: "Till five." The clock on the wall said 4:30; it was rush hour in New York City! Dad gave Frank a despairing look. Frank: "Don, go! You just gotta make it!!" Don: "Y-yes!" He grabbed his hat but left his portfolio. He raced down the street, dove into a subway tunnel and onto the train, berating himself for not reading the trades that day.

It was exactly 5:00 PM when he arrived breathless to find a man named Van Williams at the reception desk. Van said he was sorry but Mr. Rogers (Maurice Evans's associate producer and companion) wasn't seeing any more people. Don: "I begged, 'Please!' Van looked doubtful but went into the office. He came back and said, 'I'm sorry.' I almost wept. I shuffled down the subway stairway. Then I heard a voice calling after me—it was Van! He said, 'You looked so sad. I went back and pleaded. They agreed to let you audition!'"

Dad ended up getting the small role of the army psychiatrist, which he made stand out. It was his first professional theater job, and he prayed he'd be good enough. Finally, he got the courage to ask Mr. Evans if he was playing the role right. Evans looked at him slightly annoyed and said, drawing the word out, "Yes." That was all the affirmation he got.

Dad had his first conversation with Andy Griffith one afternoon during a break from rehearsal. He ambled out the stage door, and there was Andy, leaning against the wall whittling on a piece of wood.

Andy said, "Excuse me, can I ask you a question?" Don: "Sure." Andy: "Did you play the part of Windy Wales?" Dad was terribly flattered and told him he did. Andy: "I thought I recognized your voice. I used to listen to the B-Bar-B once in a while. It was a pretty good little show." They talked for a while, and Dad had a feeling that he and Andy were going to become great friends. One night after a performance, Dad put on his Nervous Guy monologue for Andy and the *Sergeants* cast, and they were in hysterics. Andy said, "Don, that's brilliant! You've got to audition for *The Gary Moore Show*," which was the *America's Got Talent* of its day. Dad took Andy's advice; he auditioned and performed the monologue on Gary's show.

It's funny how certain people pop in and out of our lives. At a future date, Dad would star in a fantasy film about a fish, *The Incredible Mr. Limpet*, and Carole Cook would play his wife. But years before, Carole had seen him in *Sergeants*! Carole: "My mother took us from Abilene, Texas, to New York, and I saw it. A friend of mine, Cecil Rutherford, was in it, and he took me backstage. I met your Daddy and Andy. I was thrilled to pieces, and the comedy they were doing, well, that kind of talk wasn't strange for me. I'm from Texas, honey, they talk the way I grew up. Maurice Evans was also a great Shakespearean actor on Broadway, and I remember your father and Andy both were laughing about how cheap Maurice was. If they needed something on stage, like if an ashtray was needed for a prop, instead of buying it, he'd say, 'Does anybody have an ashtray in the house we could borrow?' Don and Andy acted like they were a team, but I certainly didn't know they'd go on to become famous and all that!"

Andy Griffith was cast in the movie *No Time for Sergeants*, and he used his influence to get Dad cast, too. Andy left the play soon after; he had an offer to star in the movie *A Face in the Crowd*. Whoever replaced him in the play was never going to be as good as Andy. Dad lost interest and gave notice.

Dad and Andy on the movie set of *No Time for Sergeants* (1958).

In 1956, as luck would have it, NBC was launching a new Sunday-night spinoff of *The Tonight Show* and calling it *The Steve Allen Show*. It was one of the funniest sketch comedy programs ever produced. (Only a fraction of the sketches remain today, because the only recordings of live television programs at the time were low-quality films called kinescopes, which were shot off television monitors as the show was being broadcast. The film itself was often highly unstable and either self-destructed or burst into flames.) The show featured Louis Nye, Gabe Dell, and Pat Harrington Jr. They were an unbelievable team of character and sketch comedians with Steve Allen as straight man and ringleader. The show innovated many popular formats. Steve was the first to do "Man on the Street," and a segment called "The Question Man" was a predecessor to Johnny Carson's Carnac the Magnificent. In fact, Steve Allen would continue to host self-titled variety shows on multiple networks through the 1960s and '70s, and even do some episodes with Johnny Carson in 1962. Johnny later became host of his own *Tonight Show*. They were like-minded. In his opening monologue, Johnny would tell a joke for the Republicans and then a joke for the Democrats. He would alternate so nobody felt left out. Steve took a similar approach with his sketch material.

A lot of the sketches still feel contemporary today. Here's a portion of a sketch on gun control with Dad as the Nervous Guy. Steve: "You've heard the same stock answers a million times. They say that guns don't kill people, people kill people. They say that if a man wants a gun bad enough, he'll get one anyway, and if you argue with 'em, you know what they say? They say, 'Stick 'em up!'—That's what they say! Those on the opposite side are less vocal. Opponents of gun legislation are quick to point to the Constitution. They say it states in black and white that every nut has the right to a gun. The hippies, too, have their views. They favor getting guns out of the hands of the wrong people, like the police!"

The Nervous Guy appears as an expert, physically shaking. Steve: "Hello, Sir. Can you tell us your name, please?"

Don: "My name is B. B. Morrison. And I am the world's champion sharpshooter and marksman."

Steve: "And what does the B. B. stand for?"

Don: "Bang! Bang!"

Steve: "Well, if you're the champion marksman, I'd sure hate to see the guy who was the runner up."

Don: "I'm sorry to say he's not with us any longer . . ."

Steve: "Mr. Morrison, you seem to be on the shaky side. Are you a little nervous?"

Don: "*Noop!*"

Billy Harbach, the show's producer: "Don was hysterical every time; he just broke us up." Harbach misspoke in a funny way. His lines became legend when Steve Allen documented them in his book *Mark It and Strike It*. Once when Billy was referring to Charlton

Heston, he couldn't think of his name and called him Chester Moses. He once asked, "How many feet in a foot?" When Steve asked him why he was wearing a coat indoors, Billy replied, "I forgot to take it off. No! I forgot to go home!"

The television audience grew bigger as the show went on, and the program was getting tons of fan mail. The cast included Don Knotts as the nervous Mr. Morrison, Tom Poston as the man who couldn't remember his own name, Pat Harrington as Italian golf player Guido Panzini, Louis Nye as the smug Gordon Hathaway with the catchphrase "Hi-Ho, Steverino!" and Bill Dana as José Jiménez. Dayton Allen was also a regular and was known for the catchphrase "*Whyyyyy not?*" Gabe Dell, who was part of the popular Bowery Boys, was also in the cast. Near the end of its run, Jim Nabors was added. Gene Rayburn was the show's announcer, and Skitch Henderson was the bandleader.

Harbach: "At first, everything was broadcast from the Empire State Building. There were radio shows, and television was on from 5:00 till about 9:00 PM. Steve's radio program was 20 minutes long and was sponsored by Knickerbocker Beer. When we went to television we were *The Tonight Show with Steve Allen* and aired on NBC." The show's performers rehearsed in a theater about a block from the NBC Television recording studio, around Forty-Ninth Street. "Your dad was so fun to work with, it was a party every day. We would laugh all through rehearsal. I would say 'Fellas, come on, we gotta get through this.' They put the underground cable in, and the cast was so excited that they were going to be seen in Chicago, then Detroit, and a few years later they got the cable out to California!"

In spite of all the accolades, Dad was never one to rest on his laurels; he had to be nothing less than perfect. He would lie awake at night fretting about the sketches and whether he was funny enough. And since the program was live, he never got to see the shows! Dad had to rely on Kay's assessment as to whether that week's show was

At the Knotts home in Dumont, New Jersey—Kay in lower right—
about 1957.

funny. Dad's younger friend John Pyles was trying to decide whether
he should stay in Morgantown or pursue a career as a professional
singer. Dad agreed to meet him for dinner and told him, "If you want
to make it in this business, you have to come to New York and get
ulcers like I did."

Kay remembers: "Those years were relatively happy. The one
exception was Don's recurring sore throats. He dealt with them by
staying in bed, sometimes for two or three days. Coincidentally, they
seemed to occur whenever he had a live TV performance. His doctors
could find no symptoms. In those days, psychosomatic illness was not
totally accepted nor understood by the medical profession."

Dad's stomach would churn with nerves when he had a live
show to do. In 1957 *The Steve Allen Show* went to Havana, Cuba, for
a broadcast. Dad asked Ritchie, his doctor friend, to make a house
call. Ritchie opened his black bag and pulled out garlic, parsley, and

ground beef, his family's ingredients for their favorite Italian spa-
ghetti sauce. Soon they were eating, telling jokes, and laughing. The
stomach pains were history. One of the guest stars of the Havana
show was Dad's idol Edgar Bergen. He was performing with his
dummy Charlie McCarthy. At one point Edgar had to use the restroom. He turned to Dad and said "Hold this," and handed him the
dummy like a sack of laundry. Dad was in awe—he couldn't believe
he was holding Charlie!

With Kay's help, Dad began to confront his demons. Kay: "He'd
been in a depression for so long—fear and all that kind of stuff. I
kept trying to get him to go to a psychiatrist. He'd go to a regular
doctor, complaining of sore throats and things like that. They'd say,
'There's nothing wrong with you.' Finally, he went. He came home
and he had such relief, he cried. The guy treated him like a kid,
saying, 'Poor, poor child.' He gave him sympathy and understood
that he had these problems. He touched the painful part of him that
nobody could reach."

One day, Dad went to the subway and several people followed
him down to ask for his autograph. He had become famous! He was
shocked. This was something he would have to get used to. Fame is
an indicator of success and has its perks, but it also has drawbacks.
One of them is a loss of privacy, and Dad was a very private person.
I had a conversation with a great standup comedian, Katt Williams,
about fame's unintended consequences. Katt: "It changes you; you
never have time to prepare for it. It's literally one day you're not,
and one day you are. And fame takes away a part of you that made
you so good at what you did. If part of your day was sitting in the
mall observing people, that part's over. Even if you weren't regular,
you lived in a regular world. We're journalists at the end of the day.
We're telling stories that are based on true experiences."

As the technology behind television developed, more live shows
that began locally were able to expand. In the late 1950s a migration

began—New York–produced shows were relocating to Los Angeles. *The Steve Allen Show* began making trips to California, and just before one of these trips Dad came down with pneumonia. He had to be hospitalized. He insisted mother be at the hospital each day no later than 11:00 AM and stay until 11:00 PM. She had to leave us with Grandma Elsie so she could stay with Dad twelve hours a day! He had been raised as the baby of the family, and that pattern was so strong, it continued into marriage. This was a very serious illness; doctors operated, and a surgeon left a scar on his lung. He was told it might cause a problem when he got older. One day a priest came to his hospital room and asked if he would like to be given his last rights; Dad said no. The next day a doctor came by and said that a new, experimental drug had just become available and gave him the shot. The drug saved his life.

––––––––––––

In 1958 the show moved permanently to Los Angeles. In addition, the show became one of the first to be telecast in "compatible color." Our family packed up and moved to the West Coast. Kay: "When the movers came, Don said he wanted to take his briefcase himself and the moving man suggested they pack the briefcase in a wooden barrel where it would be completely safe. Don said, 'No, I only trust myself with this briefcase. I have very important papers in there.' We checked into the hotel room where we were going to spend the night; there was a big lobby. I couldn't believe my eyes when I saw the briefcase sitting all by itself in the middle of the lobby floor where anyone could pick it up. Each time we changed airplanes, Don left something behind. He lost his raincoat, his favorite hat that made him look like Sinatra, and the current book he was reading. I remember standing in the airport. I had the baby, diaper bag, you on a leash, and I just couldn't move. Pretty soon this man comes, and he takes the baby, takes the diaper bag, he takes you and he says, 'Come with me.' He took us to this room where people with means got to stay. I had no idea where your dad was. I finally found him when we got on the airplane, and I handed him the briefcase." Dad was a reluctant passenger, and Mother often wondered if his Nervous Guy persona was created from his fear of flying. One of the flights took us to a small town in Missouri where her parents were now living. Her father was the pastor there. Kay: "Don relaxed in their ample front yard, trying to ignore passerby traffic looking to see 'the celebrity.'"

It was quite a journey, but we made it to L.A., land of sunshine, palm trees, smog, and celebrities. While Dad looked for a house to buy, we moved into the Chateau Marmont. Our parents were lounging by the pool while my brother and I played in the water. One time I screamed, "Daddy! Tommy's underwater!!" I never saw Dad's legs move so fast in my life. He jumped in that pool and pulled him out. Tom sputtered a lot of water, but he was OK. Another time, Dad said to me, "I want to teach you about fire and how dangerous matches can be." He lit a match, blew it out, then touched it quickly to my hand. That was unexpected and it hurt. I yelled, "My daddy burned me with a match!" Did that come out of me?!

Mother took us to Disneyland, but Dad wouldn't go. We said, "You should wear a disguise, Daddy, like Barbara Eden did." Barbara Eden: "One time my niece and nephew came, and I took them to Disneyland with my son, Matthew. We were in line for a ride, and I had my red wig on. A woman asked, 'Are you 'Jeannie?' and I said, 'No.' My little niece stuck her thumb in her mouth and said, 'Auntie Barbara just lied!' A man came and said, 'I'm putting you at the front of the line,' and I said to Mathew, 'You see, sometimes it's good to be recognized.'"

In Dad's case, the result was more dramatic. He said, "I visit Disneyland, and if just one tourist recognizes me, I'm dead; they literally chase me." I remember when Tom and I were in London with Dad and he was chased by a group of teenage girls in uniform. They were about thirteen or fourteen years old, and I could see how that can be scary.

Don and Kay socializing in Glendale, California, early 1960s.

———

I first learned of Dad's practical-joke side on the eve of my sixth birthday. My crafty child's eye had detected no sign of a brightly colored present, and I was concerned. When Dad got home from work, he was excited. "Honey, I have a birthday present for you!" Smiling broadly, he handed me . . . an autographed picture of himself. Please don't hate me, dear reader, but I burst into tears! Dad's practical jokes were gentle kidding, never mean. Dad told Tom he foresaw a career for him as a bus driver, and he promised one day to buy him a Greyhound bus. He kept that joke running until the end of his days.

While he was doing *Steve Allen*, Dad also made an appearance on the original *Dean Martin Variety Show*, which ran from 1959 to 1960. At the top of the show, Martin was to introduce Frank Sinatra, and the silhouette of his thin frame, hat, and trench coat would come down the stairs. When the lights came up the audience would see it was Don Knotts. Don: "The sketch went well. They roared for Sinatra, and when they did a close-up on me, people fell down laughing. Someone said Sinatra came in from Hawaii and saw the stuff we did and said, 'I'm supposed to follow that?!'" The show also had a sketch with Martin that Dad didn't want to do. "I told the writer-producer, Herbie Baker, 'You've got to write me another sketch.' We got into an argument, and I got angry. I said, 'You get Louis Nye to do it.'" Sherwin Bash was Louis's personal manager as well as Dad's. Don: "I'll see you, Herbie! And I went out the front door. As I got to my car, I heard footsteps, and Herbie tackled me. We rolled around the parking lot. Finally, the manager for the show had us cross the street for a drink. Herbie agreed to fix the sketch, and I went back." Hmm, I guess that's what you'd call a comedy brawl.

Dad ran into Howard Storm, who had also moved to L.A. and was pursuing work as an actor. He told Dad, "Nothing ever happened until I came out here. I auditioned and got with Desilu Studios." Lucille Ball had a theater that Desi Arnaz had built for her because she wanted to do revues in shows, and they signed twenty-one young people. They were under an Actors' Equity union contract, because it was theater. The Desilu lot had belonged to RKO Pictures when Desi bought the studio; in later years it would become part of the Paramount lot next door.

5

THE LEGEND OF MAYBERRY: A TOWN IS BORN

"Barney is a childlike character because he is unable to hide his emotions. If he feels happy, he looks terribly happy; if he looks sad, you know that he's sad. He isn't able to hide the things that so many adults hide. And it becomes comical to see a grown man showing his emotions on his sleeve."

—Don Knotts

O NE EVENING IN 1960, Dad and mother were at the apartment of his friend Pat Harrington Jr. in Studio City, Los Angeles. Pat had been a late addition to *The Steve Allen Show*. After a long and glorious run in New York and then Los Angeles, the NBC show had come to its end, and Dad and Pat joined the ranks of unemployed actors. They were kicking around ideas about which casting directors to approach for work. Pat had turned on the TV to watch an episode of *The Danny Thomas Show*, and there was Andy Griffith in a part that Pat said was actually a pilot for a new series.

Don: "Andy has a pilot? You're kidding!"

Pat: "I'm Knotts kidding, my friend. Sheriff Andy needs to throw you a rope."

Dad couldn't wait to talk to Andy. Later that night, he dialed the phone, waiting anxiously for an answer, when finally . . . "Who's calling at this hour?" Andy grumbled.

Don: "Ange, it's Don Knotts. Sorry to call you so late. I couldn't wait to congratulate you. I saw your show!"

Andy chuckled: "Jess, as I live and breathe!"

They chatted for a bit, and Dad asked if they had completed casting. Andy answered yes, as far as he knew. Dad suggested Sheriff Taylor "ought to have a deputy."

Andy: "That's a pretty good idea! But I thought you were on *Steve Allen*."

Don: "No, the show was cancelled."

Andy: "Don, Don, Don, call Sheldon Leonard!"

A meeting was set up. Dad went in and pitched his idea for the character to Sheldon, who was the show's executive producer. "You see, I've got an idea for this deputy, and he thinks he's the best deputy that ever lived, but he's more or less exactly the opposite," and he improvised this character of an earnest but excitable deputy.

Sheldon was sold and cast him as Barney in an episode. Sheldon later said, "I never knew he would become such an important element on the show. I thought he would be there for one or two episodes" (Harrison & Habeeb, *Inside Mayberry*, 1994). But he soon knew there was something very special about Barney and the chemistry between Don and Andy. So he signed Dad to a contract making him a regular.

Sheldon was a mastermind of television comedy in the 1960s. Before he became a producer, he was an actor and must've played the epitome of a gangster in at least a hundred movies. In *Pocket Full of Miracles*, he was the gangster who came to town in his own trailer, sitting behind a desk. He was a slightly sleazy but handsome tough guy. That was Sheldon's style in real life too. With his heavy New York accent, cigar, and immaculate wardrobe, he was a smooth-talking businessman who made things happen all over town. He was also a kind man. He discovered all these great talents and made them big stars on television.

Dad said, "I've never heard a bad thing about him. How could Sheldon Leonard not be a good guy? Anybody with two first names, well . . . you just gotta be on a first name basis with."

I said, "Yeah, just like Ronny Howard!"

Many people thought the show was filmed in North Carolina, but that wasn't the case. Desilu Studios, owned by Desi Arnaz and Lucille Ball, stood at 846 North Cahuenga Boulevard in Hollywood, California. Desi had an idea that the *I Love Lucy* sitcom should be shot in front of a live studio audience with three cameras that moved with the actors, and that had never been done. He went to great lengths to create a soundstage that could accommodate his vision. It was groundbreaking, and now the small studio was bursting with talent. You could say it was the Camelot of TV comedy. In addition to *I Love Lucy*, other classic shows were filmed there: *The Dick Van Dyke Show*; *Make Room for Daddy*; *I'm Dickens, He's Fenster*; *The Red Skelton Hour*; and the pilot for *Star Trek*, to name a few. On any given day you would see big stars strolling the lot or in the commissary.

Sheldon Leonard assembled a first-rate team. He brought in Aaron Ruben to be producer and head writer. Aaron had previously written for the Milton Berle and Phil Silvers shows. Leonard brought in Bob Sweeney to direct. Bruce Bilson was first AD (assistant director). Bruce: "In those days a new TV show would start shooting long before they got on the air. We had made ten or twelve episodes, but the public hadn't seen them, and neither had we. We didn't know if we were a hit or a flop." The show finally aired on Monday evening, and the next morning they came to work, anxious to know the public's reaction. As always, they were let onto the lot by a security guard named Tiny, who was anything but tiny. Bruce:

I was in the makeup room with Don, Andy, Lee Greenway the makeup man, and Bob Sweeney, the director. We were asking each other, "What did you hear about the show last night? It was pretty good, wasn't it?"

Bob said, "Yeah, everybody I talked to said it was great."

And Don said, "Everybody I talked to loved it."

And I said, "Me too."

Andy said, "Yeah, when I came in this morning, Tiny at the gate said, 'Great show last night!'"

I said, "Well, that's who I heard it from."

Lee said, "That's who I heard it from!"

So, the five of us had decided America loved us because Tiny at the gate said it was great every Tuesday morning.

Dad later joked that Tiny was the gatekeeper of laughs.

Relaxing between setups on *The Andy Griffith Show* are (left to right) Dad, first AD Bruce Bilson, Andy, and (front) Bob Sweeney, 1962.
Courtesy of Bruce Bilson

Andy had found a dream house he wanted to buy in Toluca Lake. Every day he'd ask, "Should I buy the house?"

On this day, one of the execs said, "Ask me one more time."

Andy: "OK, should I buy the house?"

In a fake angry voice, the exec said, "You'd better, or somebody else will!" The show was a go! There was a "Whoop!" from Andy that ricocheted across the lot. Andy called his broker and got his mansion. And not to be outdone, Dad bought a scooter. The world was about to fall in love with Barney Fife.

"What was your dad like as a father?" is a question I'm frequently asked. By this, people usually mean, "Was your dad like Barney Fife?" He wasn't at all, really, but elements of Barney were inside him. There were times when Barney, the character, and Don, the man, intersected. Our house was on Mountain Street in Glendale, which was a short drive to the studio. Dad was attracted to the hills because they reminded him of West Virginia, but the steep roads were a problem. Cars sped past our house like it was a white flag to the Indy 500. Our parents worried about us crossing the street, and Dad would yelp, "There ought to be a stop sign there!"

When our boyhood friend, Paul, had a beloved dog who got hit by one of those flying autos it was traumatic for us, and the last straw for Dad. He jumped into his 1960 Plymouth and headed for the Glendale Police Department. Imagine the officers' faces when they saw 103 pounds of a quivering Barney Fife storm in and demand that a stop sign and three speed bumps be put in front of our house. The chief of police said, "Mr. Knotts, we are not in the legal position to authorize that, but if you won't tell Andy, we'll be glad to slip you a few bullets on the side." Dad had a hearty laugh with the officers, and the chief promised he'd look into it. Four months later, a stop sign and painted crosswalk were installed in front of our house. Unfortunately, we still ended up with three dead squirrels and a possum who played dead for good. Our neighbors referred to this as the "Barney Fife Stop Sign Incident."

At this point, there were only four regulars on the show: Andy, Barney, Aunt Bee, and Opie. I was fascinated with Ronny, who played Opie. Dad said the Howards were a family of actors: Rance Howard, the father; Jean, their mom; Ronny, the oldest son; and Clint, Ronny's younger brother by five years. Ronny's acting career began at the age of eighteen months, but it really took off at the age of four. Rance got a part in the Broadway production of *Mister Roberts*. He taught Ronny some lines from a scene in the show, and they performed the scene at parties for big laughs. One time, Rance went to see a casting director about work; the guy wasn't in, so he left a note and mentioned he had a son "who's a terrific little actor." That led to Ronny getting an audition and landing a role in *The Journey*, a movie starring Yul Brynner. Ronny was so good that a steady stream of parts followed.

Sheldon Leonard wanted to sign Ronny to a long-term contract, but he was so young, he didn't even know how to read. Rance worried that his son would be deprived of a childhood. Sheldon said, "We're gonna build a childhood for him right on the set." They did, and it worked! Rance and Jean rented an apartment close to the studio so he could walk home for lunch. They were determined to give him a normal childhood, which included bringing Clint to the set. They rarely, if ever, left either of them in the care of a babysitter.

Dad didn't take us to the set for at least two seasons. He didn't want us to miss school and I was getting impatient. He finally announced that when we had our next school vacation, we would make our first visit to the set. Easter was coming, and I counted the days. Having a comedy star for a dad naturally affected me; Dad and I were very close.

I used to wait for the messenger to deliver the scripts, and I'd squirrel them up to my room. I'd check the pages for any female roles so I could practice my acting. The only female who was in almost every script and had a good number of lines was Aunt Bee. I thought, *Hmm, maybe Aunt B needs a niece K!* I decided to do an audition for Dad. I found one of mother's hats and an old Easter basket and marched into the living room where my parents were sitting, and I became Aunt Bee. "Andy, Barney, there's a big basket of fried chicken and cornbread. I want you to eat it all up—don't leave a single crumb. I want everyone to be as plump as me!"

Dad chuckled. "That's a very good impression, honey, but the part of Aunt Bee has already been cast. And besides, you don't know what it's like. Being an actor is a lonely life for a child."

I asked, "Is Ronny lonely?"

Dad said that just like Shirley Temple's parents, Ronny's mother and father made sure he stayed grounded. Dad could see my disappointment, so he asked me to help him learn lines by giving his cues. I would read the other actors' parts, and he'd respond with Barney's lines. I tried to imitate the voices, but Dad told me, "Don't try to sound like the characters, just read the lines straight or it throws me off." He added, "Learn to be a great cue artist." That made the job sound important, so I was pleased.

We watched the show as a family every week. (There was an ongoing battle with the network to have the show moved to an earlier time slot so little kids could watch, but the show always lost that fight. So Tommy was allowed to stay up and watch only five shows the first year.) Watching Dad as Barney on TV was surreal at first, but he was so funny we laughed as hard as any other fans. One day, Dad announced, "You kids are going on the set next week!" Mother drove us to the studio. Dad had been at work since the wee hours.

When "Tiny at the gate" saw us, he wasn't sure who we were and asked, "Are you actors?"

Mother said, "No, we're family."

And I added, "I'm a cue artist."

We got special treatment. They had a parking spot for us on the lot, right next to an impressive-looking green car. Nobody parked on the lot except Frances Bavier, who played Aunt Bee, with her green Studebaker. Dad said the car "looked like it was coming and going."

Dad was in Makeup and Mother had to fill out some paperwork, so we walked around Stage 3 with a lady holding a clipboard. At the sides of the soundstage were big doors that rolled open and closed so sets could come in and out. Andy's house interior was on one end of the stage. There was also the courthouse and barbershop, interior sets with a small portion of the exterior to give the illusion of a street when actors made an exit. If they needed an extra set, such as the mayor's office, they'd build one. There were also temporary sets, like when they had a contest, or the set for "Barney and the Choir." These were simple sets with a lot of set dressing. When no longer needed, they were folded and stored. On the opposite end of the stage were Makeup and the dressing rooms. They called them portable, but they didn't actually move. They were small, about ten by ten, and lined up against the back wall.

At one point, it was reported that an unknown man had been seen drilling a hole in Aunt Bee's dressing room. Aunt Bee had a Peeping Tom in Mayberry—unthinkable! Everyone was on high alert, and then he was spotted again! Bruce Bilson: "So we yelled at him, 'Stop!' The guy came running, and he ran past us. A security guard, an older man named Harry, was at the other gate. All of a sudden, these guys are chasing him, and they yelled: 'Stop him, Harry, get that guy!!' Harry came out with his gun and said, 'Halt!' He fired in the air. And then he started shaking, he fell to his knees, and everyone stopped to make sure Harry was all right. The guy got away and was never seen at the studio again." (Was Harry the real Barney Fife?!) The incident epitomized the humanity of the show. Just like in Mayberry, taking care of a friend took priority. Reggie Smith, the prop man responsible for the food, joked that his famous shoofly pie was attracting the wrong sort of customer.

Part of me believed Mayberry was real, but when I went inside a building, it wasn't real at all, just a facade they called a flat. Clint had a similar reaction the first time he saw one: "At one time you could see that it was a living room, and then you'd see it all folded up. The roof overhead was there to protect cables, cameras, and lights permanently secured to light and film the set from inside. When you're two or three years old, you like to go play. So many nooks and crannies. I always wanted to go up in the catwalks. With the lights, it seemed like a great thing for me to do, but they never let me." (Thank heavens!) I noticed a life-sized cardboard cutout of the squad car. The real squad car was sometimes difficult to maneuver in and out, so Bruce had them make a fake one for times when the car was only seen in the background from the courthouse door. From one direction, everything looked real, but from the opposite view it was as exposed as Bozo the Clown without his red wig.

Dad was out of Makeup now and waved me over to where he was sitting. He still had tissues sticking out of his collar to keep the makeup off his uniform. I was surprised at how artificially tan the makeup made him look, but on black and white film it looked like normal skin tone. I said, "Dad, you're a great actor to make people believe everything so fake is so real."

He said, "That's because I don't have any fake talent. If you're looking for fake talent you have to go over to Screen Gems."

He introduced me to a man named Denny who had playful eyes and a fuzzy red beard. I decided to ask an astute question. "Are you a dolly grip?"

Dad laughed when Denny said, "When I try to grip a dolly, she gripes right back at me. Nah, I don't do anything so important. I make repairs, organize props, and so on. My most important duty is bringing coffee to the master here, your daddy." He picked up a Styrofoam cup of coffee and handed it to Dad, and the cup floated out of his hands!

I was wide-eyed. "How did you do that?"

Denny said, "It wasn't me, it was the ghost, and he never tells," and winked.

The cameras were huge, and the lights so hot they caused the actors' makeup to melt. After each shot, Lee Greenway, the head makeup man, stood off camera and applied powder to the actors' faces to keep them from sweating off their makeup. Lee kept Andy's makeup in a shoebox labeled Andy's Makeup, Size 14. Lee was a Southerner and very close to Andy. He had many talents and would often pluck his banjo with Andy on guitar.

Recently, Ron Howard told me that in today's world, Lee would be a celebrity in his own right and a frequent talk show guest. Lee was also the main instigator of practical jokes along with his coconspirator, Reggie. There was a character! He was full of pride and never ceased to tell people, "I'm a nudist—twelve months a year, hot or cold." Dad said, "When Reggie goes on vacation, he doesn't have to pack. His luggage fits in his wallet."

Denny told Tom and me they were about to shoot a scene in the courthouse, and he took us inside to watch. We got to see Dad and Andy film one of their famous "gun going off" scenes. We stood behind the cameras so we wouldn't be in the shot. Being on set was filled with voices and movement until the director called "Action!"

The scene started and at the moment when Barney's gun went off, Sween, the director, said "Bang"; the real sound effect would be inserted later. At the end of the dialogue, everyone stayed mouse-quiet until the director yelled, "Cut!" Then a roar of laughter erupted from the crew—they were laughing at Dad's performance!

This happened after each of Barney's scenes. The scene work was going beautifully. Andy went into hysterics at just about everything Dad did. I've never seen anyone laugh like Andy; it was an event. First, he'd throw his head back and laugh, "*Ha, ha, ha, ha!!*" Then, he'd start to stomp around. I was shocked at his next move—he punched a hole in a set wall. Apparently, this wasn't a one-time thing. When

I mentioned it to Dad, he said, "You know who really loves Andy's laugh? The grips on the set who make overtime pay patching up those holes."

After they got all the footage they needed from the setup, Tom watched, fascinated, while the crew began to tear down and set up for the next shot. Cables, lights, cameras, booms—everything was in motion. There was a rumble of voices combined with tuneless whistling, the hallmark of a good crew and success of another shoot. Then I heard the familiar voice of Aunt Bee. I was so excited, I turned to look . . . and she was smoking a cigarette! I said, "Aunt Bee, you're smoking!" She said in a low, husky voice, "That's right kid. I'm still a hot chick." That's not what I was expecting! I had foolishly thought of Aunt Bee as my own real auntie.

I was hungry, so Dad walked me over to a table with food spread out, and we munched on some yummy bagels. Bruce explained how the tradition of craft services got started: "Every show had somebody like a janitor who would clean up the stage, pick up horse droppings on a western, make coffee, and stuff like that." A friend of his was working on the *Superman* set. "It was cold, so the producer said to the guy, 'Let's serve some soup when they come in on these split days when they've been out in the cold.' They had the soup, and everybody liked it. Time passed, and the producer said, 'The weather's nice; let's forget the soup.' All of a sudden, they were like, 'What happened to our soup!' They'd gotten used to it."

Dad asked what I'd observed so far. I said, "Aunt Bee smokes!"

Denny piped up, "*Everybody* smokes. Even Aunt Bee is a Marlboro man." A few people laughed at his reference to the cowboy ads running for Marlboro cigarettes.

A spontaneous count started. "Let's see, I smoke, Anita smokes, Betty Lynn does, and Bob Denver . . . I've got a picture of Andy smoking at nineteen," Dad said. "Sween, you smoke."

Sween: "Yes, but I'm planning to quit."

Don: "You said that last month." Dad was also trying to quit. Public awareness of their danger was growing; the surgeon general's warning would appear on cigarette boxes two years later. Dad kept a pack of Pall Malls in Barney's shirt pocket. He might've forgotten to take it out sometimes when they were filming. Most of the crew were smokers. A few people didn't smoke anything but air; Hollywood was smoggy in those days.

Dad said, "Our makeup man is a horse trader."

Me: "He sells horses?"

Don: "No, uh, horse trading is kind of slang for someone who's clever at bargaining. He'll buy anything he can get his hands on." A handsome, silver-haired gentleman was coming toward us.

Don: "Karen, I'd like you to meet Lee Greenway. He's good at shooting the breeze and good at shooting skeet. He's good at shooting anything as long as it doesn't duck." Lee handed me an orange-haired troll doll. My first souvenir!

Don: "So, Lee, how's your golf game?"

Lee: "Pretty good."

Don: "I just bought a new golf bag."

Lee: "That's great, Don. Where's your old bag?"

Don: "It's in the car."

Lee: "I'll give you $25 for it right now."

Don: "Sure." Dad gave me a wink.

The makeup room was a comfortable place to hang out. It felt like the kitchen in our house, relaxed and casual. I met Betty Lynn and I was in heaven because she couldn't have been sweeter. I got to watch Lee do her makeup. With some actors, Lee loved to play little jokes. When he was doing Ronny, he always had a funny little thing to say or he'd pretend he had something on the back of his head. But with Betty, he had the manners of a Southern gentleman. They already knew each other. Lee had been the makeup man for a screen test she'd done for the Broadway show *Oklahoma!* with

Ray Bolger. Bolger was best known as the scarecrow in *The Wizard of Oz*, but before that he was a Broadway star. The first time Dad came to New York, he scored a rush ticket to a Bolger show and was thrilled to get it.

Lee had an instinct about people. He knew actresses could be sensitive, so his makeup station was filled with knickknacks to cheer and/or distract them. There were GI Joes, an oversized jack-in-the-box, rubber golf clubs, an autographed picture of Mel Blanc as Bugs Bunny, and a funhouse mirror that could make you look fat, skinny, or scary. When he announced her makeup was done and she could "go play" with the others, Betty peered in the mirror.

Betty: "Didn't you forget something?" And she batted her eyelashes.

Lee: "You won't be needing false eyelashes. I know you wore them in your Bette Davis pictures, but that was glamour. Andy wants it real."

Betty: "All the other actresses on the show have them."

Lee: "Thelma Lou wouldn't wear them. But you're in luck—your eyes are so beautiful they don't need any help," and he gave her a giant lollipop. Betty mentioned the conversation to a gossip columnist friend. A week later, she opened her mailbox and dozens of little packets fell out. They were false eyelashes sent to her from men all over the country! Now she had enough eyelashes to loan out to her friends, telling them, "The eyes have it."

When I went back to the stage, the crew was setting up the next shot. I heard another unmistakable voice and turned to see Jim Nabors—Gomer—and he was full of fun! He picked me up and twirled me around. I was flying through the air! He thought I loved it, but I was actually kind of scared. I was up there yelling, "Shazam!" and praying Captain Marvel would rescue me. He handed me to Dad and said, "Don, you'd better change this one, she's leaking," which is odd because I was way past my diaper years. It must've been from nervousness.

Later, Dad told me how Jim Nabors was discovered. He was doing a nightclub act at a popular club in Santa Monica called the Horn. His act consisted of singing opera and telling hillbilly jokes. Andy loved to go to the Horn, and he caught one of Jim's shows. There was a new character they had added to the show, Gomer, a gas-pump jockey at Wally's filling station. The role was promised to the actor George Lindsey. But when Andy saw Jim's performance, he went nuts. After the show he said to Jim, "I don't know what you're doing, but I like it!" Jim was brought in and hired. Poor George was out of luck, at least for the moment. (Later, he would be invited to create the role of Goober when Jim left to do his own series.)

I couldn't wait to meet Ronny. He was cute with shiny red hair. We were the same age, but he wasn't like any kid I'd ever met. He had his own little schoolhouse right on the set and a private teacher to do his bidding, or so I imagined. A PR man said, "Ronny, sit here," he pointed to a chair, and Ronny sat. Dad and Tom sat down too, and a photographer snapped their picture. Tom: "Ronny gave his perfect 'Opie look.' He was such a natural." When Ronny was younger, he loved to lie on the floor under the chairs in the makeup room. He loved hearing the stories and the laughter. Whenever Bruce needed Ronny on set, he would yell: "Ronny Hyeah!" Ronny later said he didn't mind getting the call; it got him out of school!

When Rance introduced me to Ronny, Dad said, "Be nice to him—he's going to be a big man someday." I felt so shy. I just said "Hi" and walked away.

The bathrooms on set—privies—had thin walls. Later on, I would look forward to overhearing some stories and hoped a good case of diarrhea would justify the means. I was in the privy and Andy was saying, "Don, you know I love Karen, but she is so darn slow!"

I had to smile when Dad said, "She's not slow; she's just taking her time." But then Dad asked, "Honey, do you think you're about done in there?" I realized I'd been daydreaming and Andy needed to use the john! When I came out, Dad pulled me aside and asked why I walked away when he introduced me to Ronny.

Me: "I don't know what to say to him."

Don: "He's not as different as you may think. Tell him a story."

Me: "You mean like *Jack the Giant Killer*?"

Don: "No, talk about yourself."

Dad knew I had a problem with shyness. I looked for a chance to talk to Ronny. When he wasn't filming, he was with Clint, studying lines, or shooting hoops. Then I wandered into the schoolhouse, and he was there by himself. I decided to make a go of it. "Have you ever been to public school?" I asked. "There's this weird kid at my school named Ben. He tries to impress the girls, and he does all these crazy things to get attention."

Ronny: "I only go for a couple months a year. I met some pretty tough kids there."

I felt encouraged. "When Ben loses a tooth, he gives it to one of us girls to show he likes her. When he smiles, we count his teeth to see if any more teeth are missing and try to figure out who he's gonna give his icky tooth to."

Ronny broke into a wide grin, and I saw he had three missing teeth! He pointed to one and said, "That's new." I smiled to show I had one missing, too, and we started to giggle. He said, "Don't worry, I'm not gonna give you my tooth. I can get a silver dollar for it."

The ice had broken. He took me behind the schoolhouse and showed me a shoe glued to the floor and a purple stage light that plunged the room into eerie darkness—they were remnants of practical jokes played. I picked up a Styrofoam rock, turned it over, and saw the letters RS. Reggie Smith, the prop man, carved his initials into the props he made. He was also a true artisan; he was able to make many of Lee's ideas for practical jokes come to life. Reggie also loved to cook. In the prop room, he kept an electric two-burner and a little rack with all the condiments. So if you were feeling a bit down on the set (it could happen!) he would take you into his personal dining hall, chat with you, and give you some homespun wisdom over a hot "Reggie special."

I also noticed a dart board. Ronny said they were always making bets, and Andy was always winning. Ronny showed me his latest gadgets. One of them was a gold transistor radio so small it could fit in the palm of his hand. I'd never seen a radio that small. He said that one time, Opie was supposed to eat a bowl of ice cream. He was looking forward to it, but when they shot the scene, the lights made the ice cream melt, so they replaced it with mashed potatoes. It wasn't so bad until they added chocolate syrup. Ew, gross! When Ronny got the part of Winthrop in *The Music Man*, he practiced singing "Gary, Indiana" for everyone on the set. He also had to rehearse the spit!

As our visit came to an end, Tommy and I were exhausted and finally ready to go. Tommy pointed to a woman walking toward us. She looked sorta familiar, and I whispered, "Must be a movie star. She's beautiful!" A second later, we burst out laughing—it was our mother! A couple of the makeup people had gotten bored and offered to give her a makeover. So that's where she'd gone off to. You just never know about mothers nowadays!

6

I WAS ONLY FUNNIN'

O N LATER VISITS, I learned more about how things were done. The sound-stage was used for shooting interiors and had only minimal exteriors for the courthouse, pharmacy, and barber shop. They used an area called Franklin Canyon Park, north of Beverly Hills, for the show's lake and forest scenes. Most of the exteriors—houses, downtown stores, and streets—were shot at a location called Forty Acres. It had a camp-like feel, and that's where I imagine the company first bonded. When they went "on location," everybody reported directly there. The extras and crew drove their own cars. There was a caterer, and dressing rooms were brought in. The trucks with arc lights and props came from the Cahuenga studio.

Forty Acres was attached to a studio that had been Goldwyn or Selznick Studios, where they shot *Gone with the Wind*. Just a few yards away were the remains of where they shot the train station during the Battle of Atlanta, when Scarlet goes to find the doctor and sees thousands of wounded men lying there. I can imagine them relaxing after a meal, observing their surroundings. Lee would be describing all the dummies they had laid out, probably a thousand or so, and the ones farthest away from the camera were rigged. They could pull on the dummy's wire and make a hand or leg go up and down. From a distance, it looked like they were alive, but only about one in five or six was an actual human. Dad said the dummies would've been a great audience for his ventriloquist act in the army. Andy said, "Hey, let's go see if we can find 'em!"

The two scouted the ruins and found burlap bags, shovels, and some cooking props. And sure enough, some of the dummies were still buried! Suddenly Dad got an inspiration.

He laid down with hands folded on his chest. Andy went with it:

Andy, as Preacher: "Is there anything you'd like to ask before you depart, soldier?"

Dad, as Soldier: "Do they have latrines . . . up there?"

Preacher: "You're not going to Heaven, son, so don't worry about it."

Soldier: "I see. What's the weather like . . . down there?"

Preacher: "I'm afraid it's hot as hell, son . . . but the food's pretty good."

Soldier (brightening): "It is?"

Peacher (smiling): "The devil always gets the best chefs, you know."

Soldier: "Is that why they say 'Hellzapoppin'?"

They burst into laughter. Bruce was in charge of the call sheet, which told everyone when their scenes were filming. He said it required a lot of energy for Dad to play Barney. "I always try to let your dad have an easy scene to warm up in the morning, then a major scene before lunch when he still has a lot of energy. It's better for him not to do those intense scenes at the end of a long day of work."

Dad sat in a director's chair that had his name on the canvas backing, and I asked him about it. He said, "A set doesn't have regular furniture like chairs and couches. When you aren't in a scene you need a place to sit down. All the shows supply the stars with chairs with their names so the actors have a place to sit. Otherwise the extras will sit there." It took a long time for them to get their chairs. Maybe it was a money thing, but whatever the case, nobody was going to get a chair until Andy got one. He didn't ask for one for two whole seasons. He said it was because he didn't think the show was going to last that long. But Dad had a different take on it: "There's something in Andy's nature that kept him from treating himself like a star. It was almost as if he wanted to deny that fact, and so, even the things he was entitled to, he didn't ask for" (Kelly, *The Andy Griffith Show*, 2017).

At this point the only person on set who had his own chair was the camera man, Sid Hickox, who had taken it upon himself to bring his own. After his exhausting scenes, Dad would plop into that chair until finally Reggie said, "You can't sit there, Don. That's Sid's chair."

Dad was tired and irritated. He said, "I want my own chair."

Reggie: "We don't do that on this show."

Andy heard, came over and whispered, "I want my own chair, too, with my name on it." The following Monday when they came in, there were two chairs facing each other bathed in spotlights, one with Andy's name on it and one with Dad's. Only Andy's name was spelled wrong: GRIFITH. Andy yelled: "They got my name wrong! Don, I'm surprised they didn't spell your name wrong. It would've been just as easy to leave off a *t*."

A hush fell over the group. Denny jumped up and said, "I'm gonna fix this! I'll be back before you can spell *hogwarsh*." He walked out with the chair, closed the door, opened the door, and came right back with it, with Andy's name spelled correctly! What they had done was to cover the correct name with the misspelled one, using double-sided tape.

Andy realized he had been punked and looked at Dad with chagrin. So Dad yelled at Reggie and Lee, "Hey, how come you guys didn't play that joke on me? I'm still second class around here!"

Lee: "Don't worry, Don, we're gonna make a lot of mistakes in your career, starting with your paycheck." Everyone was laughing now. The show was a whole bunch of kidding and camaraderie.

Eventually the other regulars got chairs too. One visitor who loved to play hide-and-seek among the chairs was Clint. The first time he came to the studio, it wasn't planned. Rance was always on set watching Ronny, but sometimes he'd get an audition of his own, and Jean would come down. On this occasion she didn't have time to call a babysitter, so she picked up Clint, who was playing, and brought him with her. He was dressed in a cowboy outfit complete with hat and two six-shooters. Clint was playing cowboy when he was noticed by the director. Clint: "Bob Sweeney took one look at me and saw a bit that could be created with the tiniest Mayberry townsperson offering Barney a peanut butter and jelly sandwich."

Clint was three when he got the part of Leon, close to Ronny's age when he had started. You might say showbiz was in their baby formula. Clint was a rascal, and he loved to outfox his older brother on the jail set. Clint: "Those doors really did clang shut, and when you were caught inside you couldn't open them."

When we were in the courthouse, I noticed Tommy looking up at the bars: "This is really neat." When the lights were off, it was kind of spooky, so of course we had to explore! We were about to go in the jail cell when we heard a loud "*Boo!*" We whirled around to see Denny.

"You don't want to be playing in there. The ghost won't like you messing with his stuff."

"There are no ghosts except for Halloween," I said with authority.

Denny: "There is too a ghost, and he lives right in this jail! They turned a fan on him once, hoping he'd be gone with the wind, but what they got was a ghost with a chill." I didn't know what to make of Denny. Was he for real?

Anyway, back to reality. The young actors were required to attend school every day. Ronny and Clint adored their teacher, who worked almost exclusively for Desilu. She had a special bond with each pupil. Clint said that Ron studied with Catherine Barton for eight years, and though he went to public school for a few months of the year, most of his education was in her one-room schoolhouse.

Clint: "Catherine Barton left an impression on a lot of people because she was a very consistent studio teacher. She was a great lady. For a field trip, we'd go out and look at lizards in the yard. I enjoyed studio school because if you were weak in one department the teacher could work on that. Most of the time I was by myself. Whenever there was a child on the show, I looked at that as an opportunity to hang out with another kid. But what a wonderful experience."

Another actor-student of hers was Keith Thibodeaux (stage name, Richard Keith) who played Little Ricky on *I Love Lucy*. Keith: "When that show ended, at the age of nine, I ended up on the unemployment line." When he got home, his father said, "We're taking you over to Desilu Cahuenga for an audition on *The Andy Griffith Show*."

Keith: "Great, let's go."

He was cast as Opie's friend Johnny Paul Jason. Ms. Barton told Ronny about Keith, who was a few years older, but they looked the same age. They had a common bond, of course, as they were both child stars. Keith had been the only child on *Lucy*, and it was lonely there, but his experience on *Griffith* was the opposite. When he was called in to work it was almost always in scenes with other boys—pals of Opie—so there was a gang of kids.

I began to wonder how these young actors got their start. Our housekeeper, Annie, saved me an article from the *Los Angeles Times* about child actors. It stated, "The four things that are important for a child actor, are: 1, show up on time; 2, know your lines; 3, behave and not be a brat; and 4, have the needed face for the part."

Another child actor on the show, Dennis Rush, who played freckle-faced Howie Pruitt, said, "Once a kid was in the talent pool on the lot, it was all about luck and having the right look." He overheard the casting director, Ruth Burch, tell his dad she thought he was "the right one." "I was a character actor at seven years old." Dennis's showbiz career was not planned. His mom, dad, and seven siblings moved to the San Fernando Valley from Philadelphia so his father could pursue a lifelong dream of becoming a film editor. He became one of the top editors at Universal Studios. Dennis: "It was a family rule that if you were a good kid you got to go have lunch with Dad at the studio."

Finally, Dennis's turn came up. He and his pop were having lunch, and James Cagney was at the next table. It wasn't father and son who were stealing glances; Cagney was observing them. He came over and introduced himself. Cagney said, "I'm getting ready to make *Man of a Thousand Faces* about Lon Chaney. Your son is the spitting image of me. Would you let him play me as a boy in the movie?"

His pop answered: "Well, he's never been in anything before, but if the price is right, I'll let him play your son altogether!"

They laughed, and Cagney said, "Let's take a chance, huh?" He took Dennis under his wing and taught the kid how to act. He also taught him how to tug at his pants like James Cagney and how to say, "You dirty rat." When Dennis squeaked, "You dirty mouse," Cagney roared and repeated the line all over the lot.

The adults and kid actors on the *Griffith* show had mutual respect and admiration. Ronny and Clint were terribly fond of Hal Smith, who played Otis Campbell, the town drunk. In real life, he was spectacularly sober. Dad was impressed that Hal was also one of the top voiceover talents in Hollywood. He voiced cartoons and took other acting gigs on the side. One of these was as spokesman for the International House of Pancakes—IHOP. He'd visit its restaurants as the Pancake Man. Clint: "Ron and I saw Hal on the set, so we knew him as Otis. But we made Mom and Dad take us to see him as the Pancake Man!"

The Knotts family loved IHOP, too, but Dad didn't know Hal had this gig. One Saturday morning we were sitting in the restaurant drooling over pictures of pancakes on the orange walls, when a jovial man clad in white apron, exploding chef's hat, and giant spatula appeared. Dad looked up, surprised: "Hal! What are you doing here?"

Hal got closer and said, "Don, didn't you hear? I got fired from the show. I took this gig to get things going again." Well, Dad had such a distraught look on his face, Hal burst out laughing. "Don, relax, I'm joking!"

"Thank Heavens!" Dad said. "I thought I was going to have to put my dummy in the cell to take your place!"

Hal flipped a rubber pancake with a spatula and caught it in his hat, giving a goofy look. Then he held up his fingers, which had finger puppets on them, and made them talk to him:

"What did the young pancake say to the old burnt pancake? I don't like your flip side."

"My Mum always makes the pancakes too thin. I shouldn't have to put up with this crepe."

"How do elves eat their pancakes? In short stacks."

He was doing his "Pancake Act." Tommy and I laughed till we had tears. Hal leaned in toward Dad: "Don, since you've been such a good audience, when I see you in the cell tomorrow I'm going to give you an extra hiccup." Dad laughed almost as loud as Andy was known to.

Many jokes were played, and you never knew who was going to be the next victim. Andy had a beat-up pair of loafers and took a lot of teasing about them. Lee complained, "Why don't you get a new pair of shoes? These are ready for the dumpster."

Andy: "I like them, they're comfortable."

Lee could only sigh. Then one of the loafers went missing. Andy kept looking for it but never found it. When they were wrapping the first season, Andy was presented with the loafer, which had been bronzed with a plaque that read, THE ANDY GRIFFITH MEMORIAL MOCCASIN.

Another time, there was a long wait for a setup, and everyone was bored. Dad was rambling: "When I first saw a mandolin, I thought it looked like a giant snail laying on its back." Andy and Lee stared as he went on, "My mother's birthday is coming up, and I want to get her something special."

Andy: "You gonna get her a septic tank?"

Dad smiled at this reference to the episode "Barney's First Car." Dad was very close to his mom, and jokes about Barney's mother were based on that. Don: "No, I'm serious. Every year I give her a nice check for her birthday. But this year she's turning eighty, and I want it to be special. She loves the mandolin, and I found one in a store that has a flat back instead of a round one. I'm pretty sure it's an antique." Lee and Andy exchanged glances.

Lee: "That's interesting, Don. Let me take a look, and I'll tell you if it's worth anything."

Don: "Would'ya? I have it in my dressing room. I'll get it!"

Lee took the mandolin and passed it on to Reggie, who secretly filled it with dirt and added a gaggle of purple wisteria sprouting through the hole. Lee, Andy, and Reggie presented it to Dad, who picked it up in disbelief. And that wasn't all. There was a note attached: "Happy Birthday Mommy, from your loving Donny."

The jokes served a purpose: they relieved tension for the creative team. They were having fun, but they never forgot their mission of excellence. If the jokes occasionally got off color, Frances became insulted. She would threaten to quit and have to be coaxed back to the set. Andy would usually get Lee to calm her down. Sometimes Andy himself was the instigator because he was a natural-born tease. But when he'd start in on Frances, Jim Nabors would say, "Andy, you leave that woman alone."

Dad told about the time George Lindsey was doing a scene as Goober watching a horse race. "During rehearsal, he cracked us up—he went off script and threw in some pithy bathroom humor." Suddenly, *thwack!* Francis hit Goober with her umbrella.

"We don't say things like that on this show," she said frostily. Frances had her own sense of humor. From that point on, no matter who she had a beef with, if George was on set she would give him a *thwack*. She must've enjoyed watching him stagger around, and he made the most of the moment.

Betty Lynn was not easily offended. "Your dad was very kind to me. Sometimes they had some risqué jokes they did for the crew, and he wanted to be sure I wouldn't be offended by it."

One time, Dad walked out with a brassiere in his hand and yelled back to the crew, "Can anybody get this filled for me?" He turned around and was shocked to see Betty Lynn. But Betty cracked everyone up when she yelled back, "I thought you were lactose intolerant!"

7

THE MOUNTAIN FOLK

I N THE EARLY 1950S, Richard O. Linke was handling publicity for Capitol Records, but he was hungry for more. One night in 1953, he was listening to the radio in New York City when it picked up the signal of a distant station in the South. The station was playing Andy Griffith's recording "What It Was, Was Football." The monologue was a country boy explaining the game of football. Linke thought the material was fresh and funny. He flew to North Carolina, bought the rights to the record, and became Andy's personal manager.

Another client of Dick Linke was singer/actress Maggie Peterson. When she was just fourteen, Dick had seen her sing with her brother and two other boys in a four-part harmony group. He told her to look him up when she turned eighteen. All through school she dreamed of going to New York to find the missing Linke. When she finally did, he signed her!

Later on, Andy wanted to add new characters to the show. The "Darling family" would add a rural flavor of music and humor. One of the characters was a Darling daughter who would act and sing. Dick brought Andy, Sheldon, and writer-producer Aaron Ruben to see Maggie perform. She wasn't aware that it was an audition. Maggie: "When they wrote the part, they were thinking of a voluptuous gal like Daisy Mae [of *Li'l Abner*], but Andy didn't want caricatures. They decided to go with a country girl, which was great for me, of course. And they thought it was funny that Charlene went after Andy, and she was not sexy." (In the show, Charlene famously refers to Andy as "the pretty man.") Now that they found her, they were searching for the rest of the Darling family, and because of an ad in *Variety*, they found them.

The Dillards was a bluegrass band led by two brothers, Rodney and Doug Dillard. Rodney: "We had gone on an audition when we first got to L.A. at the folk rock club the Ash Grove, where Joan Baez and Bob Dylan performed. We just sort of got our instruments out and played in the lobby, and the guy who owned the place said, 'You can't do that out here; go do it on stage.' We ended up making a record deal with them, and they put a little blurb in *Variety*."

Someone on the *Griffith* team saw the notice and invited the band to audition. Rodney: "You can imagine a country boy from the Ozarks walking on to Desilu Studios! They were shooting an episode with your father. Andy and the director, Bob Sweeney, came over. They sat down and said, 'Show us what you got.' We started playing and halfway through the song, Andy said, 'That's it!' . . . Huh? For all I knew they were kicking us out, because it was so quick. But they loved us, and that's how it started." Other members of the Dillards were Dean Webb and Mitch Jayne. Denver Pyle was later cast as Pa.

Rodney: "We were doing our second show, having lunch at the commissary, when Sheldon Leonard came by. He was holding a bunch of letters and he said, 'Each one of these letters represents about a hundred thousand people,' talking about how much they liked the show we were on." Frances loved the Dillards and brought them brownies. Rodney thanked her: "Now, that's what I call a home-cooked meal."

The Dillards continued to play local clubs, and getting up at the crack of dawn to do TV was exhausting. On top of that, they didn't all fit in their dressing room! They looked for places on the set to catch a few winks. Rodney: "If we worked a concert the night before, we'd all try to get on the beds in the jail. Denver Pyle was the only one who could figure out when to sneak in. It was his timing. He knew when the jail would be empty. He would lead us to the jail. There was always another bed in there. So the boys had to decide who was going to nap that time. They used to call us the Fearsome Foursome. Denver would often end up in the jail cell taking a nap with his hat on, covered with a sheet."

Sports was a daily part of life on set. Sheldon, Andy, and Rance had created a kid-friendly culture. Clint: "Dad encouraged Ron and me to play sports, and Andy supported that, so there was always a game of catch going on." The adult actors would participate, too. Ron: "I loved listening to the Dodgers and Lakers, Vin Scully and Chick Hearn. The show actually went out of its way to schedule so I could make those games. Your dad would take me to the backlot, he enjoyed throwing the ball around." Dennis: "They had a basketball court for us to play on; it was six feet high. It could've been 4' 7" high, and we would've dunked. We were tiny basketball players. The soundstage was our game room." When "Opie's gang" wasn't around, the challenge was to find adults to play. George Lindsey would shoot hoops sometimes. There was another source of players too. Clint: "The show would hire 'little people' to stand in for us kids. And they were great—they liked playing baseball. I had someone to play with!"

The one-hour lunch break was fifteen minutes of eating as fast as they could and forty-five minutes of horsing around. Keith: "It was a gang of us; we'd go to the commissary and see Dick van Dyke and Mary Tyler Moore sitting there. They didn't see us watching. We'd gobble down our hamburger and shake or whatever and run right back. We'd find Andy; his boots would be sticking out in front of him.

He was just so laid back. He's got the guitar going, and Lee would join with his banjo. They'd play with the Darlings and your dad would harmonize. Everybody fought to get back to just listen to music. Or you'd go to the makeup department, and there'd be these makeup men playing checkers with the tech guys." Dennis: "I couldn't have enough time with this group of people. It was just an amazing thing."

But the real kids were Andy, Reggie, Lee, and Dad. They played and refused to grow up. Some of the greatest comedians always acted like kids (think Tim Conway!). Ronny acted older than he was because he wanted to learn. So the younger the guy, the older he tried to be and the older the guy, the younger he tried to be. Their world was one big "tag-you're-it" playground.

Tommy and I were excited to watch the scenes with Opie and his friends. Keith talked about a scene from the episode "One-Punch Opie." In regard to the moment when Barney is describing prison life—"No more peanut butter and jelly sandwiches"—Keith said, "I had a serious look on my face, but underneath I was laughing. I thought he was the funniest thing in the world." He added, "When they do a close-up shot on you, a lot of times the stars don't want to feed you your lines; they'll just take a break. But Mr. Knotts, God love him, would stand off camera and give his lines for the benefit of us kids. Andy did that for us too. We really cracked up at Jim in the camping scene."

My brother recently recalled the outdoor camping scene for "Back to Nature": "It was shot indoors but dressed as outdoors because it was raining that day. In the episode, the boys go camping and learn to survive in the forest. Barney was with them and he's bragging about how good he is at camping, but of course he screws everything up. The thing I remember is Dad kept twisting the lines up. I have that stuck in my mind." I was surprised to hear that because in all the scenes I watched, Dad knew his lines perfectly, and the guest actors were in awe of him.

In the camping episode, Andy tells the "Tale of the Golden Arm." That story gave me the jitters, even when I heard it at summer camp. Suddenly I thought about Denny saying there was a ghost in the jail cell, and I thought, *That's silly!* But I decided to sneak over to the jail for a peek, just in case. It was dark in the courthouse, and I thought I saw something move. I yelled, "Dad, come quick!"

Dad soon appeared with some other folks. "Karen? What's going on?"

"There's a ghost in the jail!" I said, and pointed to Denny. "He told me, and I saw it!"

Denny said uneasily, "I was just hypothesizin'!"

"There's nothing to worry about—you'll see," Dad said. "Can we have some light?" Someone turned the lights up to half. That's when we noticed a figure shrouded in white, and it began to move. Tom and I sucked in our breath, Dad stood stalk still. Denny crouched low and slowly murmured, "Who goes there?" The figure turned and started creeping toward us. Denny made a sudden move that seemed to startle the creature, causing it to jump. Its shroud fell away, and there stood a very sheepish Denver Pyle, holding his hat and jug.

"Sorry, folks. I was just trying to catch a few winks," he said, to much relieved laughter!

———————

As Ronny got older, he learned different aspects of the show. Ron: "Friday would be a rehearsal day where we would work out staging and any other creative problems. I was witnessing scenes getting funnier, writers improving, actors getting funnier. Monday we'd do the exteriors; Tuesday and Wednesday would be filming the interior scenes."

Bruce: "I remember an interesting acting thing. We were doing the episode 'Crime-Free Mayberry,' where Don goes into the jail cell with a criminal trying to act like another criminal, and it never worked. They kept saying, 'Let's try this, let's try that.' And finally, they realized that it was Don trying to be this character and not Barney trying to be this character. When that light went on, it worked. And another thing I've never forgotten happened in the first season. We were in Aaron's office, and Don was all sort of into this thing. He had a little scrap of paper, and he kept writing stuff. And finally, he stopped and said, 'Hey, Ange, I've just memorized the lawman's code. Here, test me on it.'" That was the beginning of the lawman's code routine, where Barney couldn't remember a single word without Andy cueing him. Dad had written enough of the routine to get the idea across. It was further developed by Aaron. In this case, no one had asked him to do it, but they often did.

Dad explained, "They would call me in when they needed two or three minutes of comedy. I would frequently come up with bits. My favorite was when I did the memorization of the preamble to the Constitution." So, a pattern was established. When Dad had an idea, he'd write some lines and a general outline, Aaron would script it out, then Dad and Andy would rehearse it with the director.

Bruce: "On Saturday and Sunday the cast would be learning their lines. Our actors were good. I think our show had a reputation and a quality that the guest stars worked on their words, too."

Dad was extremely disciplined about learning lines. He said the only actor in Hollywood who rehearsed more than he did was Lucille Ball. Every weekend he'd close his bedroom door for hours to learn his lines for the next week's episode. We were forbidden to disturb him, but I used to stand outside the door and listen. It was amazing. He'd take each line and try it out a dozen ways until he found the best reading of the line. Then he'd repeat it over and over, like a concert pianist practicing chords. "Andy, we gotta do something. This is big!" He repeated each line until he got the nuances exactly right.

Ron: "One of my greatest memories, my favorite moments, would come on a Wednesday. We read two scripts, the one we were going to do the following week and the week after, so the writers could hear it. They'd get comments—they'd spend Thursday afternoon rewriting."

Bruce: "At 10:00 that Thursday, the cast came in and read that script. It was the cast plus Sheldon, Aaron, Sween, me, and Hazel Hall, who was the script supervisor, a very important person. We weren't reading this week's script; we were reading next week's script. That would be the second draft. After the cast read through, it would be discussed with everyone."

Don: "Aaron asked the entire cast for suggestions. It's called 'talking down the script.' That script went into rewrite. We would then read down the previously worked script for next week's show. We'd discuss it and make suggestions. Then Aaron Ruben, Bob Sweeney, and Andy would do a polish. They would bring me into it if a number of the Barney scenes needed fixing."

Every episode had a fully developed storyline, thanks to Aaron and especially Andy. George Lindsey said, "Andy was just about the best story constructionist there ever was." Most of the writers worked in teams. Since the show was a hit, Aaron had his pick of established comedy writers. There was one writing team that wasn't as well known, that of Sam Bobrick and Bill Idelson. They were desperate to get a meeting with Aaron. One night they were guzzling coffee and throwing around ideas for spec scripts. Bill said, "I know where Aaron Ruben parks his car, in a small lot across the street from the back entrance. I saw him go in the office through the back door." Sam was skeptical, but the next morning they watched as Ruben pulled into the lot, just as Bill predicted.

Bill: "We were scared because Aaron was a big man on the lot. So he walks up and I say, 'Aaron, can we see you for a couple a minutes, 'cause I got an idea for your show. Could you spare us five minutes sometime?' He gave us a look as he took out his keys and said, 'Come in at eleven tomorrow.' I pitched the shoplifting idea, and his eyes lit up. He bought it on the spot. He started laying out scenes right away, and we were furiously taking notes" (Harrison & Habeeb, *Inside Mayberry*, 1994).

Sam and Bill went on to write many episodes. Bill passed on in 2007. I interviewed his partner and Dad's friend, Sam Bobrick, about the writing process.

Sam: "The writers got together with Aaron Ruben in his office and pitched maybe four or five stories in the beginning of the season because we did a lot of shows then; we did twenty-two or twenty-four shows a year. Aaron would say this is a good one, work that one out, and that's a good one, you know. Everyone would take two or three shows and go home and write them."

Once an idea was accepted, they took lots of notes from Aaron, submitted many drafts, and when that final draft was in, they were done. "Aaron Ruben was one of the nicest men I ever worked with. Aaron was the first half-hour producer I ever worked for, and I was spoiled because he would tell you what he wanted, you'd give it to him. And then that's it. Whereas you got people . . . I mean you write a script they want, and they change their minds, and you never know what you're going to get. But Aaron was a solid producer. The show was sweet and everybody on it was sweet. That's the only way I can describe it. And once in a while Andy would pop in, and Andy would contribute a lot. He was very creative also, Andy."

Dad also gave a lot of credit to Andy for his all-encompassing approach to the show: As he told Bob Metz, "Andy is such a complex guy. One of the things I have always admired about him is that in addition to his acting and his superb rewrites, he keeps his eye on everything. He gets to know every member of that crew personally. He also knows who is doing what. Of course, we knew all the crew because we were living with them for years. But Andy is very political. He knows all the right people and who is pulling the strings. When he needs something, he knows who to go to. He also looks out for his people. He makes sure everyone gets credit and sees they get what they need."

Back then, writers weren't allowed on the set of a filmed show, and *Andy Griffith* was filmed. They were only there for the live shows like *Dick Van Dyke*. The writers wanted to write for Barney because they could be inventive. They also loved Dad as a person. Sam: "I don't know any downside of Don Knotts. None. People just love him, and he really earned their love. He was very respectful of everybody; he was always kind. You know, there's no dirt to dish about Don that I know of."

I asked Sam how he came up with so many great stories. Sam: "I grew up in a small town, and a couple of ideas came from my life. I remember I had an uncle, when he got mad, he used to punch everybody in the nose." That led to the episode "The Case of the Punch in the Nose." "It involved an unsolved case, and Barney wanted to open the case up again. He got everybody in town so mad, everybody kept punching each other in the nose. The first one Bill and I wrote for Barney was 'The Shoplifters.' And the one where Opie sells seeds. That was a true story. When I was a kid, I tried to sell seeds. They kept sending me letters, 'If you don't pay for the seeds, we're going to call in the federal bureau,' and all that." (I had to laugh when Sam told me that because Sam was of my dad's generation, but I also sold seeds when I was young. What kind of thrill is that for a kid? How did they ever get us hooked?) Sam passed in 2019.

Another way to kill time between set changes was doing bits. A favorite was the fake Academy Award speech. Dad would start it off—he'd pick up a spoon and talk into it like a microphone. "I'd like to thank the Academy for this beautiful—" plant, radiator, watercooler, whatever, and he'd make an acceptance speech. The cast would line up and take their turn to make a speech, getting more ludicrous and filled with playful digs at each other. Dad was in the middle of making his speech when he glanced over and was surprised to see Tommy standing in line.

Don: "Tommy, do you have someone you want to thank?" Tom nodded. Dad handed him the spoon, "Take it away."

Tom: "I'd like to thank my father for bringing me, my mother for having me, and most of all, I'd like to thank this beautiful fathility." Everyone burst into laughter (and I'm still trying to figure out how he knew the word *facility*)! It turned out to be the Academy Award of roasts. The only one who didn't give a speech was Frances; she took the spoon and smacked a bug on the table with it. Everyone kidded her and called her Aunt Beetle or Aunt Lady Bug.

8

THE WOMEN

WHEN THE SHOW was in the latter part of season 1, they realized they were going to need more characters to drive the storylines. It was time for Sheriff Taylor to get a girlfriend. The hunt was on, and Sheldon began scouting.

In those days, there were a limited number of channels, so everyone pretty much watched the same shows. I was an avid watcher of sitcoms and adored shows that featured women and girls, like *The Patty Duke Show*. Marlo Thomas in *That Girl* became a role model. I was also a big fan of *Father Knows Best*, starring Robert Young and Jane Wyatt, about two "average" parents and their three children. I was crazy about the oldest daughter Betty, played by Elinor Donahue. I fantasized about having an older sister just like her, who would be a buddy through my gawky teen years.

I never had a chance to meet Elinor until recently. I was on a shuttle to the Mayberry Days festival in 2016, where I was performing my show, and Elinor was seated across from me. She had played Andy's first girlfriend, Miss Ellie, so she was a festival guest star. I was so excited to meet her! As we talked, I remembered what Dad said about the lonely life of child actors, and I asked about her early career. She started at four years old and literally grew up on screen—she has accumulated a vast number of credits. Elinor: "I was playing younger than my age, usually, and accustomed to playing somebody's child." She was twenty-three, playing about eighteen, when *Father Knows Best* ended abruptly in the middle of their sixth year. There was a writer's strike, and filming had to stop.

"Jane Wyatt and Robert Young were tired and didn't want to continue. So we just quit and never got a chance to say goodbye. We never did a last episode, never had a party. There was no closure. It was all of a sudden, boom, we're not going to do it anymore. It was like being kicked out of a bird's nest." She had no idea how to live a normal adult life. She married, and the relationship ended in divorce and left her with a toddler to care for. "I got called into Sheldon Leonard's office for a meeting, and they were talking about a new show. They were looking for a woman to play the character of Miss Ellie. But she wasn't called Miss Ellie then, it was a woman who takes over the drugstore for—I think it was her uncle or something, who owned it. I had my little two-year-old son out in the anteroom, and Sheldon's secretary was sort of babysitting. So I was going, 'Oh how nice, that's interesting. You bet.' But actually, I'm listening for squeals and giggles and whatnot, and they said, 'Thanks very much for coming in.'" She didn't think any more about it. By the time she got home, she had an offer to play the role, which she accepted. She thought about what her duties in the pharmacy might be. She figured they would include making a soda. "One of the jobs my mother had when I was little (and in between acting gigs) was working at a Coast Currie's ice cream store in Hollywood, and she used to make sodas, so I knew how to do that from my mother." She was excited to meet the cast.

Bruce: "On Fridays the actors had their scripts; the full cast was assembled, including the guest actors. We'd sit around the table and read the script. And everybody, especially the regulars, were sort of feeling out the newcomers, and guests were feeling out what they're doing here. This rehearsal was more about relationships than 'You stand on that mark and you move over here.'"

Andy always made sure Dad's chair was next to his at the table. If anyone attempted to sit in it, he'd say, "That's Don's chair. You can't sit there." It was natural—much of the humor came from their interaction.

Elinor was excited and, of course, a bit nervous. Barbara Eden, who later guest-starred as the manicurist, said: "Doing a series is very comfortable; it's like a family. But to be a guest is different; you have to fit yourself in."

Everyone was gracious and the read-through was full of laughs. But something began to happen at the table read that undermined Elinor's self-confidence. During the discussion, Andy would say, "You know, I think that line of Ellie's would be funnier if Don said it," or, "I think that bit we're gonna do would be funnier if Don did it."

Elinor: "So he would take things that were actually written for Miss Ellie and the sheriff and give them to your dad. Certainly nothing romantic but, you know, little bits, side things, just moments. And of course, they were funny, and they made those two characters so rich and terrific. But I felt that it was because I was so terrible. And because of my emotional problems, I was having a weight difficulty. The thinner I got, the thinner I wanted to be." She began to lose weight and was becoming anorexic. "Wardrobe would bring clothes in, and if they fit, I thought I was too fat and wouldn't eat. At one point I was pretty darned sick." She became ill with pneumonia and had to be hospitalized. "They had to write me out of a few scripts or work around me. And the only person who called me from the show was your dad. He wanted to make sure I was all right. He was just absolutely precious. I was very, very touched by that. It meant the world to me at that point in time."

Eventually, Elinor got better and went back to work. Things didn't improve for her on the set, but she and Dad stayed friends. Dad had begun working with a psychiatrist, Dick Renneker, in Westwood

Village. At one point his car was in for repair, and he needed a ride. Elinor: "We'd finish in the afternoon, and I would drive him out and drop him off near Westwood Boulevard, and I would go on to my own place. This was during rehearsal days, around late afternoon. So we had a nice time, you know, the traffic wasn't horrible in those days, and it would be a nice afternoon to toodle along and chitchat about nothing. It was terribly nice." She was still having the weight issue and other problems in her life. It was becoming clear she desperately needed time to herself. "I knew that it was time for the season to end, and I had a three-year contract. I had my agent ask for my release, and they said OK. There didn't seem to be any fight about it, so I left the show at the end of the first year." But she was torn. On one hand, she needed time to work out her problems; on the other, she wanted to know that they weren't unhappy with her work.

Andy later commented: "We never did know how to write for women. Elinor Donahue was a regular in the company . . . and we were so lucky to get her, we thought. She asked to be relieved, and we were happy to oblige her because we didn't know what else to do" (Harrison & Habeeb, *Inside Mayberry*, 1994).

I also got to talk to Betty Lynn and Maggie Peterson at Mayberry Days. I was surprised to find out they never met each other until the Mayberry reunion shows, many years later. Their characters hadn't been on the same episodes. As we talked, the subject of Andy and women came up.

Maggie: "Elinor Donahue and Andy didn't really have much of a chemistry. She doesn't think so either."

Betty: "She was quite a bit younger, really. That was the thing. She was upset during a period of her life that was difficult. She thought they were gonna fire her. They weren't going to fire her."

Maggie: "I don't think Andy was very comfortable around women."

Betty: "He was with you and me."

Maggie: "But with sexy women, I think he was very flustered."

These beautiful, famous ladies were surprising me! But hey, a fly on the wall has her tiny thrills.

Betty: "There was one he got along with. The one who played Peggy, she danced for him in those shoes, almost like clogs. But then she left because she was going with Ryan O'Neil. They got married, she had two babies by him, and then he met Farrah Fawcett, and that was the end of that. Tragic."

As Barney's girlfriend Thelma Lou, Betty came on toward the end of the first year, in the episode "Cyrano Andy." Betty said, "Andy had already had two regular girlfriends on the show, Elinor and Peggy. I was kind of shocked when I got called in to read the part." Betty met Dad and they hit it off right away. "I had seen his performances in other things. He was very quiet, very smart. I'd get so excited when they'd put a hold on me"—meaning the producers expected her to be available to shoot whenever needed for a certain amount of time. "My agent would call and say, 'You have a four-day hold for *The Andy Griffith Show*.' I didn't get paid during that time, but I would be so anxious hoping I'd get to work. I loved doing it! I had never studied acting, and your daddy hadn't either. Both of us, here we are, playing side by side, and neither one of us had gone to acting school. Sometimes when we were waiting for them to set up a shot, Don would visit with me. He would tell me he was a poet; he had some poems he'd written, and he would read them to me." Hold the phone: Barney read poems to Thelma Lou's rival, the never-seen waitress Juanita! "And another thing your daddy did tell me is that he and Andy were in touch every day of their lives one way or another. I was really surprised at that. And I said, 'Well, you're like brothers.' He said, 'Almost.' But he volunteered that. I didn't ask him. I never questioned your dad but now and then."

Laura Hagen, widow of the show's composer Earle Hagen, joined us. She mentioned that Earle wrote 'Ellie's Theme' for Elinor, and he also wrote a theme for Aunt Bee. Betty said, "I never had a theme. Good ole' Plain Jane Betty."

Maggie reminded her, "Andy wrote at the bottom of your picture, 'You were Don's girl, but you should've been mine.'"

Betty: "That's right, he did!"

Maggie: "If they'd been casting Andy's girl, you would've been right in there."

Betty: "I got a lot of false eyelashes in the mail. Don got bullets."

Andy knew they needed a romance to work out. He quite honestly said, "We tried this one and that one and the other one. And finally, we realized it wasn't any of their faults, it was our fault" (Kelly, *The Andy Griffith Show*, 2017). It was a mystery. It's not like Andy was unattractive or anything.

Maggie: "When I first met Andy, I thought he was very good looking, and I was mad about him. Of course, he didn't pay any attention to me. I was too young and I'm not the type, you know."

Dad once told me, "Every year Andy says, 'I've gotta get a girl.'"

Me: "Andy's pretty handsome, for a man, and I should think he'd be popular."

Don: "He is, but Andy's shy around girls. You remember that beautiful red-haired dancer, Juliet Prowse, who came backstage to see us at Harrah's? She had a little crush on him, but nothing happened. You know, Juliet was the only one to ever turn down a marriage proposal from Frank Sinatra."

Wow! I loved how Dad talked to me like I was a grownup, even if I didn't get everything. In fact, Dad talked to me so freely that sometimes he'd get ahead of himself. Once we were talking about a lawyer show we liked to watch, *Perry Mason*. Dad started to tell me the actor who played the tough lawyer was gay—and suddenly caught himself.

Don: "In real life, Raymond Burr is—Uh, happy. I mean, he's warm."

Me: "Warm? I thought he was cold. His last name: *Brrrr!*"

Don: "You just made a joke, honey."

Me: "I did? That's cooler than cold!"

Finally, a lasting girlfriend materialized for Andy Taylor (and for his alter ego, Andy Griffith, it seems). As it often happens in real life, the romance wasn't planned. A new character they created, Opie's teacher Helen Crump, was a small role played by Aneta Corsaut. Sparks flew between them in her first episode, "Andy Discovers America." She furiously calls Andy out when he oversteps his bounds and criticizes her teaching to Opie. In real life, the actors had a similar dynamic. It turned out, the key to winning Andy's heart was to stand your ground and be absolutely fierce about it!

She became a regular as Andy's girlfriend. She once commented that she didn't have much to say in her first few episodes except "Pass the salt and pepper," but that changed, and how!

Maggie: "You know Aneta was in the movie *The Blob*."

Betty: "She was Steve McQueen's girl!"

Maggie: "She went from Steve's girlfriend to Andy's. That was a step up, I think."

Betty: "Steve starred in *The Blob* and got away at the end. Maybe that was his first great escape. People would ask me if Andy and Aneta were having an affair. I'd say I have no idea. I haven't been there since Barney left."

Maggie: "Of course they were. Who cares?"

Betty had to dress in the ladies' room outside until Aneta came on the show! After that they shared a dressing room on the set. The money came from Danny Thomas's company, which, according to Andy, was the cheapest ever. At one point, Betty asked the company for a $50 raise after she'd been on the show for four years. Five hundred dollars was all she was paid for two days' work. Her agent told her the company said it would replace her. Betty: "I said, 'Never mind, I'll stay!' I would've died if they'd replaced me." She never mentioned her need for a raise to Andy or Dad.

When Andy said, "We didn't know how to write for women," I'm pretty sure he was referring to his girlfriends on the show. The real

romance was the bromance between Andy and Barney, so female characters were mostly supportive. At a time when most of the shows depicted
women doing housework in high heels, the *Griffith* show tried to avoid
those stereotypes. Their female characters were realistic and varied.

As written, Thelma Lou existed mainly for storylines and as a foil
for Barney. But she became a great character because of Betty's acting ability, as well as the charm and personality she infused into her.
I especially love some of her reactions, like in "Barney's First Car."
In one scene, Barney proudly takes Andy, Thelma Lou, Gomer, and
Opie for a ride in the first car he ever owns; it's a secondhand car he
bought from a con artist. Of course, the car goes haywire. The actors
weren't told what was going to go wrong with the car, but they were
told they had to get the scene in one take. It would be very costly to
reshoot, so they had to be perfect. Well, when that steering column
made its snakelike ascent up into Barney's face, the actors collapsed in
hysterics and the scene had to be reshot. In the second take, Thelma
Lou does this hysterical scream when she yells, "Barney!!"

Thelma Lou's last name is never mentioned during the entire series.
That was Betty's doing. In one episode, Andy was supposed to intro-
duce Thelma Lou to a couple. He suddenly stopped and said to Sween,
"I need to know what her last name is if I'm going to introduce her."

Betty said, "No, she's always been just Thelma Lou—no last name!"

Andy said, "OK, she doesn't need it!"

The character of Aunt Bee was an authentic representation of
many women of the era. (It wasn't until the 1970s, with the women's
lib movement, that women collectively realized they had a right to
speak up.) Aunt Bee puts family first, rarely disagrees, and asks little
for herself. In "The Bed Jacket," Andy gives Aunt Bee something for
the kitchen instead of the lovely jacket she wants for her birthday. She
stifles her tears and runs upstairs before anyone can notice.

Frances was a very convincing actress because in real life she
was the opposite. She expressed strong opinions, butted heads with

Andy, and put her male cohorts in their place when she disapproved
of their behavior. She had some old-fashioned values, but they were
the values of the show.

Then there was Juanita, the waitress in the diner who is Barney's
fantasy woman. She's never seen by the viewer, nor is she mentioned
by Thelma Lou. She is "one of life's mysteries" and an archetypal
character. And there was an older single woman, Aunt Bee's friend
Clara. She's a lonely but strong-willed character; she lives to compete
for blue ribbons and usually wins.

Also, there were female criminals. Big Maude Tyler (Reta Shaw), in
"Convicts-at-Large," was a predator who pressures Barney into dancing with her in a secluded cabin where he and Floyd are held captive.
Andy is finally able to engineer an escape as Barney tangos her into
the trap. Maude's dumb female cohorts were a hoot! Another episode,
"Prisoner of Love," featured a beautiful female prisoner (Susan Oliver)
who manipulates Barney and Andy with her charm and is nearly able
to pull off a jailbreak. Another manipulator was a reporter (Ruta Lee)
who gets Barney to unwittingly give some dirt on Andy, in "Andy on
Trial." And of course, there's the widow, Mrs. Lesh (Ellen Corby), the
con artist Barney buys his car from, a very strong female character.

The show certainly didn't shy away from women looking for
romance. How could we ever forget the "fun girls," two attractive
women out on the town, looking for sex and adventure. Though
Skippy (Joyce Jameson) and Daphne (Jean Carson) failed in their
attempts to seduce Barney and Andy, there is never any put-down
of them, and it's fun to watch the two virile men wriggle away. Jean
Carson, playing another role, was barely recognizable as the character
Jalene Connors in the episode "Convicts-at-Large."

In "The Manicurist" a young, single woman (Barbara Eden) arbi-
trarily gets off a bus in Mayberry and decides to find a job there. The
manicurist's development was an interesting journey. Bruce: "When
this script was discussed after the ten o'clock reading, Sheldon felt she

should have more problems, this woman who's coming to town. He said maybe she broke up with her boyfriend, or she lost her job or couldn't pay her rent." Andy said, "Oh come on, if she had all those troubles, we'd take her home and give her a hot meal." So, Aaron read those notes, and this is what he wrote: "Manicurist: (to Andy) That's the one thing I'm looking for is a friendly place, you know where the people are friendly? I work in this big city barber shop. There was this barber and he was forever after me to marry him and I kept saying I need time to think, you know how a girl needs time to think, well he didn't think I needed so much time to think. Well, anyway we had this big fight and I just had to go away, you can see why I had to do that? And besides, I was getting awful tired of the big city, it's getting so a girl can't walk down the street anymore without being whistled at. Why do men do that? Do you know why men do that?"

Now, there was a woman with a whole lot to say! Barbara Eden was brought in to play the manicurist. This was before she starred in the long-running *I Dream of Jeannie* series, but she had done *How to Marry a Millionaire* and was on the producers' radar. She talked about the episode's appeal: "All those little men (in the barber shop) were so cute. I've had so many people come up to me and tell me the name of the manicurist" (Ellen Brown). She added, "Privately, Don told me, 'I want you to know that Andy is not comfortable with young starlets, and he thinks you're dynamite.' He was very kind to alert me." It's possible she was being considered as yet another girlfriend for Andy. She also said, "It was a very warm and gentle ambience on the set, but there was no time for conversation. I had a scene with your dad where I was doing his nails. We were talking, and he said, 'I don't know what to do about these nails.' He just started to chat as Don, and I was chatting as Ellen, and next thing I knew we were doing the scene! We were rehearsing, well we weren't really rehearsing, but we were." That approach explains to me why Dad's acting was so natural—that, and the many hours of rehearsal he put in on his own time so he would be secure in what he was doing.

Barbara Eden, who played the manicurist, kissing Dad, as Barney, between shots, 1962.

Another fun lady is Ramona Ankrum, a girlfriend created for the Ernest T. Bass character. Jackie Joseph was cast, and she realized the part delightfully. The episode is "My Fair Ernest T. Bass." Jackie: "At the read-through for [the episode] were Aaron; Howard Morris, who played my beloved; Andy; and Don. I'm just sitting in the room with them; it was such a tickle, and they enjoyed the read-through just like they were enjoying watching a show. You know they were just laughing, getting a kick out of each other. I mean it continued; it went on and on. They were enjoying it while doing it. And nobody laughed at Don more than Andy. He was just hysterical. Of course, he was funny, and you know, in your head you have a little bubble going, 'I'm in this room, and I'm with Andy and Don Knotts!' And of course, Howie Morris was comedy genius. It really felt like being, you know, with the cream of the crop."

As happy as the Mayberry set was, every now and then the outside world, a.k.a. "reality" came crashing through. Jackie: "And then the awful news came that President Kennedy had been shot. One of the assistants in the office came in and, you know, just such a pall came over the room. Everybody was stunned, and I guess Aaron or somebody said, 'OK, let's everybody go to lunch and then come back and decide how to proceed.'"

But not everyone was a Kennedy fan. Jackie: "I had to sit with Aunt Bee and Mrs. Wiley (Doris Packer). Aunt Bee and the actress who played Mrs. Wiley were saying stuff like, 'Well, he always played around.' I'm thinking, *He was our president and he just got murdered! How could these ladies have this conversation?* I'm just choking back tears, and I didn't have the chutzpah. And of course, I always knew my place. I wish I had courage back then because it was terrible to me that they would even think that way much less say it out loud. *They were playing the parts of old biddies*, I thought. *That's just acting. You're not supposed to be that way!* So many people of my generation were enchanted to the heights [with Kennedy], and to have our spirits broken so severely when he was cut down!"

Howard Morris would likely agree with her. He directed some episodes of the show after Sween left. He said that Don showed up with his conception of how it should be but was ready to pivot in any other direction if that's what Howard wanted. But he said Frances wouldn't take direction. Howard ended up with a wonderful second career as a director.

Jackie: "After that heartbreaking lunch, they decided to just read the script once, do some basic staging, and then come back after the weekend because I don't care what anyone thought, everybody was watching it on television. I mean it was just live drama. And of course, we came back to work afterward. Everybody was so professional, and Don got everybody laughing, just by acting, by just doing his part. And in between, when they were doing different setups, I was at the water cooler all the time crying with Howard, and then we'd come back and do our happy little dancing and leaping over tree stumps. Howard was bereft. And it seems we may have been the only ones who did go off into a corner."

9

DAD AND ANDY

B Y THE FIFTH SEASON, three members of the inner circle had left the show. Bob Sweeney left after a salary dispute. Aaron Ruben went on to develop *Gomer Pyle: USMC*, a show that Andy had made possible for Jim. And Bruce Bilson was offered an opportunity to do what Sween had trained him to do, and he went on to direct over four hundred television shows. These days, Bruce's mind often returns to the days of the show that was like family.

At the end of the fifth season, Dad left the show. A lot of people ask why. Andy had said he only wanted to go five years with *The Andy Griffith Show*. So Dad had signed a contract that ended after five seasons. As the agreed-upon end date approached, Dad was very practical and started looking for other work. With permission from the show, Dad had made the animated feature *The Incredible Mr. Limpet* in 1964. He got a call from Lew Wasserman, top boss at Universal Studios, asking him for a meeting. Don: "Wasserman greeted me with the comment that he had run *Limpet*, and he said, 'I don't understand why it's not a smash hit. If it was done by Disney, that movie would've made $100 million. I want you here to star in movies, and I am going to give you your name above the title. I want you to sign a contract for five years to do one picture a year. You'll have all the leeway you want. I'll see you get whatever you need.'"

Dad agreed to Wasserman's plans, but then Andy called to say he had decided to keep the show going. Dad sadly told him that he thought he'd better move on. Dad did go back and do a few episodes and won two Emmys for those. Dad told an interesting story about winning an Emmy: "Emmys mean so much. After I won my first one, I got so much press. Constant interviews. Later, I went to play golf, and in the clubhouse, the players all came over to congratulate me. I went out with my feet barely touching the ground. I met a golfer on the fairway, and I said, 'I'm Don Knotts!' and he said, I'm Bill Smith, hardware. What's your game?"

Andy was terribly sad to lose him, but he was always supportive. When Dad first came on the show, Andy realized he was not going to be the funny one as planned; Don would be taking that role. Instead of being upset or jealous, Andy was glad. He said he didn't mind being straight man because he "loved to look into Don's eyes and watch him turn into Barney."

The cast and crew were deeply affected. Betty: "I left when your dad left. They had talked to me about staying on, possibly become a hairdresser with a salon or something. I thought, well, I'd end up, what, with Goober?"

Me: "You were afraid they were going to make you date Goob?"

Betty: "Well, I figured who else would they pair me with? I'd had the best! No second, second banana! I thought, *Maybe they'll just have me be a single woman without Barney*. When Don did his last show, that was it for me, I was gone. I went to the ladies' room and cried and cried. There was another actress, and it was her first day. She came in and saw this actress crying saying it was her last day. Ron also cried. Barney was my purpose for being there. They had introduced a fellow as my husband, and I said, 'She would never do that.' But they said, 'You're going to.' I guess it was better than being shot or pushed off a cliff."

Dad knew he would miss the show, but it took enormous energy to play Barney at that level. Barney was a physically and emotionally intense character. Weekends were spent learning lines, and he was heavily featured in almost every episode. Dad said, "I would frequently have long scenes, be in every scene, and I'd pace back and forth. Andy would be sitting behind the desk all day. At the end of the day, he'd say, tongue in cheek, 'I can't understand why you're always so tired.'" Dad had come full circle. The child that raged inside him had been funneled into hilarious Barney Fife. A sturdy man emerged, ready to face new challenges.

After the last show with Barney, they had a cast party in the soundstage. Andy and Dad sat in a corner talking. After a while, they realized they were alone. The rest of the company had drifted away, leaving them a private goodbye. Dad and Andy remained close friends the rest of their lives. Dad and Andy found strength in each other to overcome their personal demons, and together they had created an amazing universe.

The 1960s was a difficult decade, with civil unrest and social upheaval. Women were pissed, kids were on drugs, there was a race to the moon! The show said, "Slow down, go and get a bottle of pop. Everything you need is right where you live."

One night after Dad left the show, I was having trouble sleeping. I'd had that problem so often as a child that Dad bought a radio for my room; the music helped me relax—but not that night. Tommy and I had just watched *The Wizard of Oz*, and the wicked witch really scared me too. Dad came in, and to get my mind off "Old Green Nose," he told me about the most awesome practical joke ever. One of the guest directors was obsessed with getting as much filmed before lunch as possible. But he was delaying lunch himself by walking off set whenever he got a personal phone call. It was happening more and more. One afternoon, the cast was still on set at 3:00 PM, and everybody was hungry.

Andy and Don during a dinner break, about 1964.

Don: "Picture this, Karen. The director walks off the set to take a call, and everyone has to stand around, doing nothing. Andy and I are next to a sink on the kitchen set, and I say, 'Hey, I'm starving! I just might take a bite out of that piece of soap.' Andy says; 'You know, Don, when I was a little tot and my Momma heard me say a bad cuss word, she'd wash my mouth out with soap. It got so that after a while, I swear I started to like the taste. And I'm so hungry right now . . .' Then, the crew sees Andy pick up a bar of soap from the sink and take a bite out of it. He chews, smiles, and says, 'Yep, still tastes pretty good.' Then he breaks it in half and gives some to me. I take a big bite and say, 'Ya know, Andy, that's mighty good eatin'.' The crew was so stunned they didn't know what to do. Pretty soon someone ran back to the director, who raced to the set yelling, 'OK, OK, we'll break for lunch now. Just stop eating that soap before you have to call in sick tomorrow!'

"Now, here's the secret behind it: that wasn't soap. It was a hunk of mozzarella cheese that Reggie had carved to look like a bar of soap.

Lee and Andy planned the prank the day before, and we made it very convincing." The director never found out what really happened. But I understand that from that day on, when the actors started to get hungry, they'd hold their tummies and say, "I sure could go for a pizza with extra soap right now."

10

A FISH, A GHOST, AN ASTRONAUT, AND A MULE

DAD LOVED TO eat out, and he finally had enough money to take us to some classy restaurants. I just adored the fine silverware, sparkly chandeliers, and elegant waiters. As soon as we were seated, Dad would start to entertain us. He'd take some dollar bills from his wallet, look at them with disdain, and say, "What are *these* doing in here!" and toss them. He'd pick up his napkin and wave it mysteriously, saying, "Watch . . . watch . . . watch!" He'd pull it away to reveal . . . his wrist-watch. That was the trick! It was also my cue to ask, "Daddy, what time is it?" He'd make a show of looking at his watch, then stop as if reconsidering: "I'm sorry honey, I bought this watch for my *own use*." He'd pick up the container of sugar packets and thumb through them: "I'm sorry folks, your photos aren't ready." He'd stand up, look out at the interior while tapping his spoon on a glass: "May I have your attention please? I'd like to make an announcement!" He'd say it in a soft voice that nobody heard, so of course they ignored him. The longer he kept this up, the funnier it got. Many years later, I was at a

121

restaurant with my friend Kerry Lee Riley, and I told him this story. He suddenly pointed behind me. I turned around, and the entire restaurant was staring at me. Somebody said, "What's the announcement?"

One of the most popular restaurants for show folk at the time was a charming Italian place in Hollywood called the Villa Capri. We loved it! It had delicious food and was run by a man everyone regarded as their personal Italian grandfather, Patsy D'Amore. He had white curly hair, a large moustache, and mounds of charm. "Welcome, Don! Hello, Karen and Tommy. You going to love the special tonight. Pini is working his magic in the kitchen. You know Pini—his parents were the chefs who invented the famous dish named for his son, Scallo. Excuse me, Juliet Prowse just came in with Andy Williams." He winked. "I tell them you say hello." He was letting the celebrities seated at tables know where other stars could be found in the restaurant.

Frank Sinatra was co-owner, and he had a table in the bar from where he could see everyone. One night we came in and we heard a booming voice: "Don, Don, Don, Don, Don, Baby!" It was Sinatra himself. Dad stopped in his tracks, turned, and gave a self-conscious wave. There were always beautiful ladies at Sinatra's table. Dad said, "He is an awfully courteous man. I used to run into him a lot. I'd stop to say hello in a restaurant, and he'd jump up to introduce the people he was with."

Our family enjoyed vacationing at a popular dude ranch near Santa Barbara called Alisal. It had activities for adults and kids—swimming, horseshoe tossing, horseback riding, and golfing. There was a bar where Tommy and I would sit and were allowed to sign for our own Shirley Temple drinks just like the grownups. After a few days, dad was shocked when he was presented with a bill for $300 for our drinks alone! Dad's friend from New York, Bob Newhart, was there, and he invited Dad to his cabin to listen to his comedy album *The Button-Down Mind of Bob Newhart*. It was all monologues on the telephone. Dad told us, "Bob's album sold over half a million copies!" He was inspired by it and recorded his own comedy album, which he called *An Evening with Me* and which had the funny monologues he'd written. The famous caricature artist Al Hirschfeld did the cover.

Tom and I simply adored each other. I was his adventurous big sister, and he was my loyal sidekick. Our neighborhood in Glendale was teaming with kids. Paul Crete lived across the street and had a beautiful tree in his yard that reached up for miles. He would dare me to follow him up the tree and I was always "in." He'd guide me up, and once we were about halfway up, he'd jump down, laugh, and run away, leaving me stuck. I would wait, hoping Tom would pass by and talk me down.

We had myriad toys to play with: a Radio Flyer wagon, Silly Putty, crayons, Play-Doh, Colorforms, Snippy Scissors, a beanie cap with propeller that launched when you pulled the cord, Slip 'N Slide, the Flag Game, yellow Remco telephones, and a Magnajector that projected pictures onto the wall. Tom also had a magic record with this riddle on the back:

YY UR
YY UB
I C UR
YY 4ME

Tom got his early engineer training by taking apart our clocks, toasters, and even the telephone receiver to see how they worked. If he couldn't figure out how to put it back, it would lay there disemboweled. When we took family trips in the car, Tommy talked all the time, and none of us would respond. We just couldn't understand what he was talking about! He finally gave up explaining to me how a battery works after about fifteen tries. Sometimes he was frustrated that he didn't have a mechanically minded dad. His favorite toy was Mr. Machine. He took it apart and couldn't figure out how to put it back together. Of course, Dad couldn't either, but our Aunt Claire was a physicist, and she was the star of the family that day.

Dad had a burglar alarm installed in a closet directly across from the front door. This thing was so loud that when it went off it sounded like you were in the center of a fire station. If you accidentally tripped it, he would be furious. He had insomnia, and there was no way to get back to sleep after that!

I had a serious problem with absentmindedness. Almost every day, mother would hand me a sack lunch and I invariably left it behind. I would daydream in class, then realize to my shock that I was holding my math book and the rest of the class had moved on to English. The kids at school knew who our dad was, of course. He was bigger than the moon! Kids would ask me questions like, "How many pickles are in Aunt Bee's pickle jar?" Huh? I haven't learned to add, and you want long division? With a famous father like that, I should've been one of the "cool kids" in school. I could've had that glory but for one thing: my name was Karen.

Dad was surprised when Mother said, "It's time for us to have kids." He didn't know if they ever would, "but then I had Karen, and I loved babies," said Dad. "I used to come home, and I couldn't wait to play with Karen. Babies are fun!" Frank Behrens had mentioned that Don had this famous dog, Susie, he loved so much. "But he found a deeper love, an even greater love with the first child, his daughter." The original plan was to name me Susan, but they couldn't have two Susies running and crapping in the house! What was it with the Greatest Generation giving their dogs human names, anyway? Whatever happened to Scout, Chip, and Bomber? My parents loved the name Karen, but the neighborhood was full of them. On our street alone,

there were thirty-three. The other Karens added nicknames or numbers to avoid confusion. In the end, my parents decided I should go
by Karen Ann, which Dad shortened to Kananny. By third grade,
Kananny wasn't so cool. I wished my parents had gone with Karen
34. These days, I go by my given name: Don Knotts's Daughter. My
close friends call me Knotts Kid. I'm kidding, dear reader, but that was
how I felt until I found my own identity. "Who is Karen Knotts?" I
would ask, but nobody knew. Everyone assumed I was an extension of
"good ol' Barn." I was trying to be what people expected of me. Most
folks think of Barney as a real person, so I was Barney's daughter.
For years I carried one lipstick, instead of one bullet, in my pocket.

Mother and Dad even managed to have an active social life in the
Glendale neighborhood. Catherine Pearce had become a close friend,
and Tom and I played with her son Cameron. Catherine: "Don and
Kay took Woody and me to dinner at the Tail o' the Cock restaurant.
Don loved the old-fashioned daiquiri, shaken not stirred. It's very
nice to say, 'Daiquiri up.'"

One Saturday morning Tommy and I were trying to figure out
what to do for Dad on Father's Day. Tom wandered over to the stack
of Dad's unsold comedy albums: "Gee, it's too bad Daddy's records
aren't selling like hot cakes. He seems kind of upset about it."

I said, "That's what we'll do for Father's Day! We'll sell his comedy albums!"

Tom: "Can we do that?"

Me: "Sure, we sell lemonade, don't we?"

Tom: "He'll be so surprised!"

We loaded the albums into Tom's Radio Flyer and pulled the
wagon to a busy intersection. We put up a sign and began hawking
"Don Knotts comedy albums available for the first time on Brand
Boulevard, only 25 cents each!" That was a ninety percent discount!
Soon we were making sales. A lady pulled over, ran up to us, and
ordered five. I said, "There you go ma'am, here's your change. Keep

it? Gee, thanks!" I told Tom, "*Now* they're selling like hotcakes!" We saw a familiar blue Plymouth go by and screech to a halt. Then we heard a familiar voice yell, "What are you kids doing?" Tom said, "It's Daddy!" We ran over to the car. I said, "We sold all your albums. Look!" I showed him the jar filled with cash . . . and held my breath.

He said sternly, "Get in the car, kids. We're going home. I've got to make a phone call."

"A phone call! Who're you going to call, Daddy?"

"I'm going to call my manager and tell him he's fired. You kids are doing better than he is." And he gave us a wink. Whew!

In 1962, word was going around that Stanley Kramer was about to make a blockbuster movie with some big-name comedians. Dad was offered a part but he turned it down, possibly out of the fear of not measuring up to such huge stars. Stanley Kramer called him at home and said, "I understand you don't want to be in my movie?" Of course, he talked him into it. The plot of *It's a Mad, Mad, Mad, Mad World* centered around a group of randomly connected people on an insane competition to find a hidden treasure. Dad was hysterically funny as a man innocently driving along when a con man, played by Phil Silvers, hops in his car and convinces him the FBI is chasing them in order to get hold of his car.

Bob Metz: "They were promoting the movie on the Jerry Lewis television show. Don was waiting in the green room, and these big comics were there: Jonathan Winters, Phil Silvers, and Milton Berle. They were all 'on,' and Don was sitting in the corner breaking up. Suddenly Phil Silvers looked over at him and said, 'See that little son of a bitch sitting in the corner there? Don't ever get on camera with him. He'll kill you!'"

The next time we were at Villa Capri, Dad was telling Patsy about Tom and me selling his comedy albums when Jerry Lewis came in. He had on a blue blazer and ascot, and on his hand was a gold pinky ring and bracelet. He stood there as if everyone was looking at him. He came over to our table. Dad hadn't seen Jerry's latest film, so he fumbled around trying to figure out what to say. Suddenly it came to him: "Jerry I'd like you to meet my kids, Karen and Tom. They're huge fans of yours!" We looked at him utterly nonplussed. We knew he was a brilliant comedian, but it just wasn't our cup of tea.

A woman was approaching the table wearing one of those 1960s faux leopard skin hats with matching gloves and, yes, matching shoes: "*Hellooo*, Don. It's *Lydiaaa*, I worked for Jane Meadows and Steve Allen! I did wardrobe on the set when you were the Nervous Guy on Steve's show. I remember the sketch where they wanted you to go into a cage with a live leopard. They told you, 'Don't worry. He's harmless!' You noticed the trainer holding a gun on the beast, and you refused to go in the cage. I admire that. Sometimes cowardice takes real courage!" I glanced at Dad; always polite, his lips were frozen in a smile. I thought, *It's a good thing the leopard can't see what a bad imitation of his coat she was wearing.*

When Dad excused himself to get a drink, Tom and I noticed we were sitting across from Desi Arnaz Jr., son of Lucille Ball and Desi Arnaz. Was he cute, or what! He and his friend started whistling the theme song to *The Andy Griffith Show*, so Tom and I hummed the theme song to *I Love Lucy*! We had something else in common. Desi and his sister Lucie used to clean out their mother's garage and sell some of the items in front of their house. I understood that. What I didn't get was how Desi went from hustling trinkets at age eleven to becoming a pop star at thirteen! He was a drummer for the popular rock group Dino, Desi & Billy. His bandmate, Dino, was Dean Martin's son. Dad came back to the table beaming. Jackie Gleason, his idol, had approached him at the bar and said, "Don, I watch you. You work from within, like me," then he had walked away.

My parents sent me to summer camp for girls, Montecito Sequoia, when I was ten. When mother took me to the bus that would take us on our long ride into the Sequoias for the summer, she noticed Debbie Reynolds with her daughter, Carrie Fisher. There seemed to be no one in charge, so Ms. Reynolds took it upon herself to round up all the girls, calling out instructions as if she were the official camp leader. In order to kill time and keep our attention, Ms. Reynolds gave us a little dance lesson—she taught us how to do the time step. We learned to tap in our tennies.

Carrie was petite and seemed very sure of herself. Later on, I saw her do some beautiful moves on the trampoline. I was too shy to introduce myself. Every morning they would wake us at seven in the morning with reveille blaring over the camp loudspeaker. (That was the closest I would ever get to serving in the army.) Each girl was assigned a chore to do in the cabin and outside in the quad. I hated camp at first, and I'm reminded me of the popular song parody sung by Allan Sherman in his heavy New York accent:

Hello Muddah, hello Faddah.
Here I am at Camp Grenada.
Camp is very entertaining.
And they say we'll have some fun if it stops raining.

I wasn't making friends; I was spoiled and didn't know it. We always had a housekeeper, so I had few, if any, chores at home. I had become lazy and self-centered. I almost failed to earn the blue scarf each of us wore on Sundays and at flag ceremonies. The cabin counselor kicked my butt, and I did earn the coveted blue scarf, just barely. The camp taught values along with the incredible activities offered: tennis, archery, riflery, water skiing, hiking, crafts, fencing, and kayaking. We were divided into two teams, the Blues and Whites. The points we made from activities were added to our team's total. It was very competitive but always in fun. Two years later I earned an Outstanding Camper Award for my age group. I was so proud, I was singing a different tune:

> Wait a minute, it's stopped hailing,
> Guys are swimming, guys are sailing
> Playing baseball, gee that's bettah,
> Muddah, Faddah kindly disregard this letter.

One year I came home from camp to a very unwelcome surprise: our parents told us they were going to separate. They still loved each other, but Dad's fame had pulled him in different directions. And in spite of how sophisticated Mother had become with their new friends and lifestyle, she was a small-town girl at heart.

Mother told me about a Hollywood party they went to: "Don and I were at Mickey Rooney's house. Standing there against a window was Cary Grant. God, yes! And there was a young woman sitting at his feet with exposed bosoms—you could see the top of them. She was leaning forward so poor Cary, he just stood there the whole time, talking to just anybody, because I think he was very embarrassed. He would've had to step over her. I don't think he knew what to do, and I think he was basically a shy man. Marge and I had a great view, and we couldn't keep our eyes off him." Was Cary Grant shy? Maybe. Of course, there are those rumors that Cary was gay and in a relationship with the actor Randolph Scott. Their mutual friend Carole Lombard once jokingly referred to the pair as having the perfect relationship: "Randy pays the bills, and Cary mails them."

When Mother and Dad separated, there was a lot of sadness and confusion. Our grandmother, Elsie, stayed with us for a while. She and Dad both loved the Dodgers and listened to all the games on the radio. Their fandom went back to when they were the Brooklyn Dodgers.

That summer, Tom and I moved with Mother into a large apartment in Westwood Village. Mother and I canvassed the neighborhood looking for kids my age, and the results were dismal. But on the first day of school at the bus stop, I met Gina, a funny, excitable girl with big brown eyes. We became instant friends, along with twins Angela and Felicia Curran and another girl, Alice Chang. Whenever Gina came to a punchline in a story she was telling, she'd kick me in the shin with her saddle shoe, causing me to buckle and giving the impression of uncontrollable laughter. Gina: "You and your dad were like a love story in a way; you guys adored each other. You were never like, 'My dad's gonna kill me.' He let you be who you were; he was very accepting. We had the biggest Beatles crush in the world. We tried everything to get tickets, radio contests, everything. Then you called me and said 'Do you want to go? Tom is sick so I got an extra ticket!'" Poor Tom, he's never gotten over that! Gina: "We sat in the last row of boxed seats at the Bowl. People were jumping in the water fountain and trying to swim across to the stage. We sat together and your dad sat behind us. Everyone around us was screaming. We were just eleven. We saw them on August 29 or 30, 1965. We spent a lot of time jumping up and down, so I guess we couldn't see anything either. You don't think of Barney Fife as a good dad; you think he's gonna drop the toast."

Gina's mother was also going through a divorce. Marcia D'Esopo was a very intelligent woman from a prominent Jewish family who refused to conform. She had pursued a career in ballet before meeting Gina's father. Now she was taking a class at UCLA and asked Dad if she could interview him about comedy. Dad usually tried to get out of interviews because they were the same repetitive questions about

Barney. But Marcia wanted to ask questions about theories of comedy, and that fascinated him. Fortunately, she recorded it.

The interview began like this: Marcia: "Hello Don Knotts, expert comedian. How do you make people laugh? I'm here to interview you for a Sociology 149 paper, which is not a very funny paper. I was hoping to start off with preposterousness and ridiculousness." Dad interpreted her question literally; his answer referenced the Theatre of the Ridiculous in New York City in the 1960s, which launched the experimental theater movement. He disliked this kind of play and refused to see any shows at the Mark Taper Forum because they did so many of that type.

Don: "They have gone back to the slice-of-life idea. Of course, it was a good form of drama, but I think it's overdone now. They've lost the feeling of giving an audience a plot, which disturbs me personally. I like to feel when I watch a play or a movie that I have seen a beginning, middle, and an end, that there is a resolution at the end of the thing, or else I feel hanging. Sometimes I think drama and comedy writers of today are just plain lazy. They don't think the audience of today expects an ending. The hardest thing to do when you write something is to resolve it, to find a punchline to go out on. It's a tough, tough job, and sometimes they just don't bother. Say they ended on a piece of symbolism. You go home and wonder what that meant. And everybody can talk about it and speculate at cocktail parties, and then when you run into the guy who wrote it, he admits finally that he didn't really know. I'm rambling on."

Kay: "When Don and I separated, we had every intention of getting back together eventually. Divorce was not an option. It was an indication of failure, considered disgraceful, and therefore to be avoided at all cost. But as time passed, we realized we had grown apart. We had made the mistake of marrying too young."

Although he had initiated it, Dad was not dealing with the divorce any better. He moved into the Sunset Marquis Hotel in Hollywood, where he moped around with that terribly lost, lonely look on his face. I slipped back into my role of amateur therapist. "Hey Dad, why don't you go down to the pool? Maybe you can make some new friends. There must be lots of other divorced celebrities here." The Sunset Marquis was *the* place where celebrities stayed through their divorces.

When Tom and I visited him on Christmas Eve, there wasn't a single holiday decoration in his suite. We decided he needed something to cheer him up, but we didn't have any money. In those days, kids weren't given cash, not even the junior movie star Jackie Coogan. We left the hotel and started walking down Sunset Strip determined to "find Christmas for Dad." We saw something green and fuzzy lying across the street. We dashed across the boulevard and, sure enough, right in front of Gil Turner's Liquor Store was a small abandoned tree. It was a Charlie Brown tree. We went through a nearby trash can and found a few cracked ornaments, a bit of tangled silver tinsel, and a red bow off a gift bottle of Jack Daniel's. Don't ask me how I knew what that was, dear reader! We set up that tree in the middle of Dad's hotel room and decorated it. Frankly, it was a pathetic bit of Christmas but it was our own.

When he finally came out of the bedroom, Dad didn't even see it until he nearly tripped over it: "What's this? What did you kids do?"

Tom: "We thought you needed a tree, Daddy."

Don: "You're right, I do need a tree. Thanks, kids. This is the nicest Christmas present I've ever had." And he hugged us.

———————————

The Incredible Mr. Limpet, which Dad made in 1964 while still on *The Andy Griffith Show*, was the first movie to extensively combine live action with animation. It's about a man who falls into the ocean and transforms into an intelligent fish who helps the Allies win World War II. We had a projector at home, and Tom would thread it up and we'd watch. Every time Dad, as Limpet, fell into the water and became a fish I'd tear up, even though he was in the room! The animators were careful to make the fish look like Dad and capture his innocent expression.

Years later we heard a rumor that *The Incredible Mr. Limpet* was going to be remade starring Jim Carrey, but it never happened. Dad and I always wondered why. Dad loved Jim and he used to say, "Jim Carrey's a big fan of mine, you know, big fan o' mine!" When I was writing this book I got to interview Jim Carrey! Jim was so excited to talk about Dad, he was yammering away and I couldn't get my questions in. Finally he calmed down, my knees stopped shaking, and I asked why he never did the *Limpet* remake. Jim explained, "We started filming and experimenting with the technology, but the process [at that time] wasn't refined enough. But because of *Limpet*, we were playing around with *Christmas Carol* and some other things. The movie started all this tech experimentation; it was a precursor to *Avatar* and motion cap." Jim was in love with the movie as a boy. He recalled, "I was sitting on the floor in my aunt's house and was just enthralled with this innocent and beautiful story."

Carole Cook, who played Dad's wife, Mrs. Limpet, remembered going to the Warner lot to audition for the part. She made a stop at the drugstore and thought, *Oh, just like Lana Turner, you go to the drugstore, and you get the part!* She had never done a film audition, but her agent called to tell her she got the part after auditioning only once. She was put under contract for two years with Warner Brothers, which was very exciting. At that time the studio contract system was on its way out, so she was lucky.

Carole: "My first day on the set I'm here with Don, your daddy, and I didn't know spit about him. I had done some television, but I was a theater baby. They said, 'Come in and hit your mark,' and your father saw the consternation. And I went, 'Hit what mark? Is somebody marked with an *X*, and I hit them?' And your Daddy came over to me and said, 'There will be a mark on the floor.' I said, 'What kind of mark?' He said, 'It'll be a big *X* you can see.' I said, 'Do I look down?' He said, 'Not if you're smart. You just go for that. You'll see it, peripherally.' Of course, that made me nervous as hell. I could tell he was being very kind. And he said under his breath so everybody wouldn't hear him, 'We now have a dummy working here with us.' And he looked at me in that funny-brilliant way, that only he could do. You know, that befuddled look? I just stared, and they were filming. Of course, the directors said, 'Cut!' And your father said, 'I think you're going to be trouble on this picture.' Because every time he looked at me, I would laugh. He was so serious about comedy."

The water tank where they filmed Carole's scene when she comes down the gangplank to put the glasses on her husband, who's now a fish, was enormous. It took up half the soundstage. They used that tank to film shipwreck scenes; it was as famous as the staircase Bette Davis came down. Eventually they had to get rid of it. All the navy stuff in the movie was shot in San Diego on the ocean.

Carole was a big inspiration to me as an actress. I was ten when they filmed that tender scene where she's putting the glasses on Dad/ Limpet the fish, and she had me so drawn in. I told her, "They were raising a cardboard box up to you with a crane and you were putting Limpet's glasses on top of the box to make it look like they were on the fish. I looked inside and there was just a bunch of junk in the box. You made it so real for me."

Carole said, "The scene where I'm saying goodbye to Limpet— well, that's a fish, OK?" They were filming in the studio tank. There was a red ball in the water. The director, Arthur Lubin, told her, "Talk to the red ball, because we'll take the red ball out of the sea and we'll draw in Limpet the fish." Carole: "Well, my problem was Don was in a little rowboat over to my right. So he would talk to me—it was his voice. I couldn't get used to talking to the red ball. My tendency was to turn right and talk to Don all the time. We were on our break, and he said, 'Somebody get a brace for her neck.'

The *Limpet* press junket in Weeki Wachee Springs, Florida; front row, Kay and Dad; back row, Carole Cook and Jack Weston, January 1964.

Your father was very quiet on the set. He'd do those asides to me, which I wanted to kill him for! But basically, he was very sincere and earnest about the work. He didn't have to prove anything. When he was on, he was funny. Don was like nobody else; he was unique and original."

She wasn't surprised when I mentioned Dad had married three times: "Whenever he gets divorced and remarries, I say, 'That's Don!'" I told her, "Some women I've talked to said they didn't know he was a ladies' man, and others asked, 'Why didn't he hit on me?'" Carole: "Now that I think about it, I'm a little put off. I'm not crazy about it." I said, "Well, he was married then." I told her that Dad was a one-woman man, and very loyal. "Each of Dad's three marriages lasted fourteen to fifteen years. Aside from a biannual trip to Las Vegas or so, he didn't cheat. An exception to that was when a relationship was failing. He would start to look around for someone before the relationship had ended because he couldn't stand living alone."

Carole became reflective: "You know, it's amazing how *The Incredible Mr. Limpet* has lasted all these years. It's like a cult movie. I remember when it had just been on television. I was getting off the plane in El Paso, and there were some teenagers. They started screaming, 'There's Mrs. Limpet!' I said, 'Kids, you're all in the will.' The fact they could recognize me after all those years—I said, 'I'm gonna adopt you all.'"

In those days, reviewers in New York could make or break a film. Don: "None of the reviewers in New York liked the picture, even though it was a pioneer feature film mixing live performances with animation. I went to a famed restaurant to eat, and the maître d' said, 'Welcome back to New York, Mr. Knotts. I understand you have a lousy movie in town.'" Nobody would give this movie a break! Dad told me with feeling that the producer, John Rose, who had realized his vision and made this incredible groundbreaking film, was so discouraged he moved to Mexico and never made another picture.

————————

Dad had starting seeing Lynn Paul, a sexy sophisticate. She wore her hair in a short bob; he was into that look. They had a torrid affair. Mother had this theory that Dad was torn between "good girls" and "bad girls." She thought Lynn fit the description of the bad girl that his brothers fooled around with, and that was her attraction. Lynn gave me some clothes that were her cast-offs; they were more chic and fitted than anything I had in my wardrobe.

After Mother and Dad's divorce, Dad and Lynn got engaged. He bought a house in the valley and took Tom and me to see it. We liked the house and the pool, but Dad was already having doubts. For some reason he was worried he wouldn't get to spend enough time with us. Also, Lynn had a jealous temper. She went through his address book and saw a couple of names she didn't recognize. In a jealous fit, she drew her leg back and was about to kick him in his bad leg. He yelled, "You kick my leg and I'll break your nose!" He had paid for her nose job and had to say whatever he could to stop her from kicking that phlebitis leg. Yeah, Dad was generous that way! He paid for his girlfriends' nose, ear, and boob jobs. But he would only pay for one per girlfriend—he was well-off, not wealthy!

Mother started a new life of her own as well. Kay: "I found a house in Brentwood I dearly loved for the children and me, and Don bought it for us. I began to date and for the first time in my adult life began to have a carefree time." She eventually fell in love with a handsome rancher, Alan Carling-Smith.

When Mother and Alan got engaged, Alan brought his two kids over to meet us. Malcolm was a popular, good-looking football player. His sister Heather was mischievous fun and a competitive swimmer. I was used to being the oldest; now I had a big brother and sister to look up to! Tom and I are close with them to this day.

After Mother and Alan married, they moved to Northern California to a rather remote town called Round Mountain because Alan was a rancher. I stayed in Los Angeles and moved in with Dad. I was old enough by California law to choose which parent I wanted to live with. Tom lived with mother and Alan, and had a tough time adjusting to the cattle ranch. He moved back to Los Angeles a few years later.

Dad rented a house on Will Rogers State Park Road, and I started going to Paul Revere Junior High in Pacific Palisades.

———————

After Dad left *The Andy Griffith Show*, he came back as a guest as he promised. The episodes were now in color, and although people were upset about Barney's departure, the show held onto its high ratings. Dad

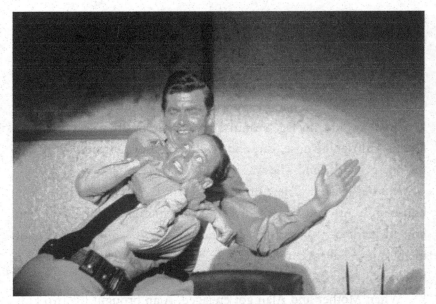

Andy and Barney getting laughs on stage at Harrah's
in Lake Tahoe, 1963.

performed in stage shows with Andy and Jim Nabors in Lake Tahoe. They sang, told jokes, and did scenes from *The Andy Griffith Show*. Dad had me out there one summer. Jerry Van Dyke was also a guest star that year and as a kid I thought he had one of the funniest acts I'd ever seen. On stage was a toy-sized mule. Jerry pantomimed whipping the mule while lip synching to the deep, booming Frankie Laine song, "Mule Train." The show also featured a popular music group, The Establishment.

Andy had a lot of moods; he was mercurial. I used to study his face before I spoke to him. One time I walked into a room where he was sitting by himself. I took a breath and said, "Penny for your thoughts!" He looked up startled, and smiled. "Well Karen, I was thinking, the game of life's not fair. Why doesn't Elizabeth Taylor like me the way I like her? Pair of deuces. Not fair a'tall."

Andy knew of my performing ambitions. One evening just before the show, he took me backstage and walked me up to the closed curtain. He said, "Put your ear against that curtain and listen to the audience. What do you hear?"

I listened and heard glasses clinking, people talking, and giggling. Trying to be funny, I blurted: "As Barney Fife would say, 'They sound like they're gassed!'"

He said a bit sternly, "Karen, I'm trying to teach you something. Now, I listen to the audience every night, and that's how I know what kind of an audience I'm gonna have." So I learned from him, and I do that before my own shows. And if I hear a lot of hiccups, I know they're gonna be a great audience!

———————————

Starring in his own motion pictures was the next big challenge for Dad. In 1966, he made *The Ghost and Mr. Chicken*. He was pacing the floor at night. Yeah, he was nervous! The script was written by a comedy team that had contributed many great scripts to *The Andy Griffith Show*: Jim Fritzell and Everett Greenbaum, known to all as Jim and Ev. Dad also contributed to the writing of *Ghost*, uncredited. He didn't take credit for the writing he offered to do on shows.

The plot centered on Dad's character, Luther Heggs, a man scared of his own shadow who gets talked into spending the night in a haunted house. Fritzell was in charge of story structure and Greenbaum had the funny ideas. They wrote a treatment that, at that time, was called *Running Scared*, which was about forty pages. Don: "It simply didn't work."

Even though Fritzell and Greenbaum had turned out a very weak treatment, the producer, Frank McCarthy, a military man who knew nothing about comedy, kept raving about how funny it was. This really irritated Dad. Fortunately, McCarthy left to do another project, *Patton*, about General George S. Patton during WWII. Don: "Wasserman gave me Ed Montagne, who was producing *McHale's Navy* for TV. Ed was tops on comedy. I breathed a sigh of relief. Andy was good at laying out plots, so I got him to come in and fix the treatment. I still wanted Fritzell and Greenbaum to write the script. I thought they were two of the best comedy writers I'd ever worked with. Universal wanted to let them go, so I went in there and used my clout at the studio to keep them. They finally caved in and said yes to Jim and Ev" (as told to Robert Metz).

Dad had an office at Universal in "the bungalows." (He even had his own secretary; I was impressed.) When Andy joined them in Dad's office, he announced, "I quit smoking!" Dad was surprised: "Really? How'd you do it?" Andy: "I just decided to quit, cold turkey. I haven't smoked since!" Don: "When did this happen?" Andy: "Just now, in the car!" Dad laughed and Andy said, "Actually it's been two solid weeks." That gave Dad the resolve to quit, too. Dad was so determined I wouldn't pick up the habit, he promised to buy me a car when I turned sixteen if I promised I would never smoke and never date a married man!

The script, now *The Ghost and Mr. Chicken*, was finally approved, and Ed Montagne began casting. Dad offered roles to as many of *The Andy Griffith Show* actors as he could, including Hal Smith, Reta Shaw, Burt Mustin, Hope Summers, Ellen Corby, Cliff Norton, Charles Lane, Herbie Faye, Lurene Tuttle, James Millhollin, Jim Begg, and Robert Cornthwaite. One actress, Jesslyn Fax, appeared in the movie and after that did an *Andy Griffith Show* episode. Dad also remembered his army buddy, Al Checco: he played the guy who was a special witness for Luther, who had his last meeting "on Mars."

Ed Montagne thought of Joan Staley for the part of Luther's love interest, Alma. Joan had acted for Ed in a series he produced called *Broadside*; she played the female counterpart to *McHale's Navy*. When he told her who was starring, she said, "Don Knotts? You bet!" She had lots of TV and film roles to her credit in the 1960s.

Before that, in November 1958, she'd been *Playboy*'s Playmate of the Month. She was a blond bombshell! So how did Mr. Fontaine sell her as the small-town beauty Luther Heggs would fall for? He put her in a brunette Claudia Cardinale wig that gave her the fresh, natural look of Alma. According to Joan, "We shot it in seventeen days. It was shot like a television show. We just made it work. We had to make sure we didn't get hit by the sets as they were moving them! We had such a short shooting schedule, Don was running from one sequence to another; there was not much time for conversation. The big hope for Universal that year was a Cary Grant vehicle called *Father Goose*. They poured millions into that. This piece we did for $750,000, and it was like, 'Eh, we'll drop it in and see what happens.' It outgrossed Cary Grant and everything else Universal did for the year."

At the table read, actors were throwing in bits to get a laugh, and as the reading went on it got a little looser and someone would try to break you up. Dad twisted the words and got everybody laughing for ten minutes; he may have done it intentionally as a tension-breaker. Joan had some challenges shooting the soup scene, in which Alma saves a table for Luther but the previous diner refuses to give up his seat, so Luther is forced to eat his soup standing up. It was difficult for Joan to keep a straight face, especially with the guy sitting at the table who was a "master of mugging."

That mug master was a short, bald, character actor named Herbie Faye. He started in vaudeville and had an act with none other than Phil Silvers as his straight man.

Tom and I were going to be extras; we were background in the park scene, sitting on a bench watching Luther give his speech. Just below the camera frame was a large fan that went off in the middle of the speech to make Luther's notes fly away. Luther tried to recover his poise by repeating the mayor's joke, "That electrician must be a Democrat." None of us were expecting to hear "Attaboy, Luther!"

from the back. That crackling voice sounded far away in the movie but was super loud in the soundstage. The extras and actors had a huge reaction; that was the voice of Everett Greenbaum. Everett got to deliver the famous line he had written when the original guy didn't deliver it right. We were shooting outdoors and the lighting was intense. Joan actually hurt her eyes from staring into the reflectors for so long and had to be taken to the hospital, but she was very brave about it.

I asked her what it was like to work with Dad. Joan: "Working with an icon, I didn't know what to expect. I didn't know if he was going to be arrogant or a dictator. I found the most incredible performer who was so giving. He was like an old friend; he made himself available as an actor. Sometimes a person's ego gets in the way, but there was nothing like that with Don. When I asked, 'Did you want me to read it another way?' He said, 'No, what you did was fine.' There were moments that I loved him and I didn't want it to end."

Joan was challenged to keep a straight face when filming the romantic porch scene. "Don would look at me and he'd do a thing that was deliberately planned to crack me up during a closeup on me. It was devilish . . . and funny. The only time I was alone with him was when we were shooting." I mentioned to her that some women think of Dad as a ladies' man. She said, "I can see why. Don was not the most handsome man, but he was so bloody bright, I would have loved to talk with him. . . . I guess I just wasn't his flavor. I got married in '67. It never occurred to me that he would hit on me because of his niceness. I've been in situations where you heard the door click behind you."

Alan Rafkin, the director, was very "New York" and an expert on comedy. He laughed a lot after the shots he was directing. It wasn't a matter of him telling Dad what to do; they had already worked it out. The park scene was shot on the Universal backlot, in

the park where they shot *Back to the Future* and many other movies. Joan: "Don was extremely fastidious—he came on set totally
prepared. He always knew his lines and he was camera savvy.
He would be in his chair checking his script, and sometimes he
would disappear to rehearse on his own. It was like we had been
working together for years. He was such a giving actor that I followed his lead. Sometimes after rehearsal he'd go, 'Yeah!' That
was the compliment—except for the occasional 'Ooh, that works,
let's use that.'"

Dad was involved in all aspects of his Universal films, including
editing. He was probably sitting in the editing room when he had
these thoughts: "Exaggeration is always funny. When somebody falls
down in a movie, people laugh for some reason. We've never been
able to figure that one out. Falling down usually gets a laugh if you fall
funny and if you make the sound effect loud enough, you exaggerate
as much as possible. If you notice when a comedian hits a comedian
on top of the head the sound effect they lay in is funny, so that you
don't take the violence seriously. He takes his fist and hits him on
the head, and you hear a *boomp* and you make it as loud as you can.
For some reason, in comedy exaggerated sound effects are funny. If
somebody walks through a plate glass, you make the glass shatter ten
times as loud as it would normally—which is sometimes difficult to
explain to somebody who's sitting in the editing room laying in the
soundtrack. He'll say to you, 'A glass won't sound that loud if you
break it.' Well, I want it to sound that loud; the audience won't laugh
unless it's louder."

When the movie was released, Dad, Tom, and I snuck into the
back of a movie theater so he could hear the laughs from the audience. They were huge! I became aware that Tom had another "extra"
bit as a boy asking for Luther's autograph outside the courthouse.
Where was I, and how did my little brother snag that gig? Hmm, I
was going to have to keep a closer watch on things!

Outside the courthouse in *The Ghost and Mr. Chicken*, Tommy asking
Dad (as Luther) for his autograph, 1966.

Dad hit a snag in a preproduction meeting when he learned they
were going to use an existing courtroom set. It was huge and inap-
propriate. Don: "Ed Montagne was usually a great help, but this time
he said, 'Use the existing one. We don't have the bucks to build one.'
The set designer quietly called me aside and said, 'You tell me what
you want.' I said, 'A small town courtroom like the one in *Inherit the
Wind*. He said, 'I'll build it, and they won't even know.'" So he did,
and they never found out.

Dad's next picture for Universal was *The Reluctant Astronaut*, in
1967. It's about a thirty-five-year-old man still living with his parents.
He plays an astronaut at a local fairground, but his father (Arthur
O'Connell) wants him to be a real astronaut. Through a misunder-
standing he ends up on an actual mission for NASA. Dad made trips
to NASA for research.

It was an exceptionally fun film for kids, and there were kid actors
in the movie. It was a lot of fun visiting the set and seeing weight-
less tubes of peanut butter rigged up on wires in the space capsule.

Pamelyn Ferdin was a child actress who was in demand at the time. She said in her soon-to-be-published book, "Squeezed into my schedule that summer was a brief appearance in a motion picture comedy, *The Reluctant Astronaut*, starring Don Knotts. As one of a group of children on a carnival rocket ship ride operated by Knotts, I interrupt an intricate 'landing sequence' with the announcement that I have to go to the bathroom. With that, the ride comes to an abrupt halt and all the children are quickly ushered out. It's a funny scene, and I got a kick out of it. Don Knotts made me laugh; he was very funny and very good to all the children."

Another kid actor was Geoffrey Mark: "I met Don on the set of *The Reluctant Astronaut* when I was eight years old. I got to be there for three hours. For technical reasons, the capsule was actually up in the air, and they had to get him up on a crane, put him there, and they shot everything with huge booms. It was way above everybody's head. He was lovely to me; he gave me his autograph and put me up on his shoulder."

———————

Dad hosted *The Hollywood Palace* three times, once in 1968 when he invited me to the taping. The music guest on the show was a trendy rock group, the Merry-Go-Round. I was a big fan of theirs. I decked myself out in false eyelashes, a poor-boy sweater, hip-hugger skirt, and white go-go boots. I looked totally bitchin'! After the show, Dad and the performers were relaxing in the performers' lounge, which had a fancy bar. One of the rockers from the band started chatting with me and said he'd like to take me home. I said, "Groovy, I'll check with my dad." I asked Dad's permission, and I'm sure my eyes were saying, "Please say yes or I'll die." Dad said yes! What a sweet and trusting dad he was!

It was still daylight and a light rain was falling when we got into his red Alfa Romeo. I couldn't believe such a worldly man was

escorting me as the car sped down Sunset Boulevard. I told a fasci-
nating story about the time I went to meet my friend Gina at Zuma,
the nude beach, but I got on the wrong bus and ended up at Venice
Beach! There was an improv group, the L.A. Connection, doing a
show. They invited people to join in, so I got up and did a scene
about a lady tattoo artist with this guy named Mark. Some clowns
on unicycles rode by—

He interrupted to ask how old I was. I gave a smug smile and
said, "Fourteen." He slammed on the brakes!! The car did a 180-degree
spin on Sunset Boulevard. It was terribly fortunate there were very
few cars on the road. The man did not speak another word all the
way to my father's house.

———————————

I was happy at school now, and I was finally old enough to take a
drama class. I didn't want to do comedy then; I idolized the great
dramatic actress Katharine Hepburn. When our class performed for
a PTA show, I did a dramatic pantomime as a mommy cockroach
struggling to find food for her babies until she gets stepped on by a
human foot. My fingers took the shape of antennae and my limbs
went flying; the audience was in hysterics. They didn't get the pathos
of the poor cockroach—I felt like a failure! Dad found me afterward:
"Karen, that was great! I don't know whether to give you a bouquet
of flowers or spray you with Raid!" I had to laugh. He always knew
what to say.

———————————

Late in 1968 Dad took me back to Morgantown to see his mother,
who was very ill, at St. Vincent Pallotti Hospital. The nurses told Dad
she had gotten up in the middle of the night, got dressed, and headed
for the main entrance. That was not going to happen on their watch!

Me, Dad, and Tommy at the Brentwood home after the divorce, 1966.

Dad had some chuckles with his mother over it. It was so endearing for me to see them relating that way. And after all his success on TV and movies, Elsie would say she couldn't understand why he didn't do his ventriloquism anymore—she missed that. We also got to see my Uncle Sid, who had pulled his life together and married a beautiful lady named Mildred. They were known as Sid and Mid, and Cousin Sandy was their daughter. Elsie did make a recovery, but she passed away the following year at the age of eighty-four, and Dad was absolutely devastated.

Tom and I found out we were going to be extras again in Dad's next movie, *The Shakiest Gun in the West*. The film was a new twist on the old Bob Hope 1948 classic, *The Paleface*. That movie in turn was a spoof of a 1946 film with Joel McCrea, which was a remake of a 1929 Western starring Gary Cooper. As you can see, it was an "original" plot. Tom and I were hamming it up on set in our western costumes. The director, once again, was Alan Rafkin. He called me over and said, "Karen, comedy is serious business—no giggles." They called, "Places!" I took my position. "And Action!" The scene was a showdown between evil gunslinger Black Bart and the town dentist, played by Dad. Black Bart tells him, "I'm gonna kill you," and Dad the dentist answers, "I'm gonna drill you!" It was so funny when they faced each other and drew their guns I almost burst out laughing. Then Dad did that thing where he pointed the gun, shaking, and I started to smile. I heard "Cut!"

Everybody was staring at me as Dad started walking toward me. He took me aside, told me I had ruined the take by smiling in the middle of the scene, and said I'd better pull it together. I assured him I would. Imagine Don Knotts telling you "knot" to laugh! He gave me a little coaching, "Honey, I want you to think of something serious, even sad." What could make me sad? That was around the time Gina and I were going to go see the Beatles at the Hollywood Bowl. I thought, *What if I got sick and couldn't go? No George Harrison?* I started tearing up. "I'm ready for my closeup, Mr. Rafkin!"

11

BEVERLY HILLS HIDEAWAY

SOON AFTER DAD'S AFFAIR with Lynn Paul ended, he met Sunni Walton. She was a beautiful and talented actress, singer, and impressionist. She had flaming red hair and wore very short skirts that showed off her amazing legs. Dad was involved with her for four years. They kept separate places, and he anguished about the relationship. He wanted to move on, and he would talk to me about it from the slant board with his legs in the air. She had two fantastic young boys whom Dad loved doing magic tricks for. He got Sunni small parts on his TV shows.

Over the years, there has been a lot of talk about Dad being a ladies' man, so I asked his leading ladies about it. Why? I was as curious as everyone else! His most prolific dating period occurred when I was in high school. Loneliness wasn't a problem then because I was there to keep him company. Once, when he was between marriages, he tried living a bachelor lifestyle. He got a swinger's pad on the beach, and I never saw him more miserable. He loved many women and was adored by them, but he wasn't always successful. He told his friend, voice actor Joni Robbins: "I've had so many weird experiences dating. Lemme tell you about Tina Louise"—the actress who played Ginger on *Gilligan's Island.* He had a thing for redheads, and she had given him her phone number. Every week, he'd call and ask if she'd like to go out on Saturday night. She'd say, "Oh, I'm sorry, I have other plans, but could you call me next week?" This went on for about a year until finally he realized how naive he'd been.

Dad made his next movie for Universal in 1969, titled *The Love God?* He played Abner Peacock, the publisher of a bird-watcher's magazine, *The Peacock.* The magazine has a financial crisis, so he takes on a partner, Mr. Tremaine, who in reality is a smut publisher known to his friends as Ice Pick Charlie. Charlie intends to use the magazine to get a fourth-class mailing license. He turns naive Abner into a national sex symbol and opens Peacock Clubs across the nation. The film was a takeoff on Hugh Hefner and the Playboy Clubs, written by one of the most respected comedy writers of the era, Nat Hiken.

In spite of the subject matter, the movie was clean. Abner stays true to his fiancé Rose Ellen, played by Maggie Peterson, Charlene Darling of *The Andy Griffith Show.* Andy and his manager Dick Linke suggested her for the part. The movie also starred Maureen Arthur, who played Tremaine's wife. She was known for her hysterically funny performance as the boss's secretary in *How to Succeed in Business Without Really Trying.* She was also married to Aaron Ruben.

The comedian B. S. Pully, who was known for his gravelly voice and tough guy persona, was in the film in the role of J. Charles Twilight. Pully was a legendary comic who influenced the comedy of Rodney Dangerfield, Milton Berle, and a host of others in that generation. When he died, Frank Sinatra paid his funeral expenses. Tom and I had the most fun hanging out with him! In the days before cell phones, he had a battery-operated telephone that would ring. He'd reach inside his jacket and pull out a phone receiver and talk. We thought it was hilarious! Later on, I found out the device was called the Phony Ring Telephone and was sold at Burt Wheeler's Magic Shop on Hollywood Boulevard for $12.50. As Dad might say, "It was a gas!"

As a lover of birds, Abner Peacock does bird calls. Dad brought home a record the studio had made for him of bird calls to rehearse because, as Abner, he had to match them in the movie. I watched his facial expressions as he practiced the bird calls and just about died laughing. The '60s was an era of extravagant clothing, and Abner's outfits parodied the styles. He wore a leopard suit, capes with matching hats, peacock pajamas, a gem-studded Nehru jacket, and a floral tapestry coat. I remember seeing those outfits in his closet; I wish I knew what he did with them!

The Love God? is a great parody and the most outlandish film he ever made. Universal studio executives paid little attention to the plots of Dad's movies since they were run so successfully by Ed Montagne. When they realized what the movie was about, they became alarmed, fearing it would upset Dad's fans because of his squeaky-clean image. Universal did only minimal publicity, and the picture was not widely seen.

Also in the 1960s, Dad guest starred on the variety shows of Red Skelton, Dinah Shore, Garry Moore, Danny Kaye, Andy Williams, the Smothers Brothers, and Kraft Music Hall. He worked on a Danny Thomas special with Sammy Davis Jr. in 1967. He said, "Sammy sort of adopted me. We hung out for a couple of days. We'd rehearse at night until 10 PM, then he'd insist I come to his house in Hollywood to watch movies. He actually had somebody there to run the projector. It was exhausting just to watch him."

He also guest starred on Andy Griffith's 1967 special *The Uptown Downtown Show*. Goldie Hawn, yet to become a star, was a dancer in the chorus line. Several more variety shows he did in the 1970s included those for Donny and Marie Osmond, Tony Orlando and Dawn, and the Muppets.

Dad appeared on *The Muppet Show* in November 1977. © *Disney*

CBS wanted Dad to do a special toward the end of his Universal contract, and he agreed, but the studio didn't have a concept. Dad's wheels began to turn. The FDA had approved the birth control pill in May 1960, and it became known simply as the Pill, as if there were no other pill worth mentioning! Before that, most women would leave the job market if they got pregnant and not return to work until their child was old enough to attend school. A sexual revolution was happening. It occurred to Dad that entertainment in the 1960s had become dirty. He said to Bill Dana, who would be writer/producer, "Why don't we do *Don Knotts' Nice Clean, Decent, Wholesome Hour*?"

This clever show aired in 1970. When the special opens, he's standing in an empty studio, and nothing is happening. He says, "Ladies and Gentlemen, I was supposed to do a special tonight, but I just couldn't get the show on. Let me show you what happened." The plot is about Dad trying to get a clean show produced. He takes his script to Broadway producers and movie executives, and they all try to corrupt him. *Don Knotts' Nice Clean, Decent, Wholesome Hour* was a brilliantly funny show and won its time slot on CBS.

I was looking forward to graduating from Paul Revere and starting Palisades High with my friends, but Dad threw me a curveball when he said he had just bought a house, and we were going to move to Beverly Hills! I wasn't wild about it. There was a popular show on the air called *The Beverly Hillbillies*. I asked Dad, "Are we gonna be *The Mayberrybillies*?" He just smiled and said, "Wait till you see the house."

It was a lovely ranch-style home on Sunset Boulevard. Dad bought it from the legendary movie star Barbara Stanwyck. The house was on the movie-star map, which wasn't updated very often. Every weekend the celebrity tour bus would go by our house and riders would yell out the window, "Hey, Barbara, love the hair!" They had no idea Don Knotts lived there. One morning, two ladies managed to slip away from the tour. They snuck around the side of our house and the gate slammed behind them. Our dog, Veer, started barking, and the noise woke up Dad. He came running out of his room with his hair all wild, like Barney Fife. He opened the door and was shocked to see this lady with her Hawaiian hat and heart-shaped sunglasses. The woman yelled, "Margaret, quick get the camera! Barbara Stanwyck wears a wig!" Dad kindly walked the ladies back to the bus, to the enjoyment of the other passengers. One lady stood up and yelled, "It's Mick Jagger!" Why did people always compare Dad, a scrawny, neurotic comedian, to Mick Jagger, a scrawny, neurotic rock star? It had to be their lips!

It didn't take me long to fall in love with the house on Hillcrest Road in Beverly Hills. Dad hired an interior designer whose name was—what else?—Max! He furnished it entirely from Sloan's furniture store. It was decorated in an elegant but masculine style in Dad's favorite color, baby blue. Tom moved in and started going to Beverly High. He made three friends who became inseparable, John Ford,

Jack Gindi, and Stan Brooks. They'd hang out at the house and Dad would join them. Dad had a lot of doctor friends and so did Tom; all three were studying to be doctors until Stan broke ranks and became a movie producer.

Once when Dad was out of town, Gina was over and I opened the door to Dad's room, causing an alarm to go off. Gina: "You were going, 'Oh my god, the security people are gonna come—they've been out here two or three times this month!' I remember thinking, *He has an alarm for his bedroom door?* The lives of people who lived in big houses were always a revelation to me. He had an old-fashioned fainting couch where he could rest like royalty, only upside down. I always felt very accepted by him; he was somebody I respected."

———————————

Bob Metz: "After he made his fifth [and final film for Universal], *How to Frame a Figg*, NBC offered Don a weekly variety show. He objected, saying he was tied to Universal for another six months. NBC said, 'Don't worry about Universal, we buy half their product.' Don said, 'I can't do this kind of thing every week.' They insisted that he could, and finally he agreed to try. They made a deal with Wasserman and got him out of the contract."

Variety shows offered a little of everything: sketch comedy, musical numbers, and movie stars from the previous era. *The Don Knotts Show* brought stars Donald O'Connor, Florence Henderson, Chuck Connors, Mac Davis, Bobby Sherman, Juliet Prowse, Dick Crenna, Robert Morse, Gina Lollobrigida, and Lesley Ann Warren to the awareness of a younger generation. Dad was uncomfortable being a host because of his shyness; he much preferred playing a character. They worked on the idea of a "host character" for him. Personally, I wish they hadn't pressured him to do that. It made him stilted and self-conscious; he was so loveable just being himself.

David Pollock was one of the show's writers. David: "A well-respected writer named Phil Sharp wrote a segment called 'The Small World of Jessie Fender.' This was a show within the show every week. Jessie was essentially Barney Fife. He was added to appease fans; Don was so loved as Barney. The great thing about Barney as a character was that you knew him so well you could predict how he was going to react. Every day my partner, Elias Davis, and I would go to our offices on Canon Drive on the second floor, two desks facing each other, and try to think up sketches. It was sort of up to us. We had a sense of what would work, keeping in mind the guest stars. The ultimate top guy was Bill Harbach with Nick Vanoff under him. Previously, there was Bill Dana and Bob Sweeney. It would be taped on Friday nights at NBC, and I remember being in Don's dressing room, but there was a chain of command. If you had something to say about a sketch, you would go to Billy or Nick—you would never go to the star—and he would never go to us directly." So they had made it from the hardscrabble days of live TV to the Hollywood caste system.

The Hillcrest home was relatively modest. A neighbor of ours had a home with a stream running through the living room! Beverly Hills High was also somewhat elaborate. The guidance office had red carpeting; it looked like a model's runway. The only thing missing was a sign saying, REMEMBER TO SMILE AND DON'T TRIP! The basketball court had a swimming pool under its rollaway floor; it had been used in the movie *It's a Wonderful Life* with Jimmy Stewart and Donna Reed. When you were watching a basketball game, the heat combined with water underneath made you sweat. It was the only basketball court with balls that literally dribbled. I was thrilled one day to see Christie Brinkley at a basketball game. She had been in a couple of my classes at Revere, and though we lived near each other, we never spoke.

I was starting to develop an inferiority complex. I told Dad, "This school is too advanced for me." He was surprised and asked what I meant. I said, "Half the kids in my class are on birth control pills." He asked, "What about the other half?" I said, "They're boys!"

My drama class at Beverly was taught by Mr. Corrigan. He had an acting exercise that became famous to us, for creating inanimate objects. He would close his eyes, dramatically raise his arms up high and hold his body taut, then relax. This was "Mr. Corrigan's Carrot."

One day a beautiful new girl walked into class; her name was Gulfiliz Kulay, or Gulo for short. Her dad was the Turkish consul general and her mother had been a child star in Turkey. We became great friends. I was terribly shy but Gulo was instantly popular. She hung out with Missy March, who had not one but two famous dads. Her birth father was Mel Tormé, and her stepdad, who had adopted her, was Hal March. We didn't know if she was Tormé, or March, or marching back to Tormé.

Multiple marriages were not uncommon in Beverly Hills. There was the story of a leading lady who yelled across the courtyard to her director husband, "Come quickly! *Your* children and *my* children are fighting with *our* children!"

Another girl I clicked with, Cecily Adams, was a year younger. The daughter of Don Adams, star of the hit show *Get Smart*, Cecily was funny, petite, and adorable, and Tom had a crush on her. Cecily and I jokingly called ourselves the Daughters of Dons. Don Adams was known for his extended families. Cecily took me to her father's house where he was living with his latest wife. It was a mansion with a swimming pool and a tennis court. I felt bad when Cecily had to ask the butler for permission to enter, but "Jeeves" did give his consent.

Barbara Feldon, who played Agent 99 on *Get Smart*, was a guest on Dad's variety show in 1970, when *Get Smart* was in its last season at CBS. I asked her about working with Dad in her sketch with him, about two lonely people who meet in Paris. Barbara said, "I remember liking the experience very much, feeling comfortable. I was sitting on a bench in the sketch. There was something about Don that was so endearing." I called Barbara recently because I had one last question for her. She said, "It wouldn't surprise me that Don was a ladies' man. I've been so naive in my life. Wow, that's interesting!"

Dad was excited when the Bridges family, Lloyd, Beau, and Jeff, made an appearance on his show. Dad worked with Beau in an airplane sketch, and with Lloyd in a sketch about two guys buying plots in a funeral parlor. Airplane humor at the time focused on fear of flying and hijackings, which were prevalent then. Beau: "I was a huge fan of your dad's. I mean, he just made me giggle so hard. My father, brother, and I, the three of us, didn't get to work together too often. We were really excited to be working with Don. He was so kind and nice to us during the rehearsal; he probably sensed we were nervous. He was very supportive, and we were having fun. When the rehearsal was done, he's walking towards the exit door of the stage and all of a sudden, he turns and just blows off! I mean he started screaming and yelling at us, incensed at how terrible we were! We looked at each other; we were just freaked. Then he gives us this big, dumb grin and walks out the door." I explained to Beau about Dad's practical-joke side. Beau: "It was really funny, because he so often plays that meek, shaky little guy. He just laid it on with this big bellowing voice. It was really funny—we laughed. I still tell that story whenever his name comes up."

When Dad told me Sonny and Cher were going to be on his show, I was so excited! Cher was my idol; we all wore our hair like hers. I went to the set on tape day. Dad was too busy to introduce me, so I went over and told her who I was, and I asked, "Do you know what I can do for acne?" Then I thought, *Geez, what a dumb question!* But Cher said, "That's a good question. Everybody thinks they know everything about me—nobody knows *anything.* I moved to Hollywood when I was sixteen, and I was so embarrassed about these zits until a friend told me about—" Suddenly there was a commotion; Sonny had taken a fall. Cher ran over to him, and I ran behind her. Cher: "Sonny, are you OK?" He was, then she turned to me and said, "Buf-Puf . . . for your acne." I bought the Buf-Puf. It didn't help my acne, but I remembered her kindness, and I understand how Dad's kindness meant so much to others.

Dad's fame, which had overshadowed Tom and me in *The Andy Griffith Show* days, seemed almost incidental in this high school "gilded cage." The Beverly High drama department was run by John Ingle, who later became an actor himself, best known for his role as a scheming patriarch in the ABC soap opera *General Hospital.* He cast all his plays around a preferred group of kids, and even though I auditioned for every show, I was never in one. A wonderful actress named Janie Murray was usually the leading lady; her father was Ken Murray. Helaine Lembeck, daughter of Harvey Lembeck, was a terrific character actress and was cast in many shows. I was too shy to get to know her then, but later I connected with Helaine when I took her dad's fantastic improv workshop at Paramount Studios. Carrie Fisher entered the drama department until her mother took her to New York to be in a Broadway show with her. I was jealous of Carrie—she was so confident, pretty, and talented. It wasn't until years later that I began to understand the struggles she was going through, and they weren't that far from my own.

Elaine Joyce was a regular who added sizzle to the show sketches. She was married to a well-known dancer, Bobby Van. They adored each other, but when they went through a rough patch in their marriage, she and Dad began an affair. Dad told me everything that was going on with her, Bobby, and him. We weren't the typical father and daughter—we were best buddies. Instead of wondering, *Should I tell my daughter this?* he would just talk to me. As Gina said, "He wasn't your typical parent; you were Mutt & Jeff. He didn't want you to become an actress, but he wanted the good things for you."

That was the only bone of contention between Dad and me; he almost cried when I told him. He knew scores of people who pursued careers in acting but ended up nowhere. He didn't want that for me. Elaine boosted my confidence, and I think she encouraged him to give me a shot on his variety show. One day Elaine took me clothes shopping at a trendy Beverly Hills boutique. I tended to hide behind the mannequins but Elaine took center stage. Here I was with this tall, beautiful blonde, ordering sales ladies from clothing racks to the dressing room. I felt like the star of my own musical! Elaine put together some darling outfits for me. Unfortunately, I lost a lot of the clothes—I was *that* absentminded.

Elaine went back to Bobby, and Dad decided to have me on his show when I was sixteen! The writers needed to come up with a bit for us. Dad told them of his concerns about my desire to act, and they wrote something that fit reality. Dad asked me if I knew any monologues. In my drama class I had learned one from Lillian Hellman's *Toys in the Attic*. I was a huge fan of the great actress Geraldine Page, who starred in the movie version. To avoid copyright issues, they rewrote the monologue so it had the same feel but was unrecognizable. The wardrobe lady found an adorable pantsuit for me, and *even I* liked how I looked. In the bit, Dad introduces me, then takes the audience into his confidence and explains rather condescendingly about my acting ambition. Then he says, "OK, honey, this is your big chance. Lights, camera, you're on!" I freeze in terror. He does an aside to the audience, "I knew this would cure her!" Suddenly I burst into my dramatic speech. It was exciting to perform with Dad, and my knees were shaking like crazy! When the speech ended, the audience applauded heartily.

———————————

Dad had met Bill Cosby through Sheldon Leonard when Dad was doing *The Andy Griffith Show* and Cosby was doing the TV show *I Spy* with Robert Culp. They became friends and hung out for a while. Dad's variety show wasn't getting very good ratings, so Cosby agreed to do guest shots on a couple of episodes. The ratings went up when he did them. Don: "He was a big draw among viewers. Variety was down his alley, not mine."

One afternoon, I called Gina and said, "We're not gonna do what we had planned tonight [listen to Beatles records and dance] because we're going to Bill Cosby's house for dinner! Ask you mom if you can go!" Gina remembers, "It was way up in Benedict Canyon. I think your Dad drove. There were about twenty people seated around a table. Cosby sat at the head of it, and I was seated next to him. There were black servants dressed like the 1920s with pinafores and funny white hats. It was constant hilarity. Bill Cosby told jokes from one end of the meal to the other. It was hard to eat because we were all laughing so much. I had the sense that he was trying out these jokes on us; we were some sort of beta testing group. But it felt spontaneous. One of the things I remember happening during dinner, and this is like a typical 'Gina, we can't take you anywhere' thing. I never learned manners—I was raised by bohemians! At one point I was laughing so hard I put down my hand and my spoon flew up in the air. He reached out his hand and grabbed it and put it on the table without interrupting his joke—he kept it going so perfectly!" Of course he caught it—that spoon was about to steal the scene!

Dad liked to go to Vegas when Cosby was doing his show and see him backstage afterward, and he took Tom a couple of times.

Tom: "One time we were all hanging out with Doug Henning, the contortionist magician. He was a small guy, and I remember Cos joking around about how flexible he was. He cups his hand over a can and goes, 'Here, pass Doug over to Don.' He was being really funny. But one time, Dad knocked on his dressing room door, Cos opened it a crack and he kind of got rid of us. Dad turned to me and said, 'I think he's got a woman in there.' So we took our seats for the show. When Cos came out he said, 'Well, before I get started I got a friend here. Ace!' And Dad would go, 'Yeah!' And he'd say, 'Don Knotts everyone!' He'd start his show that way if he knew Dad was in the audience."

Gina and I visited Dad's variety show when Cosby was a guest. Gina: "Just before they started, we came in through curtains from the back and went through the middle of the stage to get to our seats. I thought, 'Wow this is a trip, they're all looking at us. We were like, 'Hi!' We sat very close to the front."

Dad struggled with his variety show, often complaining that the sketches weren't funny enough. Although the variety show was a relatively new arrival to television, its roots went back to vaudeville. It was an example of something so old it's new again. Even good writers would use gags making a last hurrah before joining their wisecracking cousins in the resting place of tired old jokes. In 1970 Dad said in an interview, "I can't remember precise examples of sketches that didn't turn out well, usually because of my own pessimism when it comes to material. But like most comedians I tend to be on the depressed side. I pick up a script and say 'What's funny about that?' When you do a weekly variety show, because of the tremendous amount of material that you have to turn out every week, you begin to compromise in your mind because it's impossible for a team of writers to turn out solidly funny material to fill an hour every week. I just get totally depressed about the whole thing. . . . Sometimes they'll lay a sketch in front of you that's air tight; it's funny. You know it when you read it. That's a joy, because all you have to do is get up and do it."

When he found himself in an unfunny sketch, Dad would often use his Nervous Guy persona because it worked in almost any situation. Another tool at his disposal was the pantomime sketch. Audiences hadn't seen the likes of these gems since Charlie Chaplin. Certain elements had to fall into place. You needed a comedic choreographer like Tony Charmoli; a camera man who could sneak the camera through, like Bob Erbeck; and dancers who didn't dance but used movement to play shoppers, musicians, or doctors. You needed a pantomime artist whose face and body made an audience feel both pathos and humor: Don Knotts!

Don: "Facial expression is just as important for conveying to the audience what's going through your mind as what you say. I've done a lot of pantomime, and I find that's good training for any kind of acting. One of the most effective things you can do to an audience is make them laugh and cry at the same time; it's sort of an emotional catharsis. I think that's one of the reasons Chaplin was so successful. He did that probably better than anybody of our century."

The role of MC felt unnatural for him on TV. Dad couldn't relate to writers firing sketches at him and admitted, "My perfectionism began to show." The variety show was cancelled in 1971. I've often wished the industry could've had "future sight" and not destroyed thousands of amazing shows in their vaults that could still be bringing laughter today.

───────────

In my classes at school I often felt paralyzed by shyness. I began to retreat further into myself. Our new home became my teenage hideaway. I started slipping into a fantasy world. Dad had a room with a lot of portraits on the wall of women he had worked with, was friends with, or just admired: Marilyn Monroe, Carol Channing, Carmen Miranda, and others. I called this room our Hall of Dames. My favorite portrait was the one of Arlene Dahl, a pretty big movie star in the 1950s. I thought, *She's so beautiful; she's got it all together. I bet she could help me with my problem.* My active imagination brought these paintings to life, and I thought of them as my new best friends. In my mind they were talking right to me. I knew they didn't really exist, but the fantasy felt so good I had a hard time pulling out of it. Arlene's portrait would ask, "How can I help you, Karen darling?" Me: "I can't get out of my cocoon!" Arlene: "What's wrong with you?" Me: "I'm celebrity adjacent. Everybody thinks of me as Knotts' nut."

I had started seeing our family psychiatrist, Dick Renneker, but I wasn't making progress. I would sit on his couch and space out. I was unhappy, but I thought, *What can this guy do about it?* Renneker was tall, lanky, and bald. His head was literally shaped like an egg. He told a lot of corny jokes. When I met him he was chomping on some peanuts from a jar of Planters, and he said, "You want some, kid? I'm a big lover of nuts."

I kept looking for ways to fit in at school. Times and styles were changing. Even at posh Beverly High kids wanted to look like hippies. Protest marches against the Vietnam War were gaining momentum. The boys were being drafted, and some parents hired antiwar attorneys to keep their sons out of the war. The boys were advised to act crazy in the draft office. The joke was that it worked; they were immediately made generals and sent to Washington.

I was desperate to fit in, so I wore a fringed vest, headband, and love beads. But it wasn't enough just to look like a hippie, you had to talk like one too, so I practiced.

It wasn't working. I finally asked for advice from the most popular person on the planet: Dad. He looked me over in the hippie garb that covered me as completely as a Halloween costume. He said sadly, "I'm sorry you're growing up at this time. Kids these days don't know how to socialize." I didn't realize until later, when I learned about the noon dances at his high school, that he was right.

Dad became infatuated with Sandy, a woman from the Louisiana Bayou. I guess he could relate because of his West Virginia background. Dad took Sandy to a Dodger game. Her Mafia ex-boyfriend showed up and started making threats. Dad was so scared he hired guards for the front door. A hairpiece sent through the mail chute had Barbara thinking Dad had been scalped. It was crazy! The incident got attention and was the only time Dad was on the cover of the *National Enquirer* without being sick in the hospital. Comedians generally didn't make the front page of gossip rags.

Dad told me to go stay at Andy Griffith's guest house until it all blew over. I couldn't believe it! I sent Gulo a postcard: "I won't be around for a while. I'm in the Barney Fife Witness Protection Program. Dad told me he wants me to stay at Andy Griffith's in case I get stalked by White Powder Dude. I complained to Dad, 'Don't you know Andy's not a real sheriff? He lives in Toluca Lake!'"

I went to Andy's sprawling home on Camarillo Street. He welcomed me cordially and escorted me to my "hideout" with the words, "And you know why." I offered my opinion, "My dad is a weird dude. Why don't you send me to the Clampetts'? Granny has a possum gun." Andy said, "You can get the girl out of Mayberry, but you can't get Mayberry out of the girl." I rolled my eyes as he showed me to the guest house. It was a sweet little bungalow with a bedroom and kitchen. I was thrilled, I had my own place! While I was staying there, Andy got married to an attractive, younger woman, Solica. They had the wedding on the grounds. It was either a short marriage or a very long ceremony. I remember she got to keep half the wedding cake. Dad's affair with Sandy came and went just as quickly.

———————

A new fashion icon came along, and a lot of girls were cutting their hair short to look like her. All the way from Carnaby Street in London, it was boyish-looking Twiggy. She had huge eyes and never smiled on her magazine covers. On the way home from school, I dropped by the Vidal Sassoon Hair Salon and told the French hair dresser, whose name was—what else?—Pierre, to give me "the Look." He said, "*C'est si bon*, no *problème*!" He was blocking my view of the mirror. He said, "Trust me, I make you beautiful!" I felt something cold and slimy on my head—I had been *gooped*! After three hours, I left the shop a curly redhead! I was trying to look cool, and now I looked like Little Orphan Annie.

When I got home I was inconsolable. Dad probably figured in a day or two I'd get used to it, but my anxiety increased and I became unbearable. I even refused to go to school! Dad had never seen me like this. He called every female friend for advice. Dad had a coterie of gorgeous female friends, and I wondered how my looks measured up. Mother would reassure me, "For goodness sakes, Karen, you look as good as anyone!" By that reckoning, I looked as good as Sophia Loren or the Hunchback of Notre Dame. I was feeling more like the latter.

Finally, Dad had enough and gave me a stern lecture about how I was reacting to a haircut worse than men who had come home with injuries after World War II. Humbled, I went to school with my head down, determined to get over it. I was heading to my locker when I stopped dead in my tracks—I nearly ran into my heartthrob, Desi Arnaz Jr.! The last time I saw him was a few months before when he and about five members of the high school football team crashed my party. Desi had walked in the door and, without a word to me, headed straight to Dad's well-stocked bar. Desi looked me over, his gaze stopping at my curly red hair. He put on an accent like his dad's: "Karen, you got some 'splainin' to do!" I told him what had happened at the hairdresser's. Desi: "Pierre has turned more prom queens into poodles than you know. Cheer up, Shirley Temple. Free cocktails at recess!" He threw his arm over my shoulder and gave me a wink. I melted, took a breath, and asked if we could go out on a date sometime. Desi: "Well, Karen, I would've taken you for a spin, but now you remind me of my mother." Seeing my reaction, he smiled and said, "You're better off—even Liza Minelli couldn't put up with me." I was miffed: "I guess hanging out with you on the front lawn is better than nothing." Desi: "That's what you think of me, nothing? That's how I feel about myself, having two such famous parents." I said, "That's how I feel!" We both laughed, and I relaxed. He wasn't going to be my boyfriend, but we had bonded.

Women loved Dad because of his vulnerability and, of course, he made them laugh! I think John Ritter's first wife, Nancy, summed it up best: "I saw Don as the man who was quiet, kind, and respectful, warm with the greetings, self-contained; it's hard to achieve all that. He went from being a highly sophisticated gentleman to the biggest goofball with a rubbery face. There's almost nothing sexier than someone who can be hilarious. He makes you laugh when he's being a pro."

Dad enjoyed being a bachelor, but that came to an end when he started going with Loralee Czuchna. She had recently graduated from USC with two degrees, and they met on a blind date at the Beverly Wilshire Hotel restaurant. Tom was in L.A., and Dad brought her home to meet us. Loralee was twenty-five and about five feet tall, a beauty with stunning green eyes and long blond hair worn in an updo. She wore platform shoes and a pair of short shorts, like Daisy on *The Dukes of Hazzard*. She understood Dad's neuroses and wisely kept over-the-counter drugstore remedies in her purse, in an effort to keep his hypochondria at bay.

Dad hired Barbara Welles to be our new housekeeper. She was a dynamic, sixty-year-old Black woman whose innate wisdom and life experience made up for a lack of formal education. She was also an aspiring singer. That's Hollywood! She'd often say, "If only I had forty dollars, I could make me a record, honey!" I doubted that would be enough, but I was on board for the fantasy. She took me to clubs downtown where she sang with a jazz band; they called her Lady Barbara, a reference to Billie Holiday's Lady Day. That was a huge compliment, especially since she wasn't really a very good singer. Her ability to hold an audience came from what she radiated within.

When Dad entered the kitchen through the swinging door, Barbara would jump to the radio and turn down the horse race she'd been listening to, as if he couldn't hear it from the dining room! Barbara became an integral part of our lives. She recognized Dad's internal struggles. When he'd get that look of gloom and doom on his face, she'd say, "Mr. Knotts, you ain't got no cause to be depressed. You is a *worldly man*!" He'd stand prouder, a smile would brighten his face, and he'd say, "Thank you, Barbara." And when I had disappointments with friends in school, Barbara shared her disappointments with me. Barbara: "Now, honey, that's how women can be! It's like this girl Fern, you know Fern. Every time we go someplace, I always pay the bill. She says, 'I don't have no money, I ain't got no car.' So she bought her a new car. I don't know where she got the money from. I don't know how she came about it. She said, 'I just bought a car, and I paid for it cash!' Now it wasn't necessary to tell me that. She knows that little rattle trap I got downstairs ain't nothin'. It ain't nothin', honey! I do the best I can with what I have."

I was a senior in high school when Dad was cast in a Hallmark Hall of Fame remake of the film classic *The Man Who Came to Dinner*, starring Orson Welles, in 1972. It's about a celebrated author who gives a lecture in a couple's private home. He becomes injured and takes over his hosts' home while he recovers. Dad had a small comedic role as the doctor, and he was thrilled to be working with the great genius Welles. The movie takes place in Ohio, but Orson lived in Paris and didn't want to film in the United States for some reason—ahem, taxes—so the actors rehearsed in London and filmed in South Hampton. NBC was coordinating other shows in London, and executives asked Dad if he wanted to MC one, so he did that as well. Don: "The English crews didn't work very hard, and they don't work long hours. It wasn't easy to get them out of the bar after lunch."

Orson topped that; he drank wine during rehearsals. He was so insecure about his lines that a dozen people were hired to hold up cue cards so everywhere he looked he could see the cues. He didn't want to take direction, which naturally caused problems for the director, Buzz Kulik. Buzz would have to go through Dad because Orson had made him his pet. Orson would call out, "Where's Don? Where's little Don? Dammit, where is he?"

It was quite the bromance. Dad and Orson were even doing magic tricks for each other. It sounded to me like a Laurel and Hardy picture! The cast included two great beauties, Joan Collins and Lee Remick, and Lee had bronchitis. Orson glared whenever she coughed, and insisted they keep the studio at very cold temperatures. The rest of the cast were shivering, and most of them came down with the flu. Thank goodness the critics gave the cast rave reviews!

———————

By the time I was a senior in high school, I had given up on *ever* being cast in a school play. I asked Dad if I could join a private acting class, and he said yes! He talked to his beautiful actress friend, Sandra Giles, who recommended Richard Brander. Brander's class gave me training and brought me together with talented young adults who welcomed me as a peer.

Instead of high school plays and musicals, we rehearsed TV and film scripts. One evening, a bodacious guy named David Holguin walked in. I was thrilled when he and I started working on scenes, but the other actresses were working on *him*. I studied them; I had a lot to learn in the flirtation department. I hoped our rehearsals would lead to something more. I was only seventeen; David was twenty-four, and he was an honorable man. But hey, that didn't stop *me* from trying! I tempted him with alluring lines like, "Mmm, you're looking kind of down. Why don't you come up and see me sometime [*sexy pose*], get some vitamins?"

Richard Brander ran a tight ship. To keep us from overacting, he'd say, "When you drive to the dentist, you don't think, *I'm going to the dentist*, you just are." I began to find that annoying. David and I worked on a scene that was a challenge, especially for him: he was playing a blind man. The scene was from a popular play and later a movie with Goldie Hawn, called *Butterflies Are Free*. I invited David to the house to rehearse. David: "We were hanging out, running lines, and having a pretty good time. And I'm looking at you thinking, *This girl's young*. I saw a picture of your dad, and I said, 'What are you guys doing with a picture of Mick Jagger?' You said, 'That's not Mick Jagger, that's Dad.' Then he walks in the door! I think he had on a coat and tie, and you introduced me to him. And I'm like . . . you know . . . staring at him. He was the sweetest, nicest man. You mentioned to him that I was having a problem with the blindness. He takes my script, and he was so energetic, that's what blew my mind. He'd been working all day, you know? And his first impulse was to help me. He went, 'Blind, blind,' he said that a few times, and he held the script up and perused it really quick. He gets up and starts wandering around the room. And he goes up to either a coffee table or something, and he smacked his shin right on it. That had to hurt. I'm like, *Geez, one minute he's charming and nice, the next minute he's stumbling around his own living room blind as a bat and saying the lines.* He put his fingers about a foot in front of his eyes. He says, 'Imagine a red dot right here,' and he was really emphatic on saying the color. So I put my hand up like his and finally, I started to see the red dot. Then he had us run the lines, and he was watching me specifically. So I started saying the dialogue with the red dot, and it was freaky because I got it! It took him, what, three minutes to teach me that. I'd been fighting over it for hours!"

I was hoping that David would be "my first," but it didn't work out. I can't seem to remember when I lost my virginity. I should have asked for a receipt!

———————————

I met my first boyfriend after a play at Beverly High's Little Theater. His name was Etan Lorant and he went to Hamilton High. I asked what he was doing in this neck of woods. He said, teasing me in his Israeli accent, "slumming." Our dates were fun! We'd go out with about ten of his friends and in a caravan of cars. But he left me brokenhearted that summer when he left for Europe.

Mother came to visit while I was going through this. Kay: "The few weeks I spent with Karen while I was living on the ranch meant a lot to me because I had her to myself, figuratively speaking. . . . She was a teenager! She always informed me when I arrived that she wanted no structure while I was there, including meals served regularly, which she somehow managed to get on her own. She and I would connect at odd times when she felt like it, often late at night when we would watch a movie together or just curl up on the bed and talk." Yes, Mother drove me crazy in one respect: she was regimented about meals.

I found out about a summer language program in France and thought, *I'll go to Europe too!* I told Dad there was a boarding house where all the students could stay. He agreed it would be safe and gave his OK. What a generous and trusting dad he was! So, off to France. When I got there, I found out the other students learning French were from Germany or Italy and didn't speak English. I was lonely and spent many afternoons at outdoor cafés, eating chocolate ice cream. One day I was joined by a middle-age man who said he was lonely, too; his wife was away. He invited me to spend the afternoon at his house. I thought it would be fun to see how a real French guy lived. We arrived at his house, and I had to use the restroom. I went in and saw a strange-looking toilet. I went number two before I realized it had no flusher. Duh, that was a bidet! My French friend was knocking on the door: "*Ca va bien*?" Frantically, I picked up a towel, wrapped up my deposit, and hurled it out the bathroom window. From the street below, I heard a cry of "*Merde!*"

I finally resolved my problem of being unpopular at school—I graduated! I had been accepted at USC and hoped for a career in acting. Tom and I were on very different paths regarding our dad. Tom: "You know what it's like when people are treating you like a celebrity's kid. It's pretty cool, but it's addictive. I took a trip with Dad on one of his golf tours in Atlantic City. We were being treated like kings—'Whatever you want, it's yours' kind of thing. I came home and realized, 'Well, now it's me again. Nobody is going to give me any favors.' Black and white—I could see the difference. I thought, *Gotta keep your head together. This is what's gonna be my life?* I didn't care for the whole 'Don Knotts's son' thing, anyway. I thought I'd better get out of here while I still can. I went to grad school at Berkeley and never looked back."

12

IT'S ALL IN THE FAMILY

A H, **DEAR READER**, you thought my brother got away! You thought when
you turned the page that he escaped the moniker of "Don Knotts's
son." He had that intention, but it didn't quite happen that way. And
what's funny is that Tom and I never really talked about this until
now, as I'm writing this book.

Tom: "When I was at the ranch in ninth grade, the kids went
nuts when they found out who Dad was. They pointed at me in the
hall and whispered. I was insanely shy at that time in my life, and I
found it traumatic."

Me: "I know what you mean."

Tom: "It was *sooooo* nice when I transferred to Beverly High
where it was cool to act unimpressed. When I was interviewed on
the A&E Biography about Dad [2000], I 'came out.' I was relieved.
It's like, 'Ok guys, yes.'"

Me: "This book will 'out' you further. Can you handle it?"

Tom: "I can handle it as the day is long. . . . From *Casablanca*."

Me: "Oh, yeah."

Tom: "I've always had a conflict about it. On the one hand I like the attention and that it makes me unique and stand out. But I felt that in my field of engineering, my colleagues would take me less seriously. I still feel that way, truth be told. I remember when I was a student at Berkeley, the rumor started to spread after a USC friend visited me. Then when I was working at Hewlett Packard, it got back to my coworkers when my manager visited Berkeley. It just follows you around. I know the word's out when a few people call me Don instead of Tom. Still happens. That's something you don't experience because your name isn't close to Dad's. Thanks Mom, thanks Dad."

Me: "First of all, Dad wasn't famous when you were born, and, second, I may not get called Don, but I do get called Donna! Do you remember the guy who was claiming to be Don Knotts's son? He came to the door!"

Tom: "That was me. Bada boom."

Me: "Ha! The house was still listed on the movie-star map as Barbara Stanwyck's."

Tom: "They were constantly ringing the bell for Ms. Stanwyck, and it was finally too much. Do you remember when Dad put a note next to the doorbell, DO NOT RING DOOR FOR AUTOGRAPHS, PRIVACY IS DEAR?"

Me: "Yes, and I thought it was an awfully polite note to tourists who were sniffing around the yard!"

———————

Dad was usually doing theater when he wasn't working on TV or film, often in summer. In 1974 Tom and his buddy Jim went to Chicago to see Dad in the play *The Mind with the Dirty Man* at Arlington Park Theater, a "theatre in the round." His costar was Pam Britton, whom Tom and Dad loved watching on *My Favorite Martian* as Mrs. Brown.

Tom and Jim stayed down the hall from Dad and Loralee at the Arlington Park Towers.

Tom: "Jim and I would usher, then we'd go hang out backstage. When the actors were waiting for their cue light, we'd be telling jokes, and they'd miss the light sometimes. We finally got reprimanded for it. We'd go out to the lobby and walk around, chatting with the cute Midwestern girls. One night, Dad was on stage and Pam was backstage. She said, 'I'm not feeling very well.' But like a true professional she went on—and next thing we knew she was rushed to the hospital! Her husband was called; he came out and was with her when she died. The cancer had come back from when she had a mastectomy. She went from 'I'm not feeling well' to dead. Dad had to go on the next two weeks with the understudy, and he was so devastated. Can you imagine what that would be like, trying to get through an entire act? That was really hard; we were so close to her and very much affected by it."

Dad wasn't always recognized when he was on the road, because people would unconsciously think, *What would he be doing in my town?* Once, when Dad was in New York, he got into an elevator and another fellow got in, looked at him, and said, "Did anyone ever tell you, you look like Don Knotts?" Dad gave him a noncommittal, I-hear-that-so-much look. The elevator door opened, and the guy walked out, turned back to him, and said, "I'll bet you'd like to have his money."

As much as I loved Dad and was proud of his success, I longed to be in a place where I could be just *Karen* Knotts for a change. I decided to join a sorority. A few weeks later, I was standing in line for sorority rush. These girls all looked like Barbie dolls wearing identical sundresses. I looked like the Disco Kid; I had a strobe light for a hat. I put my boom box down and starting playing music from *Saturday Night Fever* and did some Travolta moves I'd practiced. Everybody was looking at me. I was finally popular! Then they turned away and

I thought, *Maybe somebody got shot.* I heard someone say, "It's Don Knotts!" I followed their heads, and sure enough, there was my father. He'd been following me!

You probably think that's sweet. But in a 1962 Ford Galaxie, the Mayberry squad car?! I ran over. "Dad, what are you doing?"

He said, "Andy brought the squad car over for old time's sake, and I thought you'd get a kick out of it."

"But why are you here?"

"Well honey, I want to make sure you're gonna be OK your first week on your own. You're independent now. But if you ever need me, I'm just a phone call away. I'm a Knotts, and that's plural, not possessive." He always knew what to say!

Dad and Loralee went to a pool party at Tim Conway's house in 1974, just before they flew to Hawaii to get married. There they met Stella Atkinson, who would become a lifelong friend. Stella's husband, Buddy Atkinson, had been a comedy writer for *The Tim Conway Comedy Hour* in 1970. Other people there were Sam Bobrick and Ron Clark; Joe Hamilton, producer of Tim Conway's show; and Dave Powers, director of *The Carol Burnett Show.* Another guest was Tim's friend Ernie Anderson, a voiceover guy for ABC.

The group was an amazing social set; they would often meet for ribald fun at restaurants and holiday parties. Stella: "Loralee is half-Ukrainian, which is what I am, so that was kind of our tie, and we used to get together quite a bit over the years. My gosh, we just laughed all the time." Don, Loralee, Stella, Buddy, and the gang were having dinner at Ma Maison restaurant, and Orson Welles was a couple of tables away. Stella: "Orson started to laugh and shake; he was such a huge man. Don said, 'Would you keep it down over there?' Orson looked up. I thought he was going to laugh so hard he couldn't stand

Dad and Loralee in Hawaii on their wedding night, 1974.

it. He came over to the table and said, 'It's nice to see you, Don.' The fact that this small man was telling Orson Welles, who was so huge, to keep it down was hilarious."

In 1975, a booker named Bob Young called Dad and said they were having a birthday dinner for Bob Hope in Indianapolis at the time of the Indy 500, and they wanted him to be toastmaster. Dad told him "it wasn't really his bag," but Young kept calling to say that Hope wanted him to be toastmaster, and they would put his family up too. Finally, Dad said he'd do it. Tom and I got to sit up in the VIP section with the mayor at the race. Phyllis Diller was there too; I loved her! She was being her crazy, funny self. Later on, Dad invited her to the Hillcrest house for a couple of parties, and she cleaned out the men at the table playing poker.

After the race, Dad bumped into Bob Hope at the hotel. Bob said, "Don, what are you doing here?" Dad said, "I'm the toastmaster!" Bob said, "Really?" Dad was floored. He and Bob had a sketch together, and they used cue cards. Don: "When we rehearsed, the guy pulling my cards was slow, so my timing was off. Hope took me aside and said, 'You're not familiar with this stuff, are you?' I said, 'Yes, I am!' Hope said, 'Well, you'd better look it over.'" Dad went to the stage manager, Barney McNulty, and told him to get that worked out. Don: "We did the show, and the guy on cards pulled them on time. When Hope brought me out for a bow, he turned to me and said softly, 'Studied, didn't you?'"

I was at USC and doing well in the drama department but still clinging to the hippie look. It hadn't won me friends or admirers, but it did something for me I could never have imagined. Dad was asked to speak at an event on campus, at Bovard Auditorium, about bringing production back to Hollywood. I showed up in my jeans, fringed vest, and hippie hat. The event host was esteemed actor Ed Asner, who would be elected to his first term as SAG president in 1981. Dad was forever upset with Ed because he kept pushing the union to go on strike. I guess Dad hadn't forgotten his frustration when he faced the Hal Roach Studios picket line in 1946. I was vaguely listening to Ed as he made his opening remarks when I heard, "Don's daughter, Karen, is a student here. Karen, stand up and let us see what *Don has done*." I wasn't expecting that! I stood up, made a quick bow, and sat down.

That evening, Dad got a phone call from the casting director Joe Scully. Dad was quite surprised when Scully said he was trying to locate *me*. He was calling in regard to a TV series produced by Universal and starring George Peppard called *Doctors' Hospital*. The show, only on for one season, was known for its sense of medical realism, which was unusual at the time. The show was set to shoot an episode called "One of Our Own," involving a hippie, Myrna, who hitches a ride with a drunk driver. The actress who was cast in the role had taken another offer and left the series in the lurch. Scully had seen me at the event and thought I had the perfect hippie look. I went to an audition and was quickly cast. The part required something beyond Acting 101.

My character, a stoned and suicidal teenager, gets into a stranger's car while holding a guitar and explains, "Each passing billboard has a line from a limerick," and she recites the lines as the billboards go by. Suddenly, Myrna realizes the car is about to crash. I had to scream in terror and throw myself at the car's windshield as if we'd been hit from behind. The windshield was made of 'candy glass' which shatters easily, but it was scary enough to make me wonder if that was why the other actress had bailed! The director, Richard Sarafian, explained to me, "We have to get this in one take because there's no way they can get another windshield." He instructed me to raise the guitar over my head, "just to be safe." We did get it in one take! Whew!!!

The producers were meticulous in their depiction of the medical situations, so there was a doctor, Milt Kogan, on set as a consultant. He explained, "In this situation they would need to operate on the girl, so she would have her head shaved." For that scene I got to wear a bald cap. It was a blast walking "bald" into the studio commissary. I meandered around the lot, relishing the "takes" and stares from people. I got praise from the producers and Dad for my acting. I guess the acting class we took with Richard Brander and his driving-to-the-dentist reference paid off.

I did several plays at USC with my good friend Kathy Easterling, who later became a writer for *Jeopardy!* We would often see John Ritter on campus, who wasn't known then. Kathy: "He had already graduated, but he wouldn't leave; he was crazy about USC. He would do impressions of the drama teachers, and when he walked into class he'd say something so funny the class would scream with laughter." He was just like Dad was in high school! John would take a class here and there, like Robert Easton's dialect class, which allowed him to act in school plays while he worked his way up in the entertainment industry. That was smart; it gave him opportunities to invite casting directors to see him. He was landing small parts then, mostly on unknown TV shows, and acted in a few shows while I was there. He was in a sketch called "Eddy's Nude Scene." John appeared to be nude, yelped, covered himself and disappeared. It was fun to compare John Ritter sightings around campus. Of course, I had no way of knowing he and I would cross paths again.

I had fears of being compared to my legendary father. Dad could tell I was uptight about my future. He thought it would be helpful if we took a family vacation, so he invited me to go with him and Loralee to the island of Oahu, Hawaii. None of us realized that I was on the verge of a nervous breakdown. After we got to the hotel, I told Dad I was going out. I remember coming out of a nightclub by myself at around 1:00 AM. I suddenly had a feeling of crushing helplessness, which was replaced by a feeling of super power. I "knew" that if I walked across this busy street, traffic would stop. I began to walk across the boulevard without looking in either direction. In no uncertain terms, I had flipped my lid.

The next thing I knew, I was handcuffed and put into a police car. I refused to answer any questions. The police took me to a psychiatric hospital, where I was checked into a room. I believed that I had been captured and taken to a prison. There was nothing in my purse to identify me, so hospital staff had no idea who I was. At the hospital, I was taken to an outdoor dining area and served a meal, but I "knew" that I was going to be tortured and refused to eat. I noticed there was a low wall surrounding the courtyard, so I attempted an escape. I jumped over the wall and made a frantic dash to a nearby house. I banged on the locked screen door, yelling that I was in danger and needed to make a phone call. The hospital attendants quickly overpowered me and took me back to the hospital, where I refused to cooperate with anyone. I believed that these people were enemies who were going to torture me.

The odd thing was, I had no idea in my mind who these enemies were, yet I believed the delusion to the point that I tried to figure out a way to "off myself" before the torturers would come for me. I even thought I was Jesus Christ for a while. Yes, I did, just like those people yelling on street corners! When I encounter them now, I look them in the eye as if to say, "I get you."

When I hadn't returned to the hotel, Dad began making calls. As two more days passed, Dad and Loralee's efforts became more desperate. On the afternoon of the third day, I was told I had a visitor, and Dad walked in. I will never forget my absolute joy and relief at seeing him! However, I was still delusional and afraid and begged him to get me out fast. Later, I found out the hospital doctors believed I was catatonic because I wouldn't speak. It's a good thing Dad showed up when he did; they were planning to give me electroshock treatment, which they hoped would induce me to talk. Dad assumed when I didn't return that night that I had hooked up with some guy and was having fun. Gee, what a . . . maybe, little too trusting dad he was?

I was twenty and had always enjoyed a lot of freedom, but he didn't understand how serious my condition had become. I seemed to return to normal and Dad was hopeful, but a couple of months later I had another episode. I was driven to Thalians Health Center, the psychiatric ward at Cedars-Sinai. This time I was committed to stay for a period of time, with a private room in the ward. I had the delusion of being all powerful again and was extremely depressed. The staff got me to attend group activities, art workshops, and exercise class. The head psychiatrist predicted I would need three months in the hospital before I would be released, but thanks to Dick Renneker I was out in six weeks.

Dick came to see me every day, and when I locked myself in the bathroom because I didn't want to hear something he was telling me, he would talk to me through the door, so I was forced to listen. Eventually he was able to break through my defenses and the feelings of false superiority began to crumble. I became so depressed it took great effort just to lift a toothbrush to my mouth. The hospital was giving me a daily dose of a drug called Thorazine, which was used to control hyperactive patients. It gave me a shuffle as I walked. Dick had them reduce the dose until I was clean, so I went through a period of withdrawal.

I was finally released from the hospital, but it was a long, slow, climb before I felt any sense of normalcy. Dad reassured me, saying, "Keep working with Dick. After a while, the good feelings will start to come." I continued to see Dick three times a week, which was reduced to twice a week, then once until I saw him only periodically.

The breakdown was the most painful thing I've been through. It made me understand how Dad lamented his father's mental illness during a time when health workers didn't know how to treat it. And the same was true for the treatment of asthma. My Uncle Shadow shouldn't have died of asthma at the age of thirty, before Tom and I could meet him. How lucky I was to be out of the hospital in only six weeks and on my way to a full recovery. Dad could afford the best treatment available, but so many people can't. I'm sure it saved my life.

I understand now why so many child actors become suicidal or addicted to drugs. They are actors before their own identity has had a chance to develop, so who they are becomes intertwined with their TV persona. When fans greet them, they are relating to their TV character. I experienced something similar. When I was growing up, people were obsessed with Dad and talked about him all the time. I felt like I had to represent him. I was more focused on his identity than my own. I couldn't define who Karen was until I started working with Dick. When I got better, I told Dad I wanted to get into a comedy group. Dad got on the phone to a friend and handed me a note with the word GROUNDLINGS and a phone number. It is still the top improv comedy group in Los Angeles. I auditioned and started taking classes at the troupe's school.

———————

For many years, Dad was uncomfortable on his birthday and at Christmas, holidays that involved gift-giving. They brought back painful memories of an impoverished childhood. At Christmas he would escape to Hawaii. Instead of a jolly Santa and reindeer, I imagined him and Loralee sitting in a canoe pulled by mechanical dolphins at the Maui Mall. Loralee did help him overcome his Scrooge-like attitude with Stella Atkinson's help. Stella: "Loralee had a wonderful imagination, and she said to me, 'Wouldn't it be nice to have a 'postcard' Christmas? Why don't we get all dressed up with fur coats and mufflers and go down to Beverly Hills and sing carols on Wilshire Boulevard?' I said, 'That's a great idea.' And we did that on the hottest night of the year! It was Don, my husband Buddy, and me; Tim Conway and his wife, Charlene; John and Joan Myhers. Andy Griffith was in the crowd, and so was Ronnie Schell. We all got dressed up and had cocktails at your house. Then we walked through Beverly Hills and sang carols. A couple of people walked by, and we heard them say, snobbily, 'Who *are* those people?' To this day, when I see Ronnie, I say to him, 'Who *are* those people!' Then Don took the whole crowd to Danny's Hideaway at the Beverly Wilshire, and we had a fun time."

As part of my ongoing therapy, Dick said I needed to follow through on some kind of project. Since USC has a great film department, I decided to make a short film. I cast my Groundlings cohorts in the parts and called my film *Citizen Kapers*. I also cast Dad, of course, and we had a lot of fun. The script I wrote called for us to do a couple of clown gags and jump in the swimming pool fully clothed; he jumped in wearing a business suit. What a Dad!

When the film was finished, I invited all the participants to a screening at the house. I even got *People* magazine to do a little feature on it. Barbara helped me lay out drinks and hors d'oeuvres to make it a happening. Phil Hartman, Paul Reubens, Edie McClurg, Tom Maxwell, Gary Austin, Victoria Carroll, Steve White, Rahla Khan,

Dick Frattali, and Kip King gave wonderful performances. Dad said it was a "good first effort." But we both knew directing wasn't my thing. It was, however, a huge step toward my psychological recovery.

On the days Barbara planned to make her best meal, she'd be grinning like a Cheshire cat. She knew how to build anticipation; "Heh, heh, you're gonna *looove* dinner tonight, Mr. Knotts! We're having fried chicken, collard greens, and grits!" Dad confided to me that he did not like Barbara's cooking. He'd been smiling through the meals, eating as little as possible because he didn't want to hurt her feelings. Cousin Bill (son of Dad's nephew, the other Don Knotts) visited for a few days, and he was there for dinner. Bill: "We were eating in the dining room, and Barbara had just cooked this meat-and-potatoes thing. There was a separate bowl for the gravy. Don poured gravy onto his empty plate and started trying to eat the gravy with a fork. Barbara comes through and says, 'Is everything all right?' Don says, 'It's a little thin.'" Afterwards, Dad would head down to Jacopo's Pizzeria on Little Santa Monica Boulevard and share a pizza with the chef and owner, Jacopo. He always had a thing for Italians and their food.

Dad may not have liked Barbara's cooking, but he respected her values. She'd say, "Karen, before you eat, you're supposed to give your thanks. Now I don't have a damn thing, but I do send a little five dollars every once in a while to them people that's sleeping out on the streets. Not all the time, but once in a while. Maybe I don't have but three; I'll send off three. That's in order for me to get a blessing. I send it to them, and somebody else will come and help me. See that's all the Book pertains to. It's to do unto others as you would have them do unto you."

When I had boyfriend troubles, my go-to person was always Barbara. She'd tell me about women friends who were having problems like mine: "This girl, Denice, she likes this man. She said, 'I'm crazy about him! I'm a business woman—I got a little money.' I said, 'In the first place, he's a musician, and I ain't seen one yet that was nothing. Now, you keep your bar filled, you got a great big king-sized bed, and he's damn near outdoors. He's a college man, he's educated, and he's gonna use his education on you. He thinks he's smarter than you, and he is! Now another thing. That word *love* has got so many people I know in the doghouse. 'I love you,'—that's all he got to say; that's a weapon in itself! There's only one kind of love, and that's infinite love." Me: "Infinite love?" Barbara: "Everybody loves a baby. If you saw a little baby out there in the streets fixin' to get run over, do you think you would sit here and just see the child get run over? You'd try to do everything you could to get that baby out the way, is that right?"

———————

I struggled to get into acting but couldn't land a good agent. Dad helped me out with a few hundred bucks a month, but I always had a job. Dad had a strong work ethic from growing up poor and always panicked about money.

One night, Dad and I were eating dinner and he asked, "Are you still working at the ice cream parlor?" I told him I was. He said, "You better quit that job. You're getting fat!" I was a good daughter, so I quit, even though I'd only tasted twenty-three of the thirty-one flavors.

Next, I answered an ad for a courier. Someone was needed to pick up a package from Tarzana and drive it to an address downtown. I looked inside, and the package contained diamonds. I told Dad about it and he said, "That's dangerous; you'd better quit that job." So I did.

My next job had the title *plant technician*, which was a marketing term for "plant waterer." I made lots of mistakes, but none as bad as when I spilled a gallon of blue-tinted fertilizer on a lady's white Berber carpet. When I came home, Dad said, "Are you still working at that plant-watering job? I can smell the pesticide on you. You better quit that job." I replied, "I beat you to it. I got fired!"

I got a job at Marie Callender's selling pies, salads, and sandwiches in office buildings. Every day at noon, I passed through a lunchroom. That's when *The Andy Griffith Show* came on a TV mounted on the wall. I thought, *Here I am selling sandwiches while my TV-star dad is hovering above me.* I felt miserable; my life was going nowhere. I didn't want to admit this to Dad, so I told him my job required me to lift incredibly massive coolers into my car, and I was in danger of injuring my back. I asked Dad, "Should I quit?" Don: "Have you got another job lined up?" Me: "Uh, no." Don: "Then you'd better keep that job."

———————

I started running with a fellow named Billi Gordon, a classmate from Harvey Lembeck's improv workshop. Billi was black, gay, and a real character. He weighed about three hundred pounds and drove a blue corvette, very low to the ground. I don't know how he got into the car. When he got out, his clothes shifted around, giving me a view a plumber's wife would envy. We were talking about trends in clothing stores, and he said, "I won't even dignify the absurd one-size-fits-all notion. Let's talk about theater seats in new malls, flying coach on any airline, small plastic or wood folding chairs. These are just a few of the natural hazards that sisters of plenty face in their everyday dealings!"

Billi was hip. I asked him to explain the difference between a thing and a thang. Billi: "Queen Elizabeth is a thing; B.B. King is a thang. The Moral Majority is a thing, the rest of us are thangs. Jane Fonda is a thing, I am a thang." Me: "I get it. Now would you explain *Green Eggs and Ham*?" Dad worried at first that Billi was a bad influence on me. Billi tended to embroider the edges of reality, but he was so much fun, who cared!?

In 1975 Dad and Tim Conway made their first feature film together, *The Apple Dumpling Gang.* Tim's son, Tim Conway Jr., has a popular radio show on iHeartRadio; one day I tuned in and he was talking about both our dads. Tim Jr: "If you were to ask my dad, he would tell you that Don Knotts was his comedy hero, and he was the funniest man in the world. Every time he could make somebody laugh without saying anything, he said he stole that from Don Knotts. I don't know if it's true or not. Maybe he was just complimenting Don Knotts, but Don Knotts was his favorite. And what was great is that he got to work with Don Knotts on *The Apple Dumpling Gang.* So he got to spend three months in a hotel eating dinner at night, working all day with his favorite comedian in the world, Don Knotts."

Dad and Tim in *The Apple Dumpling Gang* (1975).

Tim also worked and traveled with Harvey Korman. They did a live show that combined sketches from *The Carol Burnett Show*. If Harvey couldn't go, Dad would fill in. Tim Jr.: "Those were my dad's two favorite performers. And they were different guys. Harvey was really, really cautious about a lot of things in life. And Don Knotts was the most casual guy in the world. Nothing ever got Don Knotts upset, ever. My dad never saw him yell, never saw him get mad, anytime something went wrong, Don Knotts would just laugh about it." That gave me a chuckle. If *my* dad was in such good spirits on the road, it was because of *his* dad.

Dad did not like to travel. I was on tour with him in the play *The Mind with the Dirty Man*, and he checked into a hotel room that he just hated. He kept droning on: "The water is too cold." "The lighting's too dark." "The air conditioner is blowing. . . . It's blowing!" "The mirror is so dusty, I look like Tim Conway! . . . What's this?" (I had taped Tim's picture to the mirror to get him in a better mood!)

The Apple Dumpling Gang was so successful that Disney contracted them to make a sequel, *The Apple Dumpling Gang Rides Again*, in 1979. They were filming a caper in a saloon on location in Stockton, California, and Dad and Tim were disguised as dance-hall ladies. They were hysterical in their bustier corsets and bustle skirts. Dad had on a tall wig with feathers. He used to get cold in the mornings, dressing in the studio trailer. Tim said, "Why don't you have them bring the wardrobe over, dress at the hotel, and I'll drive us to the set? So every morning I'd drive him to work and he'd be in this getup. I'd stop at a light and go *beep, beep* and point to him. He'd say, 'Don't do that.' I came home one night and Don was still in costume. I told him that I'd be in the bar and when he got changed to come on over. So I'm sitting at the bar and . . . and these cowboys don't like actors. You have to be kind of careful what you say. I'm drinking a beer and in comes Don. And he's got the same dress, wig, and feathers on. He comes over to me and says, 'Tim, you got the key to that room?' I looked at him and I said, 'Well ma'am, don't you think we ought to talk about price first?'" And that's how I ended up with two cross-dressing fathers, *ba dump bump!*

Tim Conway: "He was very much like me. He was the gentlest guy I ever met; he was sensational. I don't think he ever got in a fight in his life"—not intentionally, anyway! Dad said, "Tim is so unpredictable. A reporter came out from a local paper who was anxious to record our wisdom. He asked, 'What's the name of the picture you're shooting now?' Before I could answer, Tim said, '*Tony and Her Pony.*' He went on to give him all this funny fake stuff and never did tell the guy it was phony. When I talk to the press I tend to tell the truth; Tim just says what he's thinking at the moment. I think Tim summed it up pretty well, 'Comics don't get a lot of respect. It's awfully hard to say something suave when you're sitting there in a donkey suit.'"

When Dad was between TV or film gigs, he was usually on the road doing theater. Theater audiences are more open to seeing famous actors in different roles. In fact, they get a kick out of it. Dad performed all through the Midwest doing shows that challenged audience perceptions of what was socially acceptable behavior. The trend was kicked off by Neil Simon and spanned the 1960s through 1980s. He wrote plays about middle-aged people who start to question the values they've lived by. The shows were embraced by audiences in the Midwest, even though they found them sometimes shocking. Dad had a lot of fun with Neil Simon's *Last of the Red Hot Lovers*. He played a man named Barney—but not Barney Fife. This was Barney Cashman, a man who had married his high school sweetheart, and in midlife he begins to fear he has missed out, so he decides to have an affair. Dad was absolutely hysterical in this role as the socially inept Cashman, trying to seduce three women who are utterly wrong for him. As funny as Dad was in the part, he was never Simon's first choice, for he intended Barney Cashman to be Jewish.

Dad asked if I'd like to go on the road and be in a play with him. Would I?! It would be the first of many plays I would perform with Dad, and he taught me the ropes. When we'd arrive in town, the first order of business was a technical run-through at the theater. He always tried to persuade producers to "paper the house." It simply means giving away free tickets early in the run, which spreads the word that the show is well worth seeing. If theaters did advance promotion, his shows sold out months in advance.

When Dad developed an eye disease called macular degeneration, he started losing his central vision, and he was afraid he'd go completely blind. That sent him into a tailspin of worry. It turned out he wasn't going to go blind, but fearing he wouldn't be able to learn lines, he turned down some TV roles. He eventually adjusted and developed a system for learning lines, but offers stopped coming for a while. He learned to rehearse in a way that he could tell where the edge of the stage was without seeing it, so I had to be aware of that. Dad loved doing theater because it allowed him to explore roles he would never be cast for in TV or film.

The first show I was in with Dad was *The Mind with the Dirty Man*. We were contracted for two shows, one at the Harlequin Dinner Theater in Atlanta, Georgia, and the other at the La Mirada Civic Center, California, in the fall of 1978. The cast was as follows: Wayne Stone–Don Knotts; Lucrecia Conwell–Karen Knotts; Father Jerome–Byron Morrow; Clayton Stone–Andrew Parks; and Divina–Cisse Cameron. Cisse and I became great friends in Atlanta. Cisse reminded me, "Since Don did not want to be in a townhouse—he preferred a hotel—you and I got to share the beautiful Buckhead townhome. What a blast! We prepared a Thanksgiving dinner for the cast. The show was a hit; Don's performance was always professional and funny." One weekend, Cisse's fiancé, Reb Brown, came to visit her. They were working actors, both very talented and modest about their stunning good looks. When Reb got off the plane, Cisse rushed to meet him. Some people followed, and when he kissed her, they applauded! I thought, *Guys, if this happens to you on a regular basis, count me in. I'm sure to meet my prince!*

The show was directed by Harvey Medlinsky. Dad played Wayne, the head of a censorship board. I played Lucrecia, a prudish neighbor who spies on Wayne. It was such a great vehicle for Dad, he took it on the road, on and off, for about twenty years. Andy Parks played Wayne's son, Clayton. This was Andy's first Equity job. He grew up loving Dad's work because his parents, Larry Parks and Betty Garrett, used to watch him on *The Steve Allen Show*. Parks: "I didn't care for the play. Then we opened. . . . I saw how the audience went nuts! Don knew what worked and what was good for the play. It was so great to be on stage with this crazy person and have that sweet gentle man backstage. I thought, *All I have to do is ride this boat and people will laugh at me.* Don was a master and handed me laughs on a silver platter." At one point, Dad's character, Wayne, is going a little nuts, and he's flashing everybody, opening up his bathrobe. The reaction was hysterical from the other characters seeing him! (The audience does not.) Then at the curtain call he opens his bathrobe to the audience, and he's wearing funny boxer shorts under it.

Cisse Cameron was cast in a film while we were out there. Cisse: "While I was doing the show with Don, a producer, Lang Elliott, approached me about doing a film with Don and Tim Conway, *The Prize Fighter*, directed by Michael Preece. I was booked for the costarring role as Polly. When we were filming on location in Atlanta, a cast party was given at Burt Reynolds's restaurant. That evening there was an ice storm that paralyzed the city. A stuntman who was with us, Dick Butler, had done all the oil-slick stunts for Reb in the *Captain America* TV movies, so he drove us back in the van. We were all smooshed together in the backseat. We hit a steep slope going downhill, and the van turned sideways! Don was buried underneath us, and suddenly we heard his high-pitched voice, 'Are we there yet?' The film was a 1930s period piece, and we shot in a fabulous 1920s mansion. Don and Tim's impromptu ad libs made it difficult to keep a straight face!"

The secret to success for any vehicle with Tim Conway was to have a director that allowed for surprises. Tim and Dad created their own unique comedy together. A director was needed, more or less, to enable them to do their thing. According to Tim's publicist, Roger Neal, "Sometimes directors would try to make Tim and Don sound as if they were regular, normal actors reading lines, but they were unique. Don and Tim knew how to blow the audience away. So that was a problem every now and then."

The following year Tim and Dad made *The Private Eyes*, also written by Conway and Myhers. They filmed *Private Eyes* in Asheville, North Carolina, at the Biltmore. Dad later told producer Tim Macabee, "I'll never forget how miserably hot we were. They had us in full detective suits plus these trench coats and hats, running around being detectives. Well, the Biltmore mansion was built in the 1800s, and there's no air conditioning. It was a great experience to work with Tim, but the downside was the heat."

When they were on the road making pictures, Tim would riff as he was driving and keep them laughing. If he didn't, Dad would get morose: "Look at those cows on the road. Brown cows, I hate brown cows. And those hotels, brick and mortar. If it rains they'll be brick, mortar, and mud. I hate mud." Tim got so tired of hearing it, he recorded Dad and played the tape back for him. Dad was shocked; he had no idea how he sounded.

Tim and Dad made seven movies together. They had different ways of working. Dad would rehearse diligently, but Tim thrived on improvisation. Dad used to improvise with Andy, and it started coming back to him. He began to enjoy improvising scenes with Tim, who was a master at it. Since they were both funny, they took turns playing straight man. You never knew who would deliver the punchline. Dad said Tim was the funniest man he ever knew, and Tim said Dad was right up there with Charlie Chaplin.

Billi Gordon and I were at the house around midnight in 1982, watching a replay of that night's Emmy broadcast, when Dad and Loralee came home from an Emmy after-party. Dad sat down and joined us in front of the TV. The great singer Kate Smith, who was about the same size as Billi, was being pushed out on stage in a wheelchair by Bob Hope. All of a sudden Dad started yelling at the TV: "Kate Smith, you're fat! Fat, fat, fat, fat, fat!" I couldn't believe he said that! I glanced worriedly at my friend, but Billi was laughing so hard tears were rolling down his cheeks.

Dad went on: "And look at Bob Hope. Of course, he'd wheel her out on stage to get the camera on him. I worked with her in New York, and let me tell you about her ego. She always had a problem with her weight. One day she's fine, the next day, big as a house! She had some business where she jumps out on stage. She got caught in the door because her weight had gone up, and she knocked over the whole side of the set! Instead of realizing she should just lay off the cupcakes, she has a big fit and gets this poor guy fired who made the door. She says he didn't make it big enough. She's horrible, I tell you, just horrible. If I'd have wheeled her out, I would've wheeled her right off stage!"

This was a side of Dad that was not often seen but still hysterically funny. Dad said in 1970, "There are two classifications of humor that are frequently used. One that isn't my type of comedy is insult humor. It's usually effective if the right kind of person does it, like Don Rickles. It appeals to the bully in us, I think, to see Rickles tear into somebody, and there's a certain sort of sadistic side. Everybody loves to see somebody take somebody else apart verbally. Jack Benny, on the other hand, turns the humor against himself, which is more or less what I've tried to do. He makes himself the butt of the joke. It makes the audience feel superior to this poor schmuck who's in whatever situation he's in."

Dad and Loralee's social group had expanded. Stella: "There were several people who had Christmas parties every year. Those parties that John Myhers gave were hysterical. I mean, you couldn't find that humor anywhere." Tim would be so "on," cracking jokes. Dad mostly kept quiet, laughing and enjoying Tim. Dad's style was to act as if he was going to tell you something in confidence, then, in a deadpan delivery, he'd lay a whopper on you. Once we were at the airport, and Dad brought my attention to an old woman with sagging jowls. He said, "You see that woman over there?" Concerned, I asked, "Yes, Dad, what about her?" Don: "She died yesterday."

There was a social group of comedians known as Yarmy's Army. The group started because Don Adams's beloved brother, Dick Yarmy, was terminally ill, so a bunch of comedians would meet with him for dinner regularly to keep his spirits up. After he passed away, they kept the tradition going. The group fluctuated but at one time included Don Knotts, Tim Conway, Jonathan Winters, Harvey Korman, Tom Poston, Jack Sheldon, Jack Riley, Gary Owens, Howie Morris, Ronnie Schell, Louis Nye, Pat Harrington, Shelley Berman, Chuck McCann, Ron Carey, Pat McCormick, and Peter Marshall, esteemed personality and game show host. Dad met Peter through Tom Poston, whom they both claimed as their best friend!

Loralee often included her close friend Joni Robbins. Joni: "One year on New Year's Eve, a large group, including Don, Loralee, myself, and Tom Poston, went to Le Restaurant, on Melrose Place. They took us to a table for twelve or fifteen people. We look over and there was singer Peggy Lee surrounded by men who were probably gay. She nodded hello; she recognized your dad, although they didn't know each other. We all wanted to look at her. The people on the side of the table facing her could see her, but our side couldn't. So I took out my compact mirror, looked in it, and was able to see her behind me. I passed the mirror to Tom Poston, and he looked and said, 'Ah, I see her.' That compact went all the way around to the people whose backs were to her, including Don, and he said, 'Yeah, there she is, she looks good. Look at all the guys.' When the compact came back around to me, I said, 'I'm gonna take one more look.' So I did, and she looked at me in the mirror. So then she knew!"

One evening, Tom and Dad were at a restaurant with me and my new boyfriend, Evan. They were meeting him for the first time. I was thirty-one and he was twenty-one and still in college. I decided to go young, dear reader—what could be the harm? Evan was a virgin when we met, but I took care of that. As Billi Gordon would say, "It may be the early bird who gets the worm, but it's the wise old owl that's keeping it."

Tom and Dad knew of our plans to move in together. The conversation was going nicely, and I decided to order a second glass of wine. Dad leaned in to Tom but said at full volume, "Keep that wine away from her." Tom picked up his cue and pulled my glass out of reach: "Sorry, Karen—Dad's rule!" I looked at them speechless but with my eyes saying, "You are *not* doing this!" I gave Evan a look of innocence which, of course, made me look guilty. Tom and Dad kept it up all through dinner.

Evan and I did move in together, and it was actually *his* parents who wanted us to make a commitment, so we did. We promised that when we got the Seven-Year-Itch, we'd either ditch or get hitched!

Dad loved Mickey Rooney's touring show *Sugar Babies*. The show was conceived by Norman Abbott, nephew of Bud Abbott, of Abbott and Costello. Norman inherited his famous uncle's collection of burlesque material and created a touring musical from it. He decided Mickey Rooney was the only star who could pull it off. The show had standard vaudeville sketches: a sister act, a fan dance, and a dog act. Dad took a group to see it.

Joni Robbins: "Before the show started we decided to go backstage. When Mickey saw us, he said, 'Is this the Don Knotts Tour? Mickey Rooney loves Don Knotts! [Mickey used to talk about himself in the third person.] Mickey wants to do a movie like the ones you and Tim Conway do at Disney.' And in the middle of the show, Mickey started incorporating your dad into his show dialogue. He'd say, 'And speaking of 'Don Knotts . . .'"

Tom: "We met the guy who did the funny dog act, Bob Williams. He gives a huge buildup that his dog is going to do a trick, but the dog just sits there. Bob acts real positive and says, 'He's thinking about it!' When we met the guy, he was really depressed. He said, 'Don't travel with an act with a dog.' He was genuinely depressed about travelling with the dog. It struck me that a lot of the people I met through Dad had a lot of sadness."

Dad wasn't a fan of *I Love Lucy* and he didn't care for Robin Williams, but he adored Billy Crystal. Through Women in Film, I got a job at Castle Rock Entertainment as Billy's assistant. He was working with the writing team of Lowell Ganz and Babaloo Mandel on his upcoming movie, *City Slickers*, in which he would also star.

Christopher Guest of *Spinal Tap* fame and two *SCTV* icons, Dick Blasucci and Joe Flaherty, had an office near Billy's, and they had a film project. What personalities—I loved these guys! Chris's sultry absurdity, Dick's ironic observations, and Dapper Joe's stylin' with his hats. If they hit a snafu in the plot, they'd called Billy, but not to brainstorm. Their solution to writer's block was to play a madcap game of softball in the office. Two photocopy machines and a corn plant were assigned as first, second, and third base. Neon colored nerf balls flew through the air as they kibitzed their way to home runs with jokes, howls, cheers. Assistants who needed to get across darted in between throws.

Billy wrote an entire movie, *Mr. Saturday Night*, improvising into a tape recorder in the voice of the character. Then he'd hand the tapes to me for transcribing. Occasionally he'd ask my opinion about the material. It was exciting to be on the ground floor with that project. When he hosted the Academy Awards for the first time in 1990, he had comedian and actor Robert Wuhl come to the office to help him write his opening monologue. Billy was nervous the week of the performance, of course. He's a huge Yankees fan and his approach to stage fright was to handle it like an athlete. He'd do pushups and run around in his office. Of course, he was absolutely *mahvelous* and thrilled the audience with his brilliant routines.

Billy and I sometimes had a little banter. One morning, I said, "Happy birthday, Billy!" He: "Don't get me anything." Me: "I wouldn't dream of it!"

Robin Williams and Billy worked together on *Comic Relief* for many years. When Robin would call and ask for Billy, I'd ask, "Who's calling, please?" In a serious voice that commanded respect, he'd say, "Mr. Williams." I can imagine how many wannabees tried to get Robin's attention by doing a bad impression of him.

I lost the office job when they started filming *City Slickers*, and Dad was kind of worried. He suggested I train for another career. I asked, "What else could I do?" Don: "How about becoming a librarian? Your cousin Sandy is a career librarian and she loves it!" I said, "Dad, I've been playing funny nerds since I was twenty-three, and now you want me to become a librarian? Remember that show we did where I played your secretary?" That was a TV pilot Dad did that didn't sell, called *Front Page Feeney*; it was directed by Howard

Morris, who played Ernest T. Bass in *The Andy Griffith Show*. He had a second career now and was a very good director. But it was Dad who directed me in this show; he stood behind the camera making faces while I imitated him.

———————————

One Halloween night, Loralee and Joni were handing out candy at the house, and Don was relaxing on the couch. Joni: "All the kids were coming, they could see him, and they were going, 'Oh my gosh, it's Don Knotts!' They got so excited they forgot about the candy, so he came to the door and was very friendly to them."

Sometimes, in the evenings, we'd stay home with the dogs. I had a big, beautiful dog named Veer, and Loralee had a toy poodle name Coupe Choux, or Coupie for short. Loralee liked to make her dog's dinner on the stove with meat from a gourmet grocery store, Carl's Market. The smells wafted through the house and into the receptive nostrils of Veer, who had already been fed, but he was true to the credo of the dog: they can be counted on to eat anything, anyplace, anytime. We'd be making small talk, but in reality, we were waiting for the show to begin. Loralee would put Coupie's dish on the floor. She was rarely hungry, but very possessive of her food and guarded that dish vigilantly. Veer would put on the greatest act of indifference I've ever seen in dog or human. He'd yawn, get up as though bored and plop down a few feet away, looking around idly. This gave Coupie a false sense of security. She'd wander off and Veer would make a beeline to her food and suck it up like a vacuum. Coupie would dart back, yapping furiously, but it was too late. We were all howling with laughter; Dad especially got a kick out of it. This is how the rich and famous spend their evenings in Beverly Hills.

At one point, we almost had a third dog. Tom: "One time we were sunbathing by the pool and a strange dog got into our backyard. A

man came through the gate looking for his dog; it was Roger Moore!"
He and Dad met that afternoon for the first time. Roger: "Don, I'm so
sorry about this." He was no spy in real life; his own dog had outfoxed
him! But we had no right to feel superior, as we lived next door to
an Academy Award–winning screenwriter, Carl Foreman, who was
often mad at us because Veer would get loose and tromp through
his beautiful roses. Foreman had been a partner of Stanley Kramer
and was famous for writing *The Bridge on the River Kwai* and *High
Noon*, among others. With Carl being so upset about the dog, Dad
was not about to get cast in Foreman's 1972 film *Young Winston*. It's
really a shame. Dad would've been perfect for the role of Winston
Churchill's nervous father.

Dad didn't go to many parties, except with the people he already
knew, his gang. But I do remember a time when he invited me to
a Hollywood bash, and I was so excited! The event was in a private
home, a grand estate with chandeliers on every floor. There were
celebrities galore. But the one who caught my eye was Sidney Poitier,
who played Detective Virgil Tibbs in *In the Heat of the Night*. He was
one of my favorites! I thought, *I just have to convince my shy father
to introduce me!* After some coaxing, he agreed. As we made our way
over I said, "Dad, Sidney directed that big hit *Stir Crazy* with Gene
Wilder and Richard Pryor. Maybe you could get him to put you in
the sequel!" Dad said out of the side of his mouth, "*Stir Crazy*, huh?
You're halfway there already." We arrived, and Dad cleared his throat:
"Uh, Sidney?" He turned around: "Hello, Don!" Dad: I'd like you to
meet my daughter, Karen." Sidney gave me such a handsome, mag-
netic smile, I was speechless! It occurred to me, *I'm standing between
Mr. Chicken and Mr. Tibbs, and I feel like a dumb cluck.*

I got to go on the road in *The Mind with the Dirty Man* with
Dad again, this time in Phoenix, Arizona, at the Celebrity Theatre.
I played nosy neighbor Lucrecia again, and a well-known Chicago
actress, Janice Ladik, played the other nosy. Dad's buddy Al Checco

played the priest. Randolph Mantooth, star of the hit TV show *Emergency!*, played his son, and soap opera star Shelley Taylor Morgan played Randy's fiancée.

One of my favorite stars, Rue McClanahan, played Dad's wife. I had gotten over my shyness by this time, but I was perhaps a bit overly friendly when I met her: "Oh Rue, I'm a *huge* fan of *The Golden Girls*! In real life, are you anything like that saucy Blanche Devereaux?" Rue gave me her famous sidelong glance, and said: "Well honey, I'm not going to tell you how many men I've dated, but that sign over McDonald's saying the number of people served doesn't even come close."

Janice Ladik remembered a cast party at Harvey Medlinsky's house: "We were poolside. Randolph Mantooth was there, and we were having the time of our lives. Your father was suddenly gone off the scene, and we were all wondering, *Where's Don? What happened to Don?* Suddenly he comes out, and he has his face completely scotch taped up in different directions! Up, down, sideways, horizontal, vertical. Oh, my nerves! We couldn't even talk, we were laughing so hard. And it was a joy, just a joy! I could forget my name but I can never forget that!"

After the show, the actors would go to the bar downstairs from the theater and sit under the stairs. Dad was very kind and signed autographs for everybody. Janice Ladik: "The owner of the theater was Tony De Santos. He became enormously wealthy and successful and owned all five of the Drury dinner theaters. He had a fish pond in the lobby of the theater, and he would take off his shoes and socks and get in the pool to clean it himself. One time we rode in the elevator with Tony, and an actress was giving him fits. After she got off, Don said, 'How can you work with people who give you a nervous breakdown?' Tony said, 'I don't get nervous breakdowns, I *give* them.' And he did! He said it so proudly, it was like a badge of honor for him."

Me: "Did you know Shelley Taylor Morgan was hell bent on seducing Randy?"

Janice: "Well, he was gorgeous. Come on."

I was taking improv classes at the L.A. Connection Comedy The-atre in Hollywood at Crossroads of the World, which was just a strip mall on Sunset Boulevard. I met Tim Frisbie, and we became comedy soulmates. We formed a comedy group called Side Show, and that evolved into L'Aftershock. Our favorite sketch was "Burger Hannah," a very funny takeoff on the Benihana restaurant. Tim and I also did a parody of sex therapists Masters and Johnson. I did standup as well, and Tim had a "Klutzy Superman" bit. We performed these very physical sketches on stages the size of a postage stamp.

Finally, we decided we were ready and secured a slot at the Com-edy Store Main Room for its sketch comedy show. I invited Dad. The sketches went off well, but Tim's Superman ended up being more of a klutz than he planned: he fell off the stage, taking two microphones with him! Tim: "They hit the tables and popped. Oh, boy! Your dad's big eyes got bigger." Me: "Did he say anything afterwards?" Tim: "I don't remember. I was too busy recovering from that idiotic fall off the stage."

Standup comedy was exploding in the eighties, but Dad wasn't happy with my desire to do standup. I couldn't blame him; his frame of reference for a woman in that field was Phyllis Diller, with her wild hair, cigarette holder, and clashing outfits. Opportunities in standup were opening very slowly for women. I persisted and asked him for help delivering jokes. He said, "Let's take a joke—I heard one the other day. I'll just tell it: a father in Beverly Hills said to his boy, 'Now, tomorrow I have to use the limousine and the chauffeur,' and the boy said, 'How am I going to get to school?' He said, 'You'll take a taxi like every other kid in America.' That's a short joke, and the short jokes are the best jokes, really. The biggest mistake most people make in telling a joke is they spend too much time telling it and they wear the audience out."

I appreciated the wisdom. In the 1980s I met funny man Jackie Curtiss (a.k.a. J. C. Curtiss), a beloved comedian who had become a staple on *The Ed Sullivan Show* and in major comedy clubs across the country with his partner Bill Tracy. When J.C. went solo, Hugh Hefner hired him to run the Los Angeles Playboy Club's standup comedy room in the 1980s. By adding comedy rooms to his clubs, Hefner played an important role in the development of America's standup comedy circuit. The shows provided a bridge between the old-school resorts of the Catskill mountains and the comedy club explosion of the 1980s. The new brand of comedy also helped erode the racial segregation in entertainment. J. C. Curtiss became my standup comedy mentor. I found out later he'd also been on Dad's variety show in a sketch with Sid Caeser!

Dad and Loralee's marriage started having problems; I'm not sure why. Dad would sometimes tease her about her celebrity crush on John Denver, who coincidentally had a hit song about West Virginia. It was all in fun, but once when they were in Hawaii they ran into Denver on the beach. Loralee impulsively threw off her beach coverup and stood grinning at John in her bikini. Unfazed, Dad quipped, "It's those hot flashes again, Mother."

Dad began having an affair. Barbara encouraged Loralee to speak up: "Words have wings, yes they do. And don't think when you say something that somebody don't get the message, because they do." Like my mother and me, Loralee lived in the shadow of this great man who needed constant nurturing. Loralee: "When we broke up I went into hiding and I no longer knew who I was, my identity was so intertwined with his. I felt like I was starting over, but like you I eventually got back in touch with my core, myself, and found my way to another truly productive life."

Loralee moved to Marina Del Rey, and Dad did another play. This time he did something out of his comfort zone, and he was brave to do it. A playwright-director named Jonathan Daly had an Equity-waiver theater company in Hollywood called the Stable Players. He wrote a sensitive and heartwarming play called *A Good Look at Boney Kern*, about a man who falls in love with a blind woman. The play was more dramatic than anything audiences had seen Dad perform. The group did the play in Hollywood and then took it to the Bucks County Playhouse in Pennsylvania.

Rebecca Russell was assisting on script: "Don said he was tired of always playing goofy parts. He had frustrations with Hollywood; he felt he had to always look successful. He was trying so hard to stay hip and young—maybe he was afraid of being edged out. He wore blue jeans that were pressed from the cleaners. I remember the director working to have Don resist going immediately to the funny parts. I was sitting with the director watching him work with Don to break away from old patterns."

Sometimes people ask why Dad never played a dramatic role, so I asked him about it. Dad said directors wouldn't cast him that way because he was too recognizable as a character. They should have given him a chance! They might've had to change the plot a little; it happens. Let's say Jimmy Stewart had been unavailable when Alfred Hitchcock cast his classic suspense thriller *Rear Window*. Having a thin, lanky, frame like Stewart's, Don Knotts gets the part. Instead of a stoic man spying on a murderer, we have a nervous man who fumbles with the binoculars. They fall out the window hitting a man below, knocking him to the ground. A woman screams, the police rush in, and chaos ensues in the courtyard. The murderer makes a beeline to Don, who faints into the arms of Grace Kelly. She carries him three flights of stairs in a pink chiffon gown to save her man! If that's not drama, I don't know what is.

Dad was impossible to buy a gift for; he had everything he needed and didn't want much more. Because he was born on July 21, 1924, every July, I'd trudge down to the men's department and pray for inspiration. In 1974, when Dad was turning fifty, I found myself gazing at a flat blue hat, popularly known as a "newsie cap" because newspaper boys had worn them in the 1930s. Later, golfers wore them; they had an international appeal that defied typecasting. Dad's face had naturally changed with age. When his hairline receded, he grew sideburns. To keep up with the times, he dated women in discotheques, learned to smoke pot, and carried a "man purse." None of this fit; he needed an image update. *Hmm*, I thought, *hit or miss?* I bought the cap! When the day came, dad lifted it from its box, and his face lit up. He checked himself out, and as he walked away from the mirror, I detected a little swagger in his step. I was thrilled to find something so perfect! Every July after that, I'd buy a different color newsie cap, size 7⅞. He loved every one of them.

Tim Frisbie: "Your dad had started dating a young lady. You told me he was looking for some pot. I guess he wasn't into that sort of thing, but they were having fun, and he decided to surprise her. I wanted to get a decent quality, my goodness. Who's going to give a legend seeds and sticks? Not me! I found some decent pot for Don. Here I am at Don Knotts's house with pot. *Ding dong*, I ring the bell. The housekeeper answers and lets me in. I wait in the foyer, and he walks out. I hand him the envelope, and he gives me the money. It was kind of funny—he says, 'I have to be somewhere, or I'd roll one for us.'" Me: "He said that?" Tim: "Yes, he did."

Dad was now single again, and Cousin Bill was visiting: "I was in the car with Don—he was driving his brown Mercedes to a concert at the Hollywood Bowl. I was asking him about being a celebrity and if people treat you differently. All of a sudden, he starts driving in a really annoying way, like swerving in and out. People were giving him dirty looks, but they saw who was driving, and suddenly it was funny! He gave me a look that said, 'Because I'm famous I can get away with being a dope.' After the concert, we're walking toward the restroom, surrounded by people. There was an usher wearing a bright red jacket, saying officiously, 'Please make your way courteously to the restrooms and drinking fountains.' All of a sudden Don yells out in this loud, rube-like voice, 'Where's the toilet?' People looked startled; they saw it was him and started laughing. He gives me this look, like, *Now, if you did that . . .*"

One time when we were doing a show in Kansas City, I asked: "Dad, do you ever feel uncomfortable when people are just so impressed with who you are and stuff?" And he said, "Oh, people go through that phase, and then they get over it."

When I told Tom this, he said, "I noticed that whenever he was on the phone making a dinner reservation, he'd go 'Hi, this is *Don Knotts*. . . . Ha ha ha, yes, thank you!' Me: "That was kind of a Barney Fife thing. He sounded so confident, even boastful, when he was talking to a receptionist whose job it was to make *everyone* feel special." Tom: "He was used to getting the VIP treatment. Sometimes I think he forgot how to be a regular guy." Me: "But I noticed whenever we walked into a fancy restaurant, Dad seemed insecure until the owner would welcome him in a loud voice: 'Mr. Knotts! It's wonderful to see you, how are you doing tonight, sir? Ramon, give Mr. Knotts and his guests our very best table!'"

13

MR. FURLEY LANDS, AND MAYBERRY RETURNS

I HAD STARTED GOING OUT with a filmmaker, David Hefner, who had an identical twin brother named Dan. And no, I wasn't dating them both! When the three of us dressed up and hit the town, it was an ego boost for me. But it was really their two handsome heads that were turning heads. When Dad's birthday approached, I said to David, "Dad is so generous; he treats everyone to dinner, but no one ever treats him." He said, "Dan and I will treat your father for his birthday!" They gave him the royal treatment: a fabulous dinner and a shower of gifts. When we dropped him off at his place, Dad gave them a grateful smile: "We'll do this again next week!"

One weekend Cousin Bill was visiting from Arizona. Bill: "One evening there were some people over at the Hillcrest house. I was walking thru the entryway when the doorbell rang. There was no one around so I opened the door. Andy Griffith was there. He was holding a box of Ritz crackers, and he said, as if he was doing a commercial,

'Try a Ritz, they are *goood*.' I must've looked confused because he said, 'That didn't go over.'"

Andy would occasionally drop by to see Dad when he was in Los Angeles. He had interesting quirks. Billi Gordon was in the kitchen with Dad one day. Billi: "This is a nice kitchen. I could see Aunt Bee here cooking stuff."

Don: "Andy Griffith was here with his wife sitting at my kitchen table. He said, 'Cynthia, make me some biscuits.'"

Later, Billi said, "Who goes to somebody's house and asks their wife to cook for them?" He was laughing about the fact that Andy Griffith wanted biscuits so bad his wife had to go to the store. Dad said, "She made biscuits in this house in the middle of the night!"

Three's Company, the hit comedy show that ran from 1976 to 1984, was produced by the company NRW, consisting of Mickey Ross, Don Nicholl, and Bernie West. The show centered on a guy, played by John Ritter, who shares an apartment with two beautiful young ladies, played by Joyce DeWitt and Suzanne Somers. Jack pretends to be gay so he won't get in trouble with his crusty landlord, Mr. Roper, played by Norman Fell. Audra Lindley played Mr. Roper's wife.

After three seasons, Fell and Lindley left to do a spinoff. According to John's first wife, actress Nancy Morgan Ritter, John was upset that NRW was going to spin the Ropers off into their own series to make more money for their company. He adored Norman and Audra. Gene Perret was a producer who handled the writing staff: "We had no idea who was going to replace Norman."

Bernie West was starting to panic: *What are we gonna do without Norman?* Suddenly, he said, "Why don't we get a Don Knotts type?" The casting director, David Graham, said, "Don Knotts type? Why don't you just get Don Knotts?" Bernie: "Don Knotts—is he still alive?"

David: "Yes, he is, Bernie, and he's younger than you." Dad joined the cast in 1979, and he didn't have to audition. You might say it was Don Knotts–type casting.

Gene: "Many times someone will say, 'Why don't we get a so-and-so type?' The idea is negative thinking: 'Oh, the real person will never want to do that. We're not good enough to get someone of that quality.'" Since Dad was the epitome of the second banana, they assumed that for him to go on a show that already had three stars would insult him by putting him down in the pecking order. But Dad was older now and actually relieved not to carry the weight of the show.

Joyce: "John and I were stunned; we couldn't believe Don Knotts was going to be in the cast. The first day of rehearsal, he was so polite, gracious, and unassuming. We were in shock." Nancy: "John came home, and he was extremely excited. It was a complete change. All he talked about was whether he had made Don laugh that day. Of course, Don made John laugh all the time with his asides and stories."

Gene: "When Don came on the show, we had to create a new character. We made him a wannabe ladies' man, always trying to be hip. The costume department put him in the most outlandish outfits, almost like Phyllis Diller's outfits. He said he was relieved at being able to get a laugh the moment he walked on stage in the costume." The rest of the cast didn't see Mr. Furley's outfits until he made his entrance, and when they did, the person who answered the door, which was usually Joyce, as Janet, had a hard time keeping a straight face. Dad said her timing was always perfect.

Dad would get huge laughs and applause on his entrances. Apparently, he had mixed feelings about that. According to Dad's novelist/screenwriter/TV producer friend, Phoef Sutton, "Don didn't like the applause every time he entered. It wasn't as genuine as the one-camera days, like the subtle comedy scenes on the porch in *The Andy Griffith Show*. *Three's Company* was a hard-laugh show, but he was grateful for the part." Dad felt that playing for laughs to a studio audience made it less effective for the audience watching on screen. The world of sitcom had changed a lot since *The Andy Griffith Show*, which was shot on film, like a movie. *Three's Company* was videotaped in front of a live studio audience. On top of that, they didn't use a teleprompter.

Gene: "The director was Dave Powers, who had directed *The Carol Burnett Show*, and she never used cue cards. If you use those or a tele-prompter, it almost becomes visible to the audience." Dad was insecure at first, and, true to his tradition of playing a joke when he was nervous, he pranked Dave. Joyce: "After the first read-through, Don went over to Dave and said, 'They told you about my getting the teleprompter, didn't they?' Dave said, 'What???' His face got so red. I remember your dad doing it so deadpan, I thought Dave was going to faint. I fell down laughing, and Dave said, 'I'm going to have trouble with you, I can see that.'"

Joyce: "The role of Janet, within the structure of the show, had to be straight man. At first, I felt it was impossible for me to be in a comedy without being the comedian, but the character of Janet was obliged to. When I started working with your dad is when I recognized the joy there, because with Mr. Furley, I would stand and wait and just enjoy him being hysterical; then he would take the ball and hand it back to me exactly where I needed to be. He taught me how joyous it could be to be the straight man."

Joyce explained how the work week went down. In the first few days of the week they improvised and added material to the show. On Thursday they taped a dress rehearsal for the benefit of the crew. Afterward there were notes and cuts. On Friday, they'd tape two performances in front of a live audience. They would be given more cuts and changes during the dinner break that they would incorporate into the 8:00 performance for the second audience.

Joyce: "Almost no canned laughter was ever used in *Three's Company*. It was just like doing a play." Gene: "John and Suzanne were wonderful. When we would go to meetings after rehearsal, sometimes there would be some negativity—somebody didn't like a line or whatever—so John would do something wacky, and Suzanne would go along with him, and that would relax everybody. Between takes, they were usually wearing bathrobes. John would drop a pencil, obviously on purpose, reach down to pick it up, then turn his head to look up her robe. John was the bad boy in the classroom who took some of the onus off." Once during rehearsal, Dad and John were standing behind Suzanne when John realized they were both taking in her lovely backside. Dad had to suppress a giggle when John whispered, "Forget *The Maltese Falcon*, this is what dreams are made of."

Three's Company's audience was growing, both within the industry and abroad. Actor/director Seth Green: "I was a junkie for *Three's Company*; I remember when Norman Fell left. He was a foil, but Furley wanted to be everyone's friend. He was fun, he was fashionable, unapologetic—really special. I loved all the physical stuff, the broad takes; no matter how outrageous, he always felt grounded

Dad hamming it up with John Ritter during *Three's Company*
rehearsal, circa 1980.

as a performer." Gregory Pierre Cox, vice president for the Pacific Symphony: "As a son of a diplomatic officer representing the United Kingdom, I spent my childhood moving from country to country. One constant trait of our ever-changing life experience was your father's warm, joyful humor and comedy. *Three's Company* would be playing at prime time in all of the countries we lived in—Algeria, Tunisia, Morocco, and Canada [Quebec]. The very first thing my younger brother and I did when we moved to a new consulate or embassy home was rush to the television set and look for the familiar face of Mr. Furley, which to us as children was pure, simple joy."

Bob Erbeck: "I worked as a camera operator at Metromedia on *Three's Company*. Your dad was terrific! He could keep the crew in stitches. You could always tell if the script was funny: the crew would laugh. But it's the off-script things your dad said and did that would have us rolling in the aisles. Dave Powers had such a great attitude too. As he often said, 'We're doing comedy, not brain surgery!'" Joyce: "Everyone loved working for Dave Powers because there had to be a glaring mistake for him to do a retake. By 9:30 PM, Dave would come on the loudspeaker and say, 'All right ladies and gentlemen, thank you. That's a wrap!' Our guest stars would laugh and we would go, 'No, we're done!'" Actors shooting live on other sitcoms at the time would work into the wee hours.

One morning, Joyce noticed Dad holding his cheek. He said, "I think I've got a root canal broiling." He went to see his dentist, who had hired a new assistant, Norina: "He came in and he's like, 'Hi, I'm Don. I have an appointment with Dr. McQuinn.' And I'm like, *Oh my God, oh my God, oh my God!* I said, 'They'll be right with you.' He said 'OK, thanks, dear,' you know, whatever. I couldn't stand it! I said to him, 'I was kind of wondering if you could do that thing you do.' He goes, 'What thing?' I'm like, 'You know, the thing.' And he had this look on his face. I didn't know if he was pissed or whatever, right. Then he backed away from the counter. He put his hand on his pants, and hiked 'em up, and he did that *sniff, sniff.* Yeah! He did the sniff! You know, when he's talking to Jack or the girls. He did that thing, and I almost fell over and died. I'm like, 'Oh my God, I can't believe that.' Nobody was even watching. I'm like, *Where is everybody? Where's Dr. McQuinn, where's Vicki?* Nobody saw, it was just for me! Like, somebody do something!!"

My friend Reb Brown guest starred as Elmo in the episode "Ralph's Rival." During the audience taping, just as they had rehearsed, John jumped on Reb's back, and Reb kicked the door, and, *not* as rehearsed, part of the set caved in! John whispered in Reb's upstage ear, "Way to go, Reb! You knocked the set down." John's kibitzing put costars at ease. Joyce: "Don and John were so comfortable together—Don had wonderful respect for John's talent and vice versa. They would laugh when they were working out a bit and start over again. They had a very nice-guy relationship. Dad said that John Ritter had a nice-guy complex, and he felt that John had a problem with being too nice." Personally, I saw two sides of John. I remember John kissed me on the lips every time he saw me. I also remember that I didn't mind. He had a playful way about him, but at times, he could come off like a chill pill, as in Garbo's "I vant to be alone."

Joyce: "The rehearsal hall didn't have dressing rooms; we were in that rehearsal hall every day until we got into the stage, so we told each other everything. Don would bring his radio." Jim Rice was the show's regular stage manager, but one particular episode was more complicated, so they needed an additional stage manager. They brought in Jim Smith, who was new to the position. He was instructed to cue Dad's entrance from backstage and told not to worry because "Don is very good about showing up at the right time." But the Dodgers were playing the New York Yankees in the World Series that year, 1981, and Dad had the game on. Jim Smith: "I began to get nervous when Don didn't appear from the dressing-room area. I should have gone immediately to his room, but instead, I waited and waited. He was so involved in the game that even though he finally rushed out he was too late for the cue. But Dave just stopped tape briefly, and we picked it up and moved on. I felt really bad about it, because it was my responsibility to make sure everyone was where they were supposed to be. Don was a little embarrassed, though it wasn't his fault entirely, so I learned an important lesson."

Gene: "At a rehearsal, my partner, Bill Richmond, complimented one of the performers on some business. Don Nicholl called him aside later and said, 'Don't ever give the performers a compliment. It makes them difficult to work with.' That was their attitude all along. Richard Kline, who played Larry, kept asking them for a last name, and they wouldn't give him one." He didn't get one until the second-to-last season.

Aside from NRW's condescending attitude toward the cast, things were going great, so nobody foresaw a storm brewing. Dad didn't want to involve me, so he didn't tell me about the battle between Suzanne's manager/husband, Alan Hamel, and the producers for a significantly higher salary. In my ignorance, I ended up being a pawn. Suzanne was sitting on the opposite side of the stage when she was needed for rehearsal. Little did I know, she was staging a "strike." Bernie said, "Karen, go over there and tell Suzanne she's wanted on set." Who was I to argue with the producer? I went over and said, "Suzanne, they need you on set." She gave me a haunting look.

Tom recalled coming to the set: "Dad would introduce me, 'This is my son, he's an engineer.' I always thought that put them at ease. And they were impressed. 'My brother's an engineer'—Priscilla Barnes said that to me. Dad was helping Suzanne with her Vegas act. He was coaching her, and he left the two of us sitting in her dressing room. She was eating chicken, and I felt a little awkward, but she was nice."

Tim Frisbie visited the set with me one day when Alan Hamel was there. Alan used to do a kids' TV show in Canada; he played a woodsman. Tim watched it every day when he lived in Michigan. When Tim told him he was a fan, Alan turned to Suzanne and yelled, 'Another one!' Gene: "Alan Hamel asked for more money. NRW got upset and booted her off the show. John was very bitter and upset with Suzanne; later he softened." Dad was upset about Suzanne's departure, but he felt it was her husband/manager's fault for making unrealistic demands.

Joyce: "During the transition when Suzanne left, quite often in the rewrites they'd have a great line, and they didn't want to lose it, so they'd work it so Mr. Furley could say it." According to Gene, one week there was an episode that centered on Mr. Furley—there weren't many of those. Dad was pacing the set of the bar, the Regal Beagle, waiting for the cast. It was Suzanne's birthday, and every hour flowers were delivered, causing a distraction. The only person besides Dad who was on set and ready to rehearse was Paul Ainsley, who played the bartender.

Dad headed for Mickey's office and began to yell. Gene: "We got a call to go down to the rehearsal hall because there was a problem. The only one there was Don; he was pretty upset. He said, 'This episode is my featured show, and nobody is here to rehearse. If they don't come up here and start rehearsing, I'm gonna leave.' And my partner, Bill Richmond, making a joke, said, 'I'll get my hat and go with you.' That kicked off the flood gates; as Don got angrier, the higher pitched his voice got—and it was Barney Fife. We tried to fight back laughter; he thought we weren't taking him seriously, and it just went on and on. It was a little scary too. He wanted to work hard; he wanted his rehearsal time. We called in the cast and explained. They rallied around and did rehearse." I'm sure it was a miscommunication; the cast would never had done that knowingly.

Billi Gordon noticed something really wonderful about Dad: "You and I went to a taping of *Three's Company*, and afterwards your dad took us to Greenblatt's Deli. I told him he was nice on the show, and he goes, 'Well, unfortunately I didn't do much on the show tonight. I'm sorry you guys came out for this.' I mean, he is Don Knotts! He doesn't have to explain anything. He has a legacy of a career, but in that moment what I saw was a man with his daughter, and he wanted to make her proud in front of her friend, and that was most concerning to him."

I was running late to meet Dad at Matteo's, one of our favorite Italian restaurants. Dad looked up to see Milton Berle waving him over. He said, "Don, have a seat. You see Dr. McQuinn, right? He just gave me this temporary." Milton took a tooth out of his mouth and put it in his pocket. He called the restaurant owner and told Dad, "I'm gonna put one over on Matty," who came briskly to their table: "Hello Mr. Berle, Mr. Knotts. How you doing, how's the food?" Berle: "Not bad. Matty, how long have I been coming here?" "Oh, Mr. Berle, you're a good customer. You been coming here for twenty years." Berle: "Then what is this?" He pulled the tooth out of his suit. Matteo goes crazy: "Oh my God!" He went running back to the kitchen, and they heard this screaming and yelling. Milton and Dad peeked around and saw Matty had all the employees lined up. He was looking in their mouths to see whose tooth had fallen into Berle's soup! So Milton starts laughing: "Matty, I'm just messing with you, see?" He takes the temporary out of his suit and puts it back in his mouth. Matty glared at Milton, then he slowly started to laugh. He said, "I'll get you for this. Watch your soup!" When I arrived, Dad said, "You won't believe what you missed! Don't be late next time."

One day, the NRW people called Gene and his partner into their office. They said, "You never came to the Wednesday night meetings after rehearsal." Gene: "You told us never to go to those meetings." Nicholl: "Who told you that?" I said, "Your secretary." He said, "Don't listen to her." Gene: "Our office was twelve steps away. Why didn't they just talk to us? We gave our notice."

After they quit, Gene went down the hall to talk to Tim Conway. "He asked me about *Three's Company*. I said that John Ritter was one of the funniest physical comedians in the business. Tim did a fake cough. He was out of work at the time, and I said, 'Let me change that: he's one of the funniest physical comedians *working* today.' Joe Hamilton was the executive producer of Tim's show. They had a meeting about promoting the show. We had worked with Tim on *Burnett*, so we just stopped in to say hello. Once we were off the show, they made an offer, and we took it immediately."

———————

At this point, Dad sold the Hillcrest house. He and Loralee weren't married anymore, so he decided to downsize and moved to a condo in Westwood. I went to see how Barbara Welles was doing. She had an apartment in Los Angeles at St. Andrews Place and Seventh Street. She hadn't found another job, and she was struggling. Barbara: "I keep forgetting that I'm not working anymore. I'm lucky I still got this place. I been so used to workin' and makin' a little money every week. When I get money once a month, I got to stretch it like hell. And soon as you try to buy groceries to last a damn month and pay all your little bills, you ain't got nothin' left. You got to eat the same pot of beans for a week. I went over there to the church Wednesday to get that bag of food and what was in it, just a little old bag of rice. If I'd known that's all it was, I wouldn't have embarrassed myself. Neighbors lookin' out the damn window, 'Here she come with a bag.' What's in it, nothing but that old stinkin' rice."

Not long after that, Barbara suffered a heart attack. Dad paid for the operation. She was terrified to have heart surgery so he instructed the surgeon not to tell her. She woke up the next morning and it had been done! Dad understood people's fears. I went to see her in the hospital. She did get better, but two years later, she was gone. I was shocked. I didn't keep in touch the way I should have. Dad and I went to her funeral in a small church in downtown Los Angeles. I think of her often.

Three years after *Three's Company* ended, Dad was offered a part on *What a Country*. The sitcom was about an English as a Second Language course for recent immigrants trying to pass the citizenship test. The concept was built around Yakov Smirnoff, a Russian comedian making a name for himself in the United States during the second phase of the Cold War between the United States and Russia. Yakov played a taxi driver who is in the class, along with about five other students.

A young comedy writer named Mike Scully was writing jokes for Yakov for his regular appearances at the Comedy Store. Mike: "It was a very exciting time to be at the Comedy Store with people like Robin Williams, Rodney Dangerfield, Sam Kinison, and so on." Yakov was cast in the series in 1986, and he brought Mike on board.

Dad was hired to replace Gail Strickland as the school principal after the writers decided to go another way with the character. The writing team of Martin Rips and Joseph Staretski, who also wrote for *Three's Company*, created the series. It was their idea to cast Dad. Mike: "They knew Don would be funny in the character, a guy who wasn't wild about immigrants because he doesn't know much about them. It required the audience to like the character despite his prejudices and root for him to evolve. During rehearsal, they lined up director's chairs on set. I was young and terrified, but the staff was very patient with me. I loved going to the stage because there would usually be ten to fifteen minutes before a run-through started, and that's when I usually got a chance to talk to Don. He genuinely didn't understand why people made such a big deal of him. I think he considered himself more a character actor than the star he was. He gave me advice: 'Never leave one job until you have the next one lined up.'"

The writers were amazed at the way Dad delivered a particular line when he was playing a witness in a courtroom scene. They counted four takes on one line: "That was a quadruple take!" Mike: "Don's macular degeneration was getting worse. The bright lights caused a glare. He would do his part like a pro, then immediately grab the sunglasses. When he was on set you never knew he was having a problem, but you knew he was hurting." Mike Scully went on to become executive producer of *The Simpsons*, in addition to writing for

Everybody Loves Raymond and *Parks and Recreation*, and cocreating *Duncanville* with Julie Thacker Scully and Amy Poehler.

Dad decided to hire an assistant to help him. Wendy Blair, who was on *What a Country*'s production team, lined up a few candidates. One afternoon a delightful and charming young woman, Francey Yarborough, walked in. Her first impression of Don: "He was the most vulnerable person I ever came across, like a baby with her skin peeled off, he was that vulnerable. He had no defenses! He had no calluses, somehow, in the outside world. I thought it was almost funny how vulnerable he was. Every time he'd ask me a question and I'd answer, we'd burst out laughing. I thought, *We are connecting like nobody's business!*" Francey left thinking she needed to meet more people who really understand her. When Dad called and told her she was hired, she realized he had the same reaction.

The two weren't necessarily aware of a romantic attraction because of the age difference; she was about thirty years younger. Mike first became aware that Don and Francey were an item when they showed up at a cast party together. They came arm in arm, and both looked very happy. It was a bit of a surprise. Francey: "We thought, *What harm is there in being together? No harm whatsoever. I'm single, you're single, so why not?* As time went on we kept thinking, *It looks like we're just going to stay together.*"

I was doing theater and comedy at night. I invited a friend, Mike Ruiz, to come see my show, *Kennedy's Children*. Mike: "Your dad was right there with his 1920s golf cap, and you said, 'Dad, I'd like you to meet my friend Mike Ruiz,' and he turned around. I looked in his eyes and it was Barney Fife talking to me. And he said, 'Well, nice to meet you, Mike.' He was a lot taller than I imagined, because when you see him on *The Andy Griffith Show* he's not as tall. I'm five nine, and I had to really stretch my shoulders and my head up to be as tall as he was."

Dad and Francey, 2000. © *Globe Photos/ZUMAPRESS.com*

Dad was out of work for a while, and, once again, Andy came to his rescue. After a slow period, Andy had come back on top, starring in *Matlock.* Andy went to Dean Hargrove, the producer, and pitched having Don on the show as a comic relief character, an amateur sleuth named Les Calhoun. Dean didn't want to do it; he said this show is a drama and there's no place for Don. Andy kept after the producers, and finally they relented, but they didn't want to pay Dad's salary. Andy kept after them, and finally they raised it. Later, Andy sort of realized the producers were right, Don wasn't a great fit for the show, but he was glad he had him on anyway. Francey: "Andy would try to make their interactions and characters more complex, rather than formulaic, like on *Diagnosis Murder.* They just wanted a show that worked. Andy would work so hard to do that, and they would fight him. Andy was used to being in a show that he controlled, and this time he didn't have that." Dad did a total of seventeen episodes from 1988 to 1992.

———————

Before Dad sold the Hillcrest house, I gave him a list of the furniture pieces I'd like to take, and he asked if they would all fit in my new one-bedroom apartment. I showed him a map of where each piece would be. He said, "That's fine. Now where are you gonna be?" Barbara was sad; she said, "When you get old and you can't do nothing, don't nobody give a damn about you. That's right. I see more people walkin' with sticks bent over and little groceries in their hand, just toddling along. And you know that's somebody's grandmother or somebody's grandfather, and nobody don't think enough of them old people to say, 'I'll go to the store for you.' They don't. Once you start getting old and losing all your youth, forget it. Because these young generations say after you get thirty, you're supposed to be dead anyway." I said, "I hate to say it, but I was the same way with my grandparents on my mom's side. I never answered their letters, I never called them, I never did anything. I was terrible. Just being a kid, you don't connect. And I felt really bad about it after they died." Barbara: "It was too late then! Remember how I used to remind you, don't forget to get your father something, don't forget to get a card."

When they decided to make *Return to Mayberry* in 1986, thanks to Dad and Andy, I got a speaking role! I was cast as Rudene, secretary to the now grown-up Opie, editor of the *Mayberry Gazette*. The show got high ratings and was an amazing Mayberry reunion. The only character who was not there was Aunt Bee; Frances Bavier was ill at the time. Andy and Ron visited her in her grand house, which had lots of cats. She was a cat lady! She had softened over the years, and she apologized to Andy for being a bit of a diva on set at times. In true Andy Taylor fashion, he said there were no hard feelings.

In *Return to Mayberry*, Barney and Thelma Lou actually got married! Betty Lynn was especially happy about that. She couldn't understand why they didn't have their characters marry before Barney left the show. Well, Mayberry had this quirky thing about adults in their prime staying single. There was a saying going around: "Andy, Barney, Floyd, Gomer, Aunt Bee, Helen Crump, and Thelma Lou are all single! The only one who's married is Otis, and he's always drunk!"

I was so thrilled to be part of the Mayberry legend, I couldn't believe it as I drove up to the town where we'd be filming. By this time, location shoots were becoming more common, and they were filming in Los Olivos, a quaint town in Northern California. Scenes were shot out in the town square, and people gathered in large numbers to watch. On the original show, of course, no one was allowed on set who didn't need to be there, so this was something for the cast to get used to.

I was excited to see two old friends from my childhood, Jim Nabors and George Lindsey. And there was Betty Lynn! We all hugged when we saw each other. Everybody looked the same, except with a bit more facial contouring. I was shown the anteroom to the newspaper office, where my character, Rudene, would be seated at her desk. When the scene starts, Andy enters and I look up.

Rudene: "Can I help you?"

Andy: "I'm looking for Mr. Taylor."

Rudene: "May I tell him who's calling?"

Andy: "Mr. Taylor."

Rudene: "Oh, you must be Mr. Taylor's Mr. Taylor. I mean his father!"

I was nervous about rehearsing that scene, mostly because it was with Andy and I wanted to be perfect. Andy's presence provoked both anxiety and excitement in me. People have described his personality as one extreme or the other, but any definition of Andy as one-dimensional falls flat. Andy was moody. And he felt complete fulfillment with Dad and would do anything for him. As we rehearsed, Andy could tell I was nervous. He suggested that I eat a cookie while delivering my lines. That would give Rudene naturalness and a character.

After we shot the scene, I walked by Ron Howard, who had been watching on a portable monitor. He said, "You did a fine job." I was so elated, I practically floated out of there and went to find Dad. I found him in his trailer looking deeply depressed. I asked, "Dad, what's wrong?" He looked in the mirror and said slowly, "It's not the same. Barney looks old." Me: "Your audience has aged with you, so they'll understand." Don: "It doesn't feel the same." Me: "Why would it? Twenty years have gone by. But everybody loves Barney, no matter how old he is!" He took that in and said, "Let's go find the gang and have a bite."

Dad received a letter from an aspiring actress in Morgantown, Josephine Forlini, telling him his WVU mentor, Sam Boyd, had passed away. He was sad to hear it, and he took one of his regular trips back to his hometown. Mary Callen was a Morgantown High School alumna: "I got pretty close to [Morgantown historian] John Pyles, and every time Don would come to visit, John would say, 'Mary, he's coming to town. Prepare a dinner!' Don was an extremely intelligent young man, I do remember, and he was very quiet. John would ask him a question, and he would answer, but he would never initiate. He was a very shy person. And when I told my neighbor that Don Knotts was the president of my class, she yelled, 'Oh, Mary!' He was the love of everybody."

George Laishley owned a gas station in Morgantown: "Jarvey [Eldred] was one of my very good customers. He would pick your dad up at the Pittsburgh airport, and they would stop at my service station. One year, Don was in Morgantown for a parade in the courthouse square. He and my mom were talking, and he called her by her first name, Gail, and gave her a bullet he had in his pocket. They chatted for a few minutes, and he moved on. My wife said your dad had lived on University Avenue in a house rented from the Galusha's, Leola and Sleepy, my mom and dad's best friends."

Pastor Dan Meadows: "I did a wedding for Jarvey's daughter. The wedding took place at Swallow Falls, Maryland. Don came to the wedding, and he tried to disguise himself wearing a newsie cap and big sunglasses [the same oversized pair he wore to protect his eyes]. Eventually, one of the guests recognized him, and someone asked him to autograph a bottle of beer. Don said, 'I've autographed a lot of things before, but never a bottle of beer.' He did sign it." Back in Morgantown, the pastor recalled, "Don and Jarvey would go down to the Flame [Steak House] on High Street late at night so they wouldn't be bothered by people. One time they had taken Jarvey's Cadillac; he parked it out on the street. Someone followed him home and stole the car; it was later found. Your dad was very friendly."

Lee Ann Doss: "I was an art student at WVU in 1981 through '86. I was with my fellow art students walking up the stairs at the Creative Arts Center with our portfolios and tackle boxes of art supplies. It was quite a hike up the steps. As we climbed, we noticed there were people walking down, but we did not look up. All of the sudden we heard 'Hello, girls!' We all three looked up and stopped in our tracks. It was *Don Knotts*! We could not speak. Nothing came out of our mouths. He smiled and walked by us, and we still could not say a word. He was with several people. We found out he was speaking to the theater majors. We skipped class and sat outside the presentation so we could listen. After the presentation, we followed him around the Center! It was a day to remember. We never could speak to him. We felt like we were in the presence of greatness."

Cindy DeAngelis O'Dell: "My story happened in 1969 when I was a junior and a classmate of Jenny Eldred at Morgantown High School. I was a huge fan, and as a reporter for the school newspaper, I wanted a story! Sitting around the dinner table were the Eldreds and your dad. I was so overwhelmed when I met him that I could hardly speak. Your father saw I was struggling and kindly said, 'How about I just tell you about myself?' He graciously gave me plenty of interesting details. He even walked me to the door, hoping to finally relax with his friends. When he opened the door a photographer from the *Dominion Post* was standing there. By all rights, he should have reached his limit and shut the door behind me. But no, he grinned and took me and the Eldred kids out on the front porch and posed for a picture for the city paper."

Judy Eldred: "One time when we were kids, your dad came to visit. We were in the dining room, we had chicken, and some friends were out in the yard. We took a chicken leg out there, told them it was Don Knotts's chicken leg, and we sold it."

Me: "Oh? Well, one leg isn't so bad."

Judy: "But we didn't stop with just one chicken leg. We got bones from everybody's plate. We found them on the table and in the trash. They must have thought your dad ate the whole chicken."

Me: "How'd those kids end up in the yard?"

Judy: "I have a funny feeling some of the neighborhood kids knew he was in our house. I'm sure they were just hoping to get a glimpse of your dad."

Me: "And they told their friends, 'Don Knotts's chicken bones!' How much did they go for?"

Judy: "Ten cents each. A couple of kids got in a fight over a wishbone; they broke it in two."

Me: "It was your idea then?"

Judy: "I can't say it was my idea."

Me: "How did you get the chicken bones off the table?"

Judy: "We had to be clever about it. We were terrible! And I was always the shy one."

That story was a gem, and one of many I would never have heard, had I not gone back to get stories from people for this book.

14

BARNEY TAKES
TO THE STAGE

AFTER SAM BOBRICK had written several episodes of *The Andy Griffith Show*, he started writing plays with Ron Clark. They scored big with hit comedies in the dinner theater circuit, like *Norman, Is That You?* and *Murder at the Howard Johnson's*. Sam knew an actress named Dodie Brown who was a big theater star in Kansas City. She performed most often at the New Theatre & Restaurant, a gorgeous dinner theater with a great reputation for comedy and musicals. One day Sam called Dodie and said, "I want to get you to meet Don Knotts." At the same time, he told Don, "I want you to look at this wonderful actress."

Dodie was so excited. Her dad said, "Dodie, that's big time!" Dodie: "We first met at the read-through for the play *Harvey*, about an invisible rabbit who can only be seen by Don's character, Elwood. I was reading the part of Veta Louise, Elwood's sister." This was Dodie's audition. Francey told her later that the director, who was very British, had taken her aside and said, "Listen, if that gal playing Veta Louise isn't any good, we're out of here." They started to read. Dodie: "Don was cute and he was funny. We started reading the sides, and we clicked. Don said, 'I knew we were gonna be great, because we both really saw the rabbit.' Then he added, 'Dodie, what you could've done if you'd been in California when you were younger.' I said, 'Nobody would've wanted me—my nose was too big.' Don knew every line in the play, and not only did he memorize all these lines, he had to learn them verbally. Francey would read him his script, and that's how he learned it. We would find little things to touch on, to keep his vision on track. He loved playing Grandpa because he could sit in the chair and not have to worry about blocking. I always thought he had the sexiest mouth and eyes since Frank Sinatra. I said, 'I love you, Don.' He said, 'I love you, too, Dode. You know, you're a good-looking woman.' What a great compliment from a blind man!"

Pat Paton was the PR man for the theater. Pat: "He used to call me around five o'clock and say, 'Hey, Pat, are you hungry?' There was a steakhouse he liked. I'd go and pick him up, and it was kind of fun, because a lot of people would recognize him. I told Don, 'I know you want to sit in the back where people can't see you.' And he says, 'No, I want people to see me!' One time a gal comes over and says, 'You look an awful lot like Don Knotts.' He says, 'Well, a lot of people tell me that.' She'd talk for a while, then, 'You sure look a lot like him.' He says, 'Well, I give up. I'm . . . I am Don Knotts.' And she says, 'Oh, how wonderful,' and she goes over and sits down. He looks at me and says, 'See, once you tell them, they leave.'"

Pat: "I took him to my doctor; he was seeing bubbles running around the outside of his eye. The doctor checked him up and said, 'Well, it's your condition; there's nothing I can do. You're going to have that on occasion.' Don gives him a look and says, 'What kind of a doctor are you?' He says, 'A good one.'"

It is not atypical for comedians to score with women in doctors' offices, partly because they spend so much time there. In Hollywood, Dad and Tom were in a doctor's waiting room in Beverly Hills where

Groucho Marx saw Dad and said, "What's this quack doing for you besides giving you his bill?" A woman started gushing over Groucho. Then she turned to Dad and said, "You're Don Knotts." Groucho said, "He's always known that!"

There was also a pretty lively social set at the New Theatre. Dodie: "It's a good thing Don had a good appetite—I guess he was tired of being skinny. All his exes would show up at the stage door to surprise him. He wasn't a party guy necessarily, but we would all go out for ice cream." Pat: "He was so good to me. We went up to the Chinese restaurant, and I said, 'Now it's my turn to pay.' He said, 'No, you brought me here. I'm paying.' And I said, 'No, I'm paying today.' Then he says, 'OK, I'll get even with you.'"

Francey got raves for her role as Bobbi Michele in *Last of the Red Hot Lovers*. Francey: "It was fantastic. We had the greatest time, and he taught me this amazing thing about how you should stop the laughter from getting out of control. It was the scene where Bobbi Michele is smoking pot and Barney Cashman is freaking out about his mother coming home. I thought, *If people are laughing hysterically or going wild, don't stop them, let them laugh.* But he said, 'No, stop them.' He was afraid they would laugh themselves out, they'd be so exhausted. He said he learned that from the show on Broadway with Andy in *Sergeants*, that if you let them laugh themselves out, they're not going to laugh anymore. We had to walk across the stage and make a big movement to make them stop laughing, and we could not make people stop laughing! They would get more and more out of control; they were laughing and laughing, and it was really fun!"

I got to perform with Dad in Kansas City when he was doing *You Can't Take It with You*. The theater went through a few name changes before it settled on the current name, the New Theatre. Dad and I were joking about it, and we came up with a little patter:

Don: "It used to be the Newer Theatre."

Me: "Before it was the Newest Theatre!"

Don: "Now they're opening the Brand-New Theatre."

Me: "What if it goes bust?"

Don: "It'll be the Foreclosed Theatre. When they did shows for the Indians here in Kansas—"

Me: "It was the New Tent Theatre." Notice how I snagged the last punchline? I always got my licks in with the Master! One nice thing about the New Theatre was that every two weeks it had a Grand New Opening.

In *You Can't Take It with You*, Dad played Grandpa, who made a game of not paying his taxes. Dodie played Penny, his excitable playwright daughter. I was cast as an alcoholic actress named Gay Wellington who enters in the first act, passes out on the sofa, and stays face down through the rest of the act. I wondered, *How can I get more mileage out of this part?* I thought, *Since Gay is drunk, it would be natural for her to fall off the sofa.* I didn't let on to Dad or the director, but during rehearsal, I rolled off the sofa and landed on the floor with a thud. There was a pause, then a scream of laughter from the cast. The director, Richard Carrothers, yelled, "Keep it!" For the next twenty-six performances, I fell off that sofa. It had not occurred to me there was no plush carpeting to soften my fall. I ended up with some bruises on my elbows, but getting that big laugh was worth it. Everybody loves physical comedy, but nobody thinks about the poor comedian! Comedian Katt Williams: "I'm not nearly as physical as I'd like to be. I do standup, and the joke is hilarious if I fall to the ground; that would be the funniest way to do it. But after seventy-five shows and I've fallen seventy-five times, I often end up hurting myself."

In *Norman, Is that You?*, Dad and Dodie played a married couple. There was a scene where they were supposed to kiss. Dodie would play a trick on him and move away from her spot. He would find her by following her voice. It was funny for the audience to see a bare cheek and a big pucker going all around the stage. It wasn't a romance made in heaven; it was a make-believe romance made in the third act.

Dad as Grandpa and Dodie Brown as Penny in *You Can't Take It with You* at the New Theatre in Kansas City, circa 2002.
Courtesy of Dodie Brown

The two went on tour with the show *On Golden Pond*. Dodie: "They would line up around the block to get his autograph. Everybody that came by would give him a bullet. Every person said, 'I'm your biggest fan!'"

Once when I was visiting Dad at his hotel in Orlando, I said, "Dad, the desk clerk wants to know if you'll autograph a picture for him." He said, "Sure honey." He reached for a pen, but the drawer wouldn't open. Finally, he gave that drawer a yank and all these bullets came flying out! A lot of people from the autograph line had given him a bullet in honor of Barney Fife. He said, "What am I gonna do with all these bullets? I don't own a gun, bless their hearts!"

————————

Dad was getting older, but he never stopped working. He wrote a book, toured with his one-man show, and did voice-overs for animated features. Then there was exciting news. Dad was going to get his star on the Hollywood Walk of Fame! Francey, Tom, and I got to go to the ceremony. Andy Griffith and John Ritter were there, and Hollywood Boulevard was filled with Dad's excited fans. A lot of celebrities paid tribute to Dad, and they still say amazing things. Four of my favorite comedians, Jim Carrey, Katt Williams, Craig Shoemaker, and Dana Gould, do impressions of Barney Fife. I've either got a daddy complex or a comedian fixation. If any of these fine "gentlecomics" asked me for a date, I'd have to say, "*Noop!*"

Ron Howard said that when he was directing *How the Grinch Stole Christmas*, Jim Carrey was depressed because of all the hours he had to spend in the makeup chair. Ron called Dad and asked him to make a surprise visit to the set. When Jim looked down from the

At seventy-five, Dad got his star on the Hollywood Walk of Fame; (left to right) Tom, Dad, Francey, David Hefner, and me, 2000.

top of Grinch Mountain and saw Dad, he launched into a Barney Fife impression while wearing the Grinch costume. Ron said if only he had kept the camera rolling.

Jim Carrey: "It was an incredibly difficult shoot, every day, a couple of hours in makeup. I was covered in this horrible suit. Ron had told me Don was gonna come. When I saw him down there I started doing impressions of him in *The Shakiest Gun in the West* and a risqué impression of Barney talking to Thelma Lou. Don made my heart sing. I got to meet my hero and to see what kind of man he was: so kind. He created something so strong—it continues to bring joy. He affected things and left a beautiful fragrance."

Dana Gould: "I grew up in a tumultuous childhood—six kids, two adults. The number of times everybody would shut up I can count on one hand . . . very few things would shut everyone up, and *The Andy Griffith Show* was one of those things. So the show means a lot to me because it was my family growing up and everybody was together. There were catch phrases I didn't realize came from the show. 'Bless his heart'—that was from your dad. There are very few people who are always as funny as the situation could be. There's never a time where he's on camera and you think that could have been funnier, or played differently. It's such comfort food. You could tell those people loved each other—they were having a great time. Being a fan of your dad is like a secret handshake."

Craig Shoemaker: "My career really exploded with *Comic Relief* in 1986, when they were honoring *The Steve Allen Show*. Tom Poston was there, your Dad, and Steve Allen. They introduce me, I go out doing Barney, I'm killing it. And Don is watching me on the monitor. The audience was fascinated watching him watch *me*, doing my impression of him. Don turns to Steve Allen and says, 'He does Barney pretty good.' Steve says, 'Well, yes, exactly like him.' Someone said, 'Let's put them next to each other.' They whisked him over to live television, and it was just the two of us doing a press conference.

Afterwards, we talked privately. Don said, 'You know, I can't do that anymore. You do me better than I can; you really do sound like me.' It still brings a tear to my eye. My dad left when I was born and my mom wasn't ever around, so I was left with the television set. I just wanted a father so bad. Now, my own son is doing Barney Fife impressions like me!"

Katt Williams: "When I see him as Barney, he's working every angle, every part of his uniform, the posture . . . the stance. The older I got, the more I'm realizing this is a real professional, all the way through *Chicken Little*. When Tim Conway came into the mix, it made it even more wonderful. *The Ghost and Mr. Chicken* is, like, textbook. You could watch that and see how comedy is done, scene by scene, in one man's hands. Comedically, there's no way for you to care about physical comedy and the name Don Knotts not to come up in the conversation. To say you are 'Don Knotts-esque' would mean you have complete control, as well as perfect comedic timing. This guy is funny to everybody. It doesn't matter what age, group, or race. That's when you get into rarefied comedy air."

John Waters is a filmmaker/actor best known for the cult film *Pink Flamingos* and more recently the musical *Hairspray*. I always thought Dad and John knew each other, but when I talked to John I found out they had never met. John: "I've always thought Don and Mick Jagger looked exactly alike. I often get mistaken for Steve Buscemi. When I told that to Steve, he said, 'If you think that's weird, I always get told I look like Don Knotts.' So there's a trifecta: John Waters equals Don Knotts equals Steve Buscemi!

"I always thought Don was really sexy. Now that Don has passed, I had to move on to Alvin the Chipmunk as having a type. When I was a kid, he was my secret friend. He was nervous all the time and acted weird, so he was like a role model. I still have pictures of him in my house that I look at every day. I tried to get him to be my date at the premiere of one of my movies. His manager didn't see the humor;

he said, 'Don is a married man.' Like I was trying to come on to Don Knotts! It was hilarious." When I told Francey, she said, "John Waters was letting it be known that he had a big crush on Don. I had a gay friend he told all this to. John tried to get Don to go with him to a gala in New York, but Don was getting ready to go on tour and the usual nerves were kicking in, so he turned it down." So Dad wasn't only a ladies' man, he was man's man, too.

Jim Carrey: "Don had so many levels. Barney was a fully formed character, fully informed in his choices and a totally real, believable character. You could run into this guy. . . . I found it so funny that he thinks he knows what he's doing. Nothing funnier than ego combined with ineptitude. I felt incredibly lucky that he knew who I was and some things I had done. Finding out how kind he was is hard to describe, when he is off the screen and he's human." I asked Jim what was the trigger to his impersonation of Barney Fife. He said Barney had a musicality the way he punched certain words, and a cadence: "The melody of his voice is pleasing to the ear."

Dad did quite a few voice-overs during this time. At this point, his macular degeneration was at its worst, but he always managed to work around it. Actor/director/producer Seth Green had a new animated show called *Robot Chicken* in 2005 and convinced Dad to do a role in it. Seth: "This was the first season, so we didn't have a sample to show him. We were luring performers to Santa Monica. I pitched it to him as an animated *Saturday Night Live*; it's acted out with action figures and pop culture. It's demanding—we need experienced and willing performers. I got him to say yes because I got Phyllis Diller to do it, and plus it would be an iconic guest appearance, a callback to his character on *Scooby-Doo*." (He cameoed in a couple episodes of the animated series in the 1970s.) "As a director, you want to help people get their best. He's so easy, so pro. He was like, 'Show me the mike. Let's do it.' I talked to his agent; they said he wasn't doing this kind of work because of the macular degeneration. He can't read, you'd have to feed him. That would be great for me; I'd be next to him in the booth, and there'd be almost a Cyrano dynamic."

———————

Dad went back to Morgantown to celebrate with his friends when they had the ribbon-cutting ceremony to open Don Knotts Boulevard, which had been approved by the city council with the help of John Pyles: "When your dad appeared here at the dedication, he pointed out on the highway and said, 'And I want my toll booth put right about there.' He said Richie [Ferrara] had given him that idea. Whenever I talked to him, he asked, with a twinkle, if we had his toll booth set up yet so he could collect some money. After the dedication we went down to the Glasshouse Grille. Richie and Jarvey were there; we were back in this room singing. Your dad liked to sing the old-time songs. The waitress came back and said people were wondering who all these old drunks were back there. Don said, 'You just tell them that you don't have to drink or smoke to have a good time and that we aren't drunk—we're just having fun.'"

In the 1990s, fandom was exploding over the fictional town of Mayberry. *The Andy Griffith Show* hadn't been filmed in decades, but people still watched it daily on rerun channels. To this day, in fact, Mayberry is vibrantly alive in the hearts and minds of millions of Americans. A regular part of many peoples' lives is discussing the show and answering each other in the characters' dialogue. Many fans will say, 'I want to live in that show!'

Tanya Jones started the first Mayberry Days festival in 1990 in Mount Airy, North Carolina, which is Andy Griffith's hometown. Mayberry Days has drawn as many as fifty thousand people at a time, and there are now dozens of Mayberry festivals all over the country. A big attraction for fans at the festivals is interacting with tribute artists who take on the show's characters. They dress, talk, and act

like Barney, Floyd, Otis, Aunt Bee, the Fun Girls, and so on. Many of
them are so good that they have a following of their own.

———————

In the early 1990s Dad also started touring with a one-man show
Bill Dana had helped him put together called *An Evening with Don
Knotts*. In the show he performed a classic monologue he developed
on live TV, in which a weatherman's report is missing, so the poor
guy has to make stuff up. He also performed his classic baseball pantomime. He would show clips from his film and TV career, then tell
behind-the-scenes stories and take questions. Dad performed the show
in 1991 at the Geo Amphitheatre, produced by Phil Stegner. There
were Mayberry tribute artists on the grounds to provide atmosphere.
Among them was David Browning, who had been performing as a
Barney Fife tribute artist at events like churches and county fairs. He
was entertaining the crowd as 'the Mayberry Deputy,' as he billed
himself, when to his surprise Francey Knotts approached him and
said, "Mr. Knotts would like to see you." David was sweating bullets
as he followed her into the theater's backstage area to meet Dad.

Afterward he said, "We had a wonderful conversation in his dressing room! Don said that I was doing a good job with the crowd and
he was enjoying what I was doing, improvising with them. He asked
if I had a routine. I told him that I had about ten minutes of stuff. He
said that was good, but thirty minutes would be better. I asked what
he meant, and he said that if I was interested, when he traveled east
again I might open for him. I was thrilled and thanked him. I guess the
conversation lasted no more than about ten minutes, but it changed
my life, for sure. When we initially worked together the first time at
Milligan College in East Tennessee in 1994, I had my routine ready
and opened for him. We had eleven hundred people in attendance,
and the evening went very well from beginning to end. Afterward

we had a brief talk, and he simply said, 'You need to get out there and do what you do.' He said that I could bring Mayberry directly to people and keep the memory alive. The next week, I resigned from my full-time job and a month later began performing the Mayberry Deputy as my full-time work. I would not have made that decision had it not been for your dad. I'm forever grateful for his friendship and inspiration." David has had an amazing career with it since, and has MC'd for many years at Mayberry Days.

Dad performed the one-man show in Bradford, Ohio, for the Mayberry Squad Car Rendezvous, a fundraiser for cancer, in 1995. A man named Kenneth Junkin was in charge of security and transportation for the show. David Browning and Floyd tribute artist Allan Newsome kept calling him Otis. Ken stood by Dad at the stage after the show, talking to him as he signed autographs and taking pictures with every person who wanted one.

Ken: "The very last lady said, 'I'm so glad you stayed. I know you're so tired.'"

Don (deadpan): "The only problem is all the flashes turn these white shirts yellow."

Ken escorted him and Francey out the back way. Francey: "Ohh, it's so dark out here."

Don (sniff): "That's show business."

Ken: "Don talked about how the producers on *The Andy Griffith Show* wouldn't let him drive a motorcycle off a four-inch curb when Barney says, 'Aunt Bee, you're jaywalking!' He said, 'I had one in high school. I weighed about 115 pounds. I looked like a zipper riding around on a motorcycle.' I told him one of my favorite sayings was with Gomer and Opie about the Miracle Salve, [in] 'A Deal Is a Deal.' He did that whole thing for me; he quoted it!" Don: "That is correct, U. T. Pendyke VDM, practice limited to small animals, dogs, cats, birds of all kinds, and small sheep. Mr. Taylor Sr. here brought me some of your ointment, and I tried it on six of my mangy animals, and it cured them within a twenty-four-hour period. An absolute miracle. By the way, that's a fine name you have for your company, Miracle Salve Company, and much better than the ointment I've been using, Molly Harkin's Mange Cure. Yeah, much better. So we thought we would like to buy from you and sell it to other veterinarians." Ken: "You ought to have seen my face. And then I got to escort him!" Ken became a regular tribute artist as Otis.

Dad performed his one-man show for the University of North Carolina School of the Arts in 1996 in a performance produced by Steve Davis. Before Dad arrived, a schoolteacher came to Steve and said, "I teach down at the elementary school in Arcadia-Midway, and I use things from *The Andy Griffith Show* in my lesson plan. I ask them, 'What would Barney do?' Well, you know Barney; he might make mistakes, but he always did what was the honest, right thing to do. I told the students he was coming to town, and they've all written Don a letter." He put a stack of four hundred letters from his students on Steve's desk. When Dad came in, Steve showed him the stack and asked him if he'd like to go down to the school and meet the students. Dad said he would as long as Barbara Eden was included. He was also on tour with Barbara with *Last of the Red Hot Lovers*.

Dad and Barbara had taken the show to Lake Tahoe, West Virginia, and now North Carolina. I asked her about the show. Barbara: "Don had macular degeneration, and he told me, 'I can't see you in front of me but I can see you on the side.' His vision was peripheral but he dealt with it beautifully. He was a dream to work with. Andy Griffith came to see us when we did the show in North Carolina. It was lovely to see them together." I asked if she saw Dad as a ladies' man, and she said, "Our relationship was strictly professional," and added she heard he "had fun."

When Dad and Barbara arrived, the entire student body was in the school auditorium. Steve introduced Dad and all four hundred kids sang the "Fishing Hole" song. Steve was delighted—he didn't know there were words! When Dad got up and spoke to them, they fell apart. After the show, Steve said, "I really appreciate you doing that." Dad said, "I wouldn't have missed it for anything. I've got something I want to show you. I really always wanted to be a magician." He pulled out a dozen cards and started doing magic tricks. Steve: "The tech guys were going, 'Don Knotts is here . . . doing magic tricks . . . while we're eating lunch. . . . This is a great job!' This was back when everybody had an answering machine, and it was a big deal to have a funny outgoing message. I said, 'How about you and I make a recording on my phone?" Dad said, "OK, I'll do it." This is how it turned out: *BEEP*. Don: "Hi! Steve can't come to the phone right now. This is Don Knotts. I'm taking all of his messages. Leave your message, and I'll see that he gets it." Steve: "Instead of pushing the OFF button, he leaves it running and says, 'OK, where's the fifty bucks you promised me? I want my money.' And I answered, 'I don't have fifty bucks.' And he says, 'Well, I'm gonna have to erase this.' *Click*. And that's the way it ends."

Steve brought Dad out for another show with twenty-three original actors from *The Andy Griffith Show*. Cast members were coming in on flights at all different times, so there was very little time to run lines. Steve: "The Darlings and Charlene [Maggie Peterson] came in. They rehearsed their songs, and in fifteen minutes they were ready. Betty Lynn [Thelma Lou] was there. Aneta Corsaut [Helen Crump] was very sick at the time. She was going to try to come, but she couldn't make it." Betty asked in front of the audience, "Can we get her on the phone?" Steve answered, "Let me see if I can get a phone." (This had actually been prearranged.) A guy in a tuxedo brought a silver tray with a phone out and handed it to Betty. She told Helen, "I'm here with about sixteen hundred of your friends that want to say something to you." Steve held the phone up, and Helen heard them cheering. At the end, the performers came out and sat in rocking chairs that had their autographs on the back. They all ended up on the "front porch" rocking, and the audience went crazy. He auctioned off the chairs. They went for $1,200 to $1,400 per chair; the money was donated to the School of the Arts.

Producer and concert promoter Tim Macabee brought Dad out to do his one man show at the Southern Nights Theater in Sevierville, Tennessee, in 1999. Phil Stegner and Jim Clark were friends of Dad's and both lived in Tennessee, so they came by to watch a rehearsal. For the baseball pantomime, Dad was accompanied by a drummer playing sound effects. The drum emphasizes when a ball is caught—or dropped—and the emotions of Dad as the pitcher. As Dad and the drummer rehearsed, it became clear the musician was struggling to get the sound effects right. After rehearsal Dad and his friends went out for a meal. Phil asked, "Do you think he's ever gonna get it?" Dad took a bite and said "Nope!" It was only natural for a drummer to be nervous accompanying Don Knotts on a tricky solo bit such as this. And while there were many great musicians in the Nashville environs, this was a specialized kind of accompaniment. Finding a drummer who could do this and learn it quickly was a challenge for Dad. Phil contacted someone he knew of, and this fellow got it right. Dad was relieved and Tim was delighted. Tim: "Right before showtime, Don made the comment 'Well, it's about time for me to get over here and start getting nervous.' And he did—he kinda walked the floor." The show was a huge success.

Tim had Dad back to do a show in 2000 at the Country Tonite Theatre in Pigeon Forge. Tim: "Your dad performed the same one-man show as before, but Betty Lynn and Howard Morris were also on the bill. Each performed a short set leading up to your Dad's performance." Tim had rented cabins where the performers could be near each other. Betty Lynn was the first to arrive. Tim and his helper Chris Osborne showed her around and took her upstairs to see the view from her balcony. Tim: "At the time, Betty was a smoker. The three of us stepped out onto the balcony so she could smoke. When she finished her cigarette, I went to open the door. It was locked! It had just gotten dark; there was no way to get down and no cell phones then. They were stuck there all night, but Betty kept them entertained with stories of working with Lucille Ball and the Three Stooges, doing shows on Broadway, and starring in the movie *June Bride* with Bette Davis.

"At dawn we could see well enough for Chris to hoist me over the side of the railing. I shimmied down a beam, got in the front door, and let Betty out." Dad, Betty, and Howard put on a great show that night. Tim: "It was around your father's birthday. David Browning was hosting the Q&A. He said, 'I have Tim Conway on the phone,' and everybody hears Tim Conway singing the *Andy Griffith Show* song, or whistling it, and he comes in with a joke about your father and your dad dies laughing. There was a great banter between them. Tim said, 'I know you're doing this show, and I'm still in L.A. and wanted to call and wish you happy birthday. I wish I was there. Have a great night!' And it just thrilled the audience. Don wore Barney's original salt-and-pepper jacket. You know, that's cut 'perfect for dips,' as Barney said on the show. It was amazing to me that forty years later it still existed and Don held on to it."

The next day, a limo headed to the Grand Ole Opry for a big Mayberry reunion performance. The party included Dad, Francey, and Tim along with Dad's manager Sherwin Bash, and Phil Stegner. The rest of the cast would be arriving separately. Tim wasn't directly involved with this show but had volunteered to help out, just as Phil helped with Tim's show; it was the Mayberry way. They made a stop at a Cracker Barrel restaurant, because Dad wanted breakfast and they serve it all day. Tim: "I remember Don saying to the waitress, 'I'll have bacon, and I want it on the crisp side.' Well, that's exactly how Barney always ordered his food, bacon on the crisp side, so I giggled to myself across the table because Don just said that. Don said, 'I'm in a draft. The draft is gonna bother me. Do you care to move and switch with me?' I said, 'Of course, I'd be happy to. I was just hiding you from the public—you're going to be facing them.' He's like, 'I gotta get out of this draft.' So we switched sides, and he was comfortable. I learned there was always something he was coming down with. Tim asked Sherwin, 'How's Don feeling this morning? Is he OK?' Sherwin just looked at me and said, in his dry New York voice, 'If you ask, you're gonna get an answer. I've learned not to ask.'"

Tim: "Your dad started talking about his family in West Virginia. Someone in the Knotts family had been arrested for something, and it was not something to be proud of, but he got the biggest kick out of telling this. Back in the 1600s, one of the family members was put in the stocks for fornicating with a maid in the bushes. But he took pride in telling that he had come from a long line of West Virginians, and that was one of his ancestors."

In Nashville the cast met at the Gaylord Opryland Hotel in the green room of the Presidential Ballroom to rehearse. They included the *Andy Griffith Show*'s famed bluegrass band, the Dillards (Rodney and Doug Dillard, and Dean Webb), along with Maggie Peterson Mancuso, Betty Lynn, Howard Morris, Elinor Donahue, Bernard Fox, George Lindsey, Jean Carson, LeRoy McNees, George Spence, and David Browning as host and MC. Dad and several cast members were at one table, Tim and the crew at another. Tim: "Somebody came to our table and said that Don wanted to see me, so I approached the table. He had a serious look on his face. I knelt down and said, 'Hey Don, I heard you wanted to see me.' Don said, 'So I heard you and Betty spent the night out on the balcony.' Everybody at the table was in on it, and they died laughing. Somebody had told him, and he had to rib me about it. And it was classic Don—a totally dry delivery, and the expression was so serious."

David Browning: "While we were in rehearsal, one of the ballroom doors opened and this young, dark-haired guy introduced himself as Brad Paisley, an up-and-coming country western singer and a huge

Mayberry fan. He met your dad, and he was in seventh heaven." To promote the show, Phil Stegner had scheduled an interview at the Gaslight Theatre for a TNN talk show. Dad, Jack Dodson, and Hal Smith appeared.

Phil also promoted the show by having the cast make an appearance on the Grand Ole Opry showcase. For decades, this show had brought together rising talent, superstars, and country legends. David: "We were all gathered backstage, and right before the show, Don asked the stage manager how they were going to get us onstage. The guy said, 'We'll cue you.' Don said, 'You mean we're not going to be introduced?' He looked at me and asked, 'Can you get us onstage?' I said, 'Absolutely.' Allan Newsome got everybody lined up." The audience had no clue what was in store. Country music legend Porter Wagoner was MC, decked out in his customary sequined attire. At the top of the show, David interrupted him: "Excuse me, buddy, I got some people that want to see what this Grand Ole Opry is all about. That's a pretty jacket you got on. I've got some important people."

"Well, who are they?" Porter asked.

David: "I've got Malcolm Merriweather . . ." Bernard Fox walked out and the audience was surprised. He continued, "I've got Ernest T. Bass over here . . ." Howard Morris came out, and the audience started applauding. He introduced singer Whisperin' Bill Anderson, who looked around and said, "What's going on?" David: "Can you speak up, buddy?" That got a laugh. Then he announced Charlene Darling, the Darling boys, and Goober. The audience was thrilled! Betty Lynn appeared, then David announced, "The one and only Barney Fife!" and Dad came out. There was a *roar!* People came running down to the stage.

David: "Three minutes is a long time for people to keep applauding! Don would just smile and look at the audience."

Dad and David had developed a patter for their shows, part of which they performed here. David was dressed in his Barney uniform, Dad in his street clothes.

David: "Hello, Mr. Knotts, it's nice to see you."

Don: "Haven't I seen you somewhere before?" That got a laugh. Then David did a bit from his funny Barney monologue and introduced Don as "the real Barney Fife."

Don: "Isn't that David Browning *something*?" After the applause died Dad said, "I wish I could do that."

After the show everybody went back to the bus. They were seated and waiting . . . and waiting. Tim was sitting across from Dad and saw him suddenly say, "Let's go!" with a wide-eyed look as if he was shocked and trying to figure out who said it. Tim: "Everybody on the bus died laughing. I'll never forget seeing him do that and pretend he didn't. They were laughing because they felt like, yeah, they wanted to go, too. And, actually the driver did go ahead."

Dad's last year performing Mayberry reunion shows was 2004, at the Roy Acuff Theatre. According to Phil Fox (Ernest T. Bass tribute artist): "We were backstage, away from the big ballroom where they were having the show. I was walking with your father down to the stage area, just chatting about life, strolling along. Someone from Opryland came up with a wheelchair and said, 'Mr. Knotts, they need to get you down to the stage; they're about ready for you.' He said, 'OK, I'm on my way.' He and I kept walking, and they said, 'Well, they want you to use the wheelchair.' And he said, 'No, I'm fine, I don't need a wheelchair. I'll just walk.' So we walked a few more feet, and the woman said, 'Well, they really kind of wanted me to get you in the wheelchair and take you down there.' You know, the man is preparing to go on stage—he's in his element; he's got his mind cleared. She insisted one more time: 'But, Mr. Knotts, they really want you to get in there.' He said, 'I told you I don't need a damn wheelchair.' Then he turned around and sat down. He just plopped down in it. And I knew that you don't mess with someone before they go on stage. You don't give them good news or bad news because they're preparing to go on stage, and it upset him. A lot of people think of octogenarians like they're feeble. He was not feeble at all, so that kind of blew my mind and his at the same time. They wheeled him down to the stage, and it held the show up for a few minutes because he had to recompose himself." David observed, "Don would sit so quietly backstage, and you knew the wheels were turning. He was prepping himself to control that audience. He was a genius."

Later on I asked Brad Paisley what appealed to him most about *The Andy Griffith Show*. Paisley: "I come from a town of fourteen hundred people in West Virginia: one barber shop; volunteer fire department, which my dad was in; and a drugstore. I would save up and get candy or comic books—it was an ideal existence. The neat thing about a small town is that when you want to be an artist, by golly, they'll make you one. There was this great place I used to eat in college, these nice, older, caring ladies would say, 'Honey, are you alright?' If I was having a bad day, they'd give me another piece of pie. It was just like Mayberry. I wanted to live in that show."

I asked Brad about the music video "Waitin' on a Woman" he made with Andy Griffith. Paisley: "Andy was everything I hoped he'd be. He wasn't exactly sure what a music video was. He showed up to shoot that day, and he had learned the entire song. The first time, we flew to his house and had lunch. He loved driving this little off-road vehicle. His favorite part of doing *The Andy Griffith Show* was the music; he loved playing and singing bluegrass. We talked a lot about your dad; he was so devastated about losing him. He also said he tried many times to get Blacks on the *The Andy Griffith Show*, but couldn't get past the powers that be."

––––––––––

Dad had an annual tradition of spending Thanksgiving at the Mark Hopkins Hotel in San Francisco, where our whole family would convene. It would be Dad and Francey, Kay and (her then husband) Burt, me and my date, and Tom and his son, Stephen.

The first time Stephen came, he was five years old. We were in Dad's hotel suite, and Stephen discovered the fax machine. He instructed us to draw pictures and pass them to him so he could run them through the machine. We didn't know what we were doing, but we made an excellent production team under young Stephen's guidance; it was just like a real Hollywood production! Today, Stephen is studying for his computer science degree and also shows talent for the arts. When he was at Palo Alto High School, his fine arts teacher said he was very gifted at directing. I don't have any kids, but if I sound like a proud auntie, I am!

Irascible Ronnie Schell has been a staple at Mayberry Festivals for years. He's best known for playing Duke Slater on *Gomer Pyle: USMC*, and Bernie, the Furrier, on *The Andy Griffith Show*. Dad really enjoyed his friendship. Ronnie: "Every time I saw Don, he would say, 'This is the guy that taught me how to roll a prophylactic on yourself with one hand.' I did, I taught him that because, you know, the other

Dad fussing over his grandson Stephen, not yet one year old, 1993.

hand's busy. We had a running gag that I was his VVVBP, very, very, very best pal. What always surprised me is that he wasn't Barney Fife. Women loved him. There was one woman who used to beat him up, Andy Griffith's secretary—she used to hit him. One time, I walked into a Du-pars coffee shop about six o'clock at night. And there, sitting all by himself in a booth, was Don. And I think geez, everybody's gonna recognize him. I don't think he was aware that he was so popular, do you? When I was with Andy, it was almost like being with Don—bigger than life, popular, iconic. Don loved Andy. I remember him saying to me, 'You know, a lot of people criticize Andy for his temperament, but he's always been good to me, and I love him.'"

Ronnie: "We were both hypochondriacs. One time he had phlebitis in the leg. He was in the hospital, I went to visit him, and I walked down the hallway with Andy. The door to his room was open, and I said very loudly, 'Have they told him the truth yet?' He loved it. Cancer, sore throat, strokes, heart attacks—those are things we all imagined we had."

A conversation I once had with Lucille Ball puzzled me, so I asked Howard Storm about it, because he knew so many people. I had met Lucille at a seminar in comedy she was teaching at Cal State University, Northridge, in 1977. I went up to her after the class, and I said, "You've worked with my dad, Don Knotts." She said, "Oh! That *poor man*!" Howard: "What a strange thing to say." Me: "Thank you! I was so taken aback, I couldn't bring myself to ask, 'What do you mean?'" Howard: "You know, Don was a powerful personality. People had to be naive to believe that he was *that guy*, the character he created. He was a strong-willed, solid guy who was not afraid of anything. That fear was all part of the character. But that's the danger of playing characters—people start to believe that's who you are."

I recently chatted with the former "Mrs. Limpet," Carole Cook; we were sharing observations about Dad. Carole: "Don seemed preoccupied, like there was something else on his mind. Maybe that's what gave him that distant feeling. You had the feeling he was playing another movie inside his head. That's one of the reasons I thought he was complicated. Extremely polite to me always, very gentlemanly. He'd always help me." Me: "Sometimes he was distant because of his neuroses and things." Carole: "He had a dark side." Me: "Yeah. He had a dark side, and he was constantly battling that. Sometimes I'd be telling him things, and he wouldn't remember any of it. He was there for me, but not always tuned in."

Dad was a hypochondriac, but he had another problem that was real. He remarked in 2001, "I felt I was dependent on alcohol. I never got a good night's sleep. I would toss for hours. Then I overdosed on sleeping pills, which I had taken for thirty years. I was in the hospital two years ago. The doctor said drinking interferes with sleep patterns. I quit drinking and pills. I sleep fine now." But Dad returned to the pattern of liquor followed by a sleeping pill. Tom and I used to laugh because Dad had a lovely bar at the house, and he would say, "Good night, kids." We would just look at each other because we knew he was going to come back and make another drink. We never counted how many; we just thought it was funny that he kept coming back. It never occurred to us two eggheads that our dad might have a drinking problem. He would drink, then he'd have to take a sleeping pill to fall asleep. It was the same pattern from his early New York days when he had the stress of live television.

The sleeping pills that Dick had prescribed for him went off the market. They were replaced by another product, and the prescription dosage was slightly higher, which was not clearly indicated. What he thought was a normal dose was actually an overdose, and he ended up in the hospital. Two years later, he overdosed again, and it was scary because he was "out" for quite a while. We didn't know if his brain would be affected. It was unharmed, but Dad was in denial about the problem.

Dad's doctor told Francey and me the only thing that would cure him was a twelve-step program, which would require two weeks with other patients in a hospital unit, without contact from the outside. The program had a high success rate and was developed by Bill Wilson, the same man who started Alcoholics Anonymous. In order for the program to work, an acceptance and belief in God was required. Dad refused to go through with it. Francey and I did an intervention with him, and we both insisted. He fussed at us, argued, and yelled. He could be very tough, but we knew all his tricks! Finally, he relented but said he would only stay for a few days.

After he got into the program, he immediately turned around. Not only did he stay the whole time, he talked other patients out of leaving! When he got out, he was a new person. He never touched another drink, and he was upbeat and even-tempered. He had come full circle from his beginnings in a dysfunctional, alcoholic family. I was so proud of him!

———————

My mother Kay has had a long, eventful life. She and Alan Carling-Smith weren't suited to each other, and they divorced. Then she married a geologist, Burt Amundson, and they lived happily in Sacramento until his passing in 2015. Now she is ninety-four, and the little hottie is currently in a relationship with a wonderful man named Doug Dean. Mother is in assisted living, and despite the COVID-19 pandemic, she is enjoying life.

Loralee has been happily married to Dr. Howard Murad for years.

By 2005, Dad was having trouble with his lungs and had to carry a small oxygen tank with him, but that didn't stop him from doing voice-overs on several animated films, including *Air Buddies* (video short, 2006), *Chicken Little* (movie, 2005), *Hermie & Friends* (TV movie, 2004), *Johnny Bravo* (TV series, 2004), and *Cats Don't Dance* (movie, 1997).

My friend, comedian Dana Snow, was asked to house-sit when Dad and Francey were away. Dana: "There was a pile of fan mail, and I was given instructions or permission to give out some of the photos of him that were there. And two or three times someone did buzz from downstairs and say they were a fan. I'd say, 'He's out now, but I can give you a photograph.' There was a pool table, and . . . to be in the condo with five Emmys! It was weird to walk from one room to another: *There's an Emmy . . . oh, there's an Emmy.* There was the big bedroom, a TV, and on the computer was a big magnifying glass which had a plastic tentlike thing to help his breathing at night. The water didn't work in the bathtub, and there was a grinding sound that happened if you pressed the button that was supposed to make the water come out, and you just sort of had to put up with the grinding noise. I learned that at this late date, when he was offered a part, it was usually also offered to Bob Newhart, and I hadn't thought about them as being similar types, vulnerable older men. Don had an oversized dummy that someone had given him."

Dad had named him Danny, in honor of his army dummy, and kept him in a rocking chair by the window. When Dad and Francey were away, the condo's private security officers were instructed to keep an eye on the place. On one of their rounds, they noticed a figure rocking in the chair and they quietly let themselves in. One of the officers pulled his gun and yelled, "Freeze!" Suddenly, he realized he was in Barney Fife's apartment holding a gun on a dummy!

Over the years, Dad told different versions of how he lost his dummy in the war. I finally asked, "Did you leave him on an island, did the army lose his suitcase, or did you throw him overboard? You're eighty years old—what's the story?" He said, "I can't remember. You should've asked when I was seventy-two!"

Dad and Francey continued to live happy, comfortable lives together. Francey: "Don loved Country Gentleman [a variety of white corn, instead of yellow corn]. He was absolutely adamant that it be that corn. He wanted to make it without butter and salt; he was really proud of it. And I finally realized that's because he grew up on those corn farms. He used to say, 'Oh I didn't want to work and pick corn.' But the truth is, Don loved that white corn.

"He was quite the Anglophile. He was very, very proud of the fact that he understood British humor. He talked about the time he saw a play in England and said he wanted to go back. He just never quite made the time to do it."

Dad still made regular visits to Morgantown to see his pals. Judy Eldred: "Don was there at the time my father was dying. I told him how grateful I was that they have been friends all these years and that he had come. Both their birthdays were in July, so they were celebrating, and they played their ukuleles. When he was on hospice, Don gave it to him, and my dad played it." Me: "Andy Griffith gave my dad three ukuleles. . . . Giving each other ukuleles is a bit of a mystery."

———————

It occurred to me one day that for many years I hadn't heard Dad tell his stories of growing up in the boarding house. I decided to write them down, along with other precious memories from childhood. That led me to write my one-woman show, *Tied Up in Knotts*, which I started performing after he passed. I have performed the show now for ten years and taken it to thirty-two states. It has been an exciting experience to help Dad continue to spread the love and laughter!

Mother helped me get my first bookings. She wrote: "Karen's show, *Tied Up in Knotts*, is meeting successful engagements all over the county. She uses her acting talent in this presentation. Her father, knowing how difficult it is to succeed in show business, tried to dissuade her from pursuing acting. But I am sure he would be very proud of her current accomplishments."

Sometimes when I asked Dad for advice, he didn't know what to tell me. He'd simply say, "When in doubt, smile. A good joke or a funny story can get you through just about anything." He was such a loving father.

It's strange how things happen out of the blue. One day I was working at the library, and I got a call from Francey telling me that Dad was in the hospital. Andy Griffith was on his way, too, so I knew his condition was serious. When I got to the hospital, he was in the pulmonary unit. It turned out to be lung cancer.

I visited every day. One time I was running late. I hurried into his room, and he was lying there with a mask over his face! I didn't know what could've happened. I touched his hand, and started telling him how much I loved him and that the whole world loved him too. Then Francey came into the room. I didn't want to hear any bad news, so I turned away. She said urgently, "Karen, I'm trying to tell you, your Dad was moved to another room this morning!" Oh! Well . . . some poor patient got an extra dose of love from a daughter he didn't know he had!

Francey: "I noticed there was a certain pride that you were going to be there for him. He was a hundred percent sure of that. It just made him so happy." Later, I said something in an interview that surprised me by how much attention it got. I was talking about what it was like to be at Dad's deathbed. I told the interviewer, Ed Gross, "Dad had this funniness that was just completely, insanely natural. When he was dying, he was making us laugh; we were in hysterics. He did or said something that caused Francey and me to go into fits of laughter, and I ran out of the room. I thought, *I don't want to be standing there in front of this man, my dearly beloved father who's dying, and laughing.*" I told Howard Storm about it. He said, "You should have stayed and laughed out loud. That's what comedians live for." Hmm. Maybe he was right. But if Dad was being serious, he didn't want to be laughed at, so it was a tough call.

Francey: "He was in great humor all the time, really. He talked about the Great Wizard taking him away. But I also remember him laughing and cutting up and being in a great state of mind. This is the time most people would think, *Oh, who would be in a good state of mind now?* He was in a fantastic state of mind! He insisted one night that I tell him a story. I didn't have a story—what the heck was I gonna tell? He insisted, so I made up a story! It was that two guys went to a hot dog stand. They were on a break from their job. They were saying, 'I can't believe I have to go back to work.' The other one said, 'I don't either. Why don't we just cut out. I dare you! Listen, right now, we're going to get on a plane, and we're just going to take off for Africa.' The first guy said, 'No way are we going to do that!' But they decided to go. When they landed in Africa, they heard some music—the drums were beating in the background. They got off the plane, started walking toward the drums, and they started to dance.' He screamed with laughter! We laughed and laughed, and I never saw him laugh harder in my life. He doubled over, that I had made up such a silly story. The part that finally sent him over the edge was when they were dancing and going toward the music. It was one of those things that literally someone's going to die laughing."

When the end neared, we were with him. Andy was alone with him, then he left, and it was Francey, Tom, and me. He was hooked up to a machine and wasn't feeling any pain. I asked him how he was doing, and he said he was "waiting for the Wizard to take him away." I knew who he meant. Everybody has their own name for God; his was the Wizard. Sooner or later we all have to get behind the curtain with him.

I said, "Dad, are you going to pull through this, are you going to be OK? Come on, you can nip this. Nip it in the bud!"

He said, "No time. The Wizard is here."

Tom, Francey, and I each kissed his cheek and said goodbye. He passed away at UCLA Medical Center at about 8 PM on February 26, 2006.

We went to the condo. We could feel his spirit still there. We knew we had only a few precious hours to absorb what had happened until the world found out; then the phone would not stop ringing.

Mike Ruiz: "I was at the sink washing dishes, and I heard a voice come on TV. I thought, *I know that voice; that's Karen Knotts.* I watched and found out your dad had passed away. It was the Larry King show. What I couldn't understand or believe was how strong you looked. You were stronger than I was. And I know you had already gone through the horror, and you were still feeling sad. But I couldn't believe how strong you were on television."

I wasn't as strong as I appeared. I felt like I had lost an arm or a leg, we were so attached. In my dreams I felt Dad's presence. We communicated but didn't speak. I took long walks in the hills, looked up at the sky and asked, 'Where did you go?' Finally, I stopped running and sat down to think. When a baby comes into this world, we call it a miracle. Why is it not the same when a spirit leaves it? I thought about a conversation I once had with Barbara Welles in her apartment on a chilly autumn day.

Me: "What do you suppose happens to us after we die?"

Barbara: "You come back as five generations of people."

Me: "What are the . . . five generations of people?"

Barbara: "First you come back as the *red* man, then you come back as the *brown* man, then you come back as the *black* man, then you come back as the *white* man, and then you come back as the *yellow* man."

Me: "Oh. What happens after that?"

Barbara: "That's the end. Then you're *dead*. You don't come back no more."

Me: "So it's final, then."

Barbara: "You know, Karen, I look out that window, and every day I see something different. That poor little tree, it's just barely hanging on. In a little while there won't be no leaves on that tree at all. But *soon* as springtime comes, brand new stuff come out! See that tree across the street, that big pretty one? That's what God gave us; that's for shade. That's to keep you cool when it's hot. Everywhere you look you see God in action. Man ain't made those! Only God can make a tree—ain't no lie about that."

EPILOGUE

I WAS A LATE bloomer; it took me a long time to develop. But I'm proud of who I've become and of my generation. We baby boomers have always redefined ourselves, and we'll continue to do so. It's not our fault we got stuck with that dumb name! The media reminds us of our advancing years and implies that we'll become irrelevant. The idea has even been put forth that we should quit our jobs to make way for the young! Well, I don't think millennials would be too interested in flying across country to perform *Tied Up in Knotts* in theaters like I have for the past decade.

I've come to realize that every person comes to fruition at their own pace. Each moment of life has infinite possibilities!

Performing my stage show, *Tied Up in Knotts!*, 2015.

ACKNOWLEDGMENTS

Research

Margaret "Peg" Brennan

Professor Neal Brower

John A. Cuthbert, director of the West Virginia & Regional History Center, WVU

Dominion Post, especially David Raese and Pam Queen

John and Larry Gassman

Josephine and William Aull Center

Andrea Mankey

Harold McQuinn, DDS

Morgantown High School Library

Morgantown History Museum

David Pollock

John W. Pyles, former Monongalia County commissioner

Jon "Jack" Raese

Karen Lemley Ruckle

Harold Max "Swifty" Shaver

WAJR Radio

Morgantown Friends

Beege Bowers

Janet Capiola

James Carabasis

Rose Anne Childs

Karen Cira

Jason Croston

Jeff Davis

William F. DeVault

Denise Powers Fabian

Sean Malone

Kay Fanok

Matt Marino

Scott Giessman

Dr. Maynard Pride

Adrienne Goff

Heidi Pride Mallory

Carolyn Goff

Sue Reed

Jeffrey Goff

Patty Ryan

Greg Grapsas

Ida Hadden Seggie

Deborah Smyth Green

Gary Simmons

Lenora Grosselin

Reba Smith

Sandra Hanford

Michelle Taft

Betty Barnard Holden

Paul Edward Templeton

Richard Jacobs

Roberto Tottori

Al Jasper

Jim Truman

Mark S. Johnson

Amee DeFere Tuggle

Tiffany Johnson

Leslie Thorpe Wileman

Kieran Johnston

Matthew Wilson

Michelle Kinsley

Marjorie Wolfe

Janis Lewis

Entertainment Friends

Tim Behrens

George Lindsey Jr.

Troy DeVolld

Jerome Pohlen

Brenda Feldman

Marilyn Sands

Sandy Hackett

Marvin Silbermintz

Cary Kozlov

Bobbi Stamm

Marleah Leslie

Gordon Warnock

Special Thanks To

"Uncle Bob," a.k.a. Robert Metz, renowned author and journalist, for the memories

Thanks, as well, to all the contributors mentioned in the text, and to everyone else who provided help and support—too many to mention here.